# COME UP HERE:

## THE UNVEILING OF JESUS CHRIST

# COME UP HERE:

## THE UNVEILING OF JESUS CHRIST

AN EXPLORER'S GUIDE TO REVELATION CHAPTERS 1-5

*BOOK 2 OF THE UNVEILING OF JESUS CHRIST SERIES*

MICAH PAUL GAYLOR

Come Up Here: The Unveiling of Jesus Christ
By Micah Paul Gaylor
Copyright © 2025 Micah Paul Gaylor


All rights reserved.
www.theunveiling.org
www.micahpaul.com

Edited by: Rebecca Hershberger
Cover design by: Micah Paul Gaylor
Cover Image: Adobe AI tools were used in the creation of the cover image.
Book layout by: Micah Paul Gaylor
Chapter title artwork by: Jamie Gaylor

International Standard Book Number: 979-8-9877560-6-5
Ebook ISBN: 979-8-9877560-7-2
Hardcover ISBN: 979-8-9877560-8-9

Library of Congress Cataloging-in-Publication Data: An application to register this book for cataloging has been submitted to the Library of Congress.

Bolding in scripture quotations was added by the author for emphasis only.

# TABLE OF CONTENTS

## CHAPTER 1

# WHERE WE'VE BEEN

G ood morning, fellow explorers! I hope you are rested, refreshed, and ready to go! Yesterday's training (i.e., the material covered in book 1 of this series) was focused entirely on preparation for what promises to be an utterly unique journey into the book of Revelation. During that time, we expanded our perspective of God's plan for the universe, anchored our vision in Christ alone, and introduced the necessary tools for a successful foray into end-time prophecy. And here we are, finally ready to embark on a life-changing study of the book of Revelation that will further unpack the Word of God in us and move us closer to the season of His Unveiling!

If you haven't already read book 1, *Face to Face: The Unveiling of Jesus Christ*, I recommend doing so before moving forward. Otherwise, it may feel like you are stepping into the middle of a deep conversation with no context. We'll do a quick review in this chapter, but without the full experience of book 1, you may miss, or at least not fully appreciate, many of the greatest treasures we'll discover in this book.

One lesson book 1 should have taught you is the importance of savoring every step of the quest. Our pilgrimage through Revelation isn't a race. True, there is a prize at the end, but the journey itself is every bit as important as the culmination. The very process of searching for Christ in the narrative of Revelation is one of the ways we heed its message and hasten its unfolding.

To that end, we will take our time in this book to unpack the first five chapters of Revelation. Too many eschatological studies rush through these introductory chapters to focus on the more predictive and "exciting" sections. Eager to find comfort or legitimacy in the knowledge of future events, some have built confident timelines and rigid doctrines while missing the main point of the prophecy, which is to know Christ and be transformed by that experiential knowledge.

The first five chapters of Revelation provide essential context to help us keep our eyes fixed on Jesus throughout the journey, and they establish the anchor point around which everything else in Revelation revolves. Extra time spent on these fundamentals will pay massive dividends down the road.

Even with this mindset, it's not always easy to avoid the common pitfalls of Revelation. John knew this better than anyone. Near the end of the vision, he got so caught up in excitement about promises of future glory and eternal comfort that he started worshiping the wrong person:

> The first five chapters of Revelation provide essential context to help us keep our eyes fixed on Jesus throughout the journey, and they establish the anchor point around which everything else in Revelation revolves.

> Then he [an angel] said to me, "Write, 'Blessed are those who are invited to the marriage supper of the Lamb.'" And he said to me, "These are true words of God."
>
> Then I fell at his feet to worship him. But he said to me, "Do not do that; I am a fellow servant of yours and your brethren who hold the testimony of Jesus; worship God. **For the testimony of Jesus is the spirit of prophecy.**"

> And I saw heaven opened, and behold, a white horse,
> and He who sat on it is called Faithful and True, and in
> righteousness He judges and wages war.
> —*REVELATION 19:9-11*

Notice the angel corrected John's temporarily distracted focus with a simple redirection: "The testimony of Jesus is the spirit of prophecy." In other words, he was reminding John that everything in Revelation reveals something about Christ. Also, notice that after this adjustment, John was able to see the Lord's return. How much more should it be our goal to listen intently until we can hear what each verse declares about Him. Otherwise, like John, we'll elevate a lesser concept and risk missing the entire point of the vision ... that is, the appearance of the Bridegroom who makes it all happen.

In this book, we'll attempt to listen intently, to stare intensely, and to search deeply for often-overlooked treasures. On the way, we'll be drawn down paths that are less traveled but absolutely vital for the journey.

Like inextricable gemstones embedded in surrounding rock walls just out of reach, some of the truths we'll inspect may feel impractically complex or useless for the daily grind of life. You may be tempted to pass them by with little more than a sideways glance. But remember that the book of Revelation is written for bondservants. It isn't a simple story of practical wisdom for the mildly interested. No, it's a profound encounter for those who have devoted—or at least desire to devote—every aspect of their lives to pleasing the Lord.

Besides, simplicity and practicality aren't always the best metrics of utility. It takes faith and patience to engage with the majestic complexity of the mysterious, and that is how we'll find some of the most transformational paths through Christ's Unveiling.

We shouldn't be afraid to stare into the mysteries in Scripture. As long as we remain within the boundaries of the

> The book of Revelation is written for bondservants. It isn't a simple story of practical wisdom for the mildly interested. No, it's a profound encounter for those who have devoted—or at least desire to devote—every aspect of their lives to pleasing the Lord.

written Word of God and don't attempt to wander off its trail, we can confidently engage our imaginations to visualize the nebulous and complex scenes described in Revelation. We'll even exercise some healthy speculation—as all good treasure hunters must from time to time. Doing so is an act of sonship that awakens our spirit and grows our soul's ability to perceive God's character. And both of those are necessary ingredients for experiencing Christ's Unveiling.

Having said that, I recognize that some people are designed by God to savor the elegance of simplicity. Their relationship with Jesus is most enriched by the thousand little kisses He sends throughout the day— those beautifully profound encounters with the divine in nature and friendship and family. If that's you, I celebrate your design, but I also encourage you to approach the daunting complexity of Revelation with the same childlike wonder. The process may grow you in ways you don't expect and enhance the simplicity of your devotion to Christ.

## WHERE WE'VE BEEN

In preparation for the exciting path ahead, let's quickly review how we got here. In book 1 we found ourselves standing on the edge of a dark forest, looking for an entrance into the foreboding narrative of Revelation. We started by clearing away the fallen brush of common misconceptions. Remember, Revelation is not a prophecy about future cataclysm and harrowing escape. It is not about the antichrist, the mark of the beast, or a one-world government. It's not even a revelation *about* Jesus. *He* is the revelation. All prophetic experiences in Revelation facilitate His Unveiling.

We also learned there is a blessing for heeding the book of Revelation. Heeding doesn't mean preparing to survive by stockpiling food and provisions. Heeding the Revelation of Jesus Christ means learning to see Him in every step along the way: in the mountaintops and valleys, the meadows, and the wildernesses of life. The very act of looking for Him hastens His coming (see 2 Peter 3:11-12), so the blessing of heeding the book of Revelation goes far beyond survival, salvation, protection, or escape. The blessing is getting to experience and participate in Christ's Unveiling, which includes the total and complete transformation of all things, first in us and then through us.

After clearing the debris and locating the starting point for our journey, we spent most of our time in book 1 tarrying at the forest's edge to familiarize ourselves with a map. We found the map's border to be a single crimson thread representing God's plan for creation from eternity past to eternity future. This thread established the boundaries of our quest. It tracked the lifecycle of the seed of the Word of God from its initial sowing at the dawn of time until the end when everything in heaven and earth will be summed up in Christ so that God can be all in all.

While following the crimson thread around our map, we learned something about God's reason for calling light out of darkness, life from sacrifice, and maturity from suffering. He uses all these things to refine human free will and fashion a suitable companion for Christ out of creation.

In addition to its glorious border, we found that our map also has a legend for interpreting the symbols and numbers in Revelation. The legend is made up of fractals, which are derived from biblical patterns. In our discussion of fractals, we learned to look beyond the simple data points of biblical truth to identify the principles they reveal about God's essence. We introduced the fractal of one (God, alone in His holiness), the fractal of two (the giving and receiving postures of God), and the fractal of three (Father, Son, and Holy Spirit). However, most of our time was spent unpacking the fractal of seven, especially in light of the seven days of creation, the seven Spirits of God, and the seven portions of the human spirit. The fractal of seven is the fingerprint of God and one of His primary tools for unveiling Jesus Christ to creation. Don't worry, we'll review the details of the fractal of seven again before we encounter it in Revelation.

Next, we examined Daniel's seventy-week prophecy to gain a general understanding of the scale and timing of end-time events. It was a deep discussion that required wading through some thick "underbrush" full of numbers and dates. The prophecy revolved around the perfection of the people and the land of Israel, and it followed the growth of the seed of the Word of God from the time of the prophet Jeremiah all the way to the season of Christ's second coming. The seventy weeks represented a total of 490 years of discontinuous time that was split into multiple sections based on whether or not Israel was living in their homeland and connected to the root of their messianic promise.

We tracked the starting and stopping of the seventy-week prophecy through history like an hourglass in the hand of the Creator. We learned that the final week of the prophecy (the seventieth week) revolved around Christ's new covenant, with the first half tracking the 3.5 years of His earthly ministry during His first coming and the second half set aside for the period of His Unveiling at the end of the age. We also concluded that we are currently living somewhere in the middle of an indeterminate pause between the end of the first half of the seventieth week and the beginning of the second half of the final week.

Finally, we studied the topography of our map by unpacking Revelation chapter 12 as a parable foretelling the general shape of events that will unfold during Christ's Unveiling. We learned about the birth of the male child, the casting of the dragon out of heaven, the flight of the woman into the wilderness, and the dragon's persecution of the woman's other children. We interpreted these symbols through the lens of the nation of Israel (the natural olive branches of Christ's Body) during the first half of the seventieth week, and through the lens of the Gentile Church (the wild olive branches of Christ's Body) during the second half of the seventieth week.

Okay, hopefully that rapid-fire, fifty-thousand-foot review was enough to grease the gears of your memory. Every step of the journey ahead will build upon the principles learned in book 1, but don't worry if some of these topics still feel rusty in your mind. As we move forward, I'll try to be sensitive when a more detailed review of a particular concept is necessary.

That's enough about where we've been. I hope you're as excited as I am to step onto the path and find out where we're going ...

# CHAPTER 2

## PARALLEL TRACKS

With a whistle on our lips and a new spring in our step, we approach the forest edge with mixed expectations. The path ahead is dimly lit, and rumors of its precariousness still echo all around us. The journey will be exhilarating, but it won't be easy: Revelation is not for the faint of heart.

But we have a map. And that map holds promise. And that promise skips through the shadows of our trepidation, enchanting our hearts with indescribable colors and melodies that beckon our spirits ever deeper. And so we embark with confidence toward the mystery of Christ.

To be clear, our confidence is not rooted in our map. It is rooted in our faith in God's character and the majesty of His plan. Indeed, our map is not even a physical map that we can literally hold. It is more of a mental construct used to organize the deep spiritual principles we'll use to navigate the book of Revelation. It's a way of framing everything we know about God and His eternal plan so we can recognize the trail of His endgame, even in the darkest parts of the forest.

This may be surprising given how much time we spent building it, but we won't often refer back to our map for this leg of our journey. At least not in a literal sense. It's not that we don't need a map to stay on track, but we've already learned many of its lessons. We spent so much effort consuming its principles in book 1 that it has largely become part of us. It has already expanded our view of God's plan. We are already on the lookout for the symbols defined in its legend—especially those fractal patterns of seven and three. It has already given us a general sense of the topography of the book of Revelation. So we won't need to keep pulling it out and referring to it by name—it's in our hearts and will continually guide us as we move forward.

## PARALLEL PATHS

With that in mind, let's talk about what's ahead. One of the first things you'll notice as we enter the forest of the book of Revelation is that the path has many branching trails. Some lead left, some lead right, some end abruptly with no obvious purpose, and others loop around to reconnect with the main path unexpectedly. Sometimes, the main path itself forks into parallel paths before reconverging further down.

In other words, the narrative of Revelation doesn't always unfold chronologically from beginning to end. Charting the best course can feel very daunting. But don't worry! What we've already learned from our map will provide enough contextual markers to lead persistent seekers like us to the treasure, even if we don't explore every trail or always take the shortest route.

The truth is, there are many ways to traverse the book of Revelation. Multiple courses lead to the ultimate treasure of Christ's Unveiling. Sure, some only lead to smaller treasures, while others lead to frustrating dead ends. Even so, we don't need to cover every possible step nor coerce other travelers that ours is the only legitimate way.

Consider everything we learned in book 1 about the seed nature of the Word of God. Seeds germinate. They send down roots and send up shoots that break through the surface and reach toward the sun. Branches expand, leaves grow, and flowers eventually appear in season. Each of these stages takes time, and some stages overlap. Likewise, biblical prophecy unfolds on multiple levels, often in a cyclical fashion. The challenge is knowing which stage we're looking at. Even when fruit of the prophecy appears, are we observing the first fruits or the final harvest of the entire crop? No wonder even the wisest struggle to discern the phases of prophetic fulfillment.

**B**iblical prophecy unfolds on multiple levels, often in a cyclical fashion. The challenge is knowing which stage we're looking at. Even when fruit of the prophecy appears, are we observing the first fruits or the final harvest of the entire crop?

Our goal in this series is to focus on the final harvest so we can chart a course consistent with the grandeur of God's plan. But just because we don't explore every possible path doesn't mean they hold no value. For instance, much of our time in this book will be spent walking through the letters to the seven churches described in Revelation chapters 2 and 3. Were the letters intended for seven specific churches in Asia Minor during the first century? Yes. Were they describing seven aspects of the Body of Christ relevant for every generation? Yes. Were they representing the seven chronological phases of Church history from the first century until Christ's return? Yes. Are they invitations to the seven portions of our spirit (on the individual level) and to the entire body of Christ (on the corporate level) to engage with the process that leads to us experiencing Christ's Unveiling? Yes. And that's the application I'm most excited about!

Each perspective is a piece of the puzzle—one of many legitimate paths through Revelation. However, since it would require a huge expenditure of time and energy to address them all, we'll focus on the path most congruent with our desire to see and experience Christ's Unveiling. We'll leave the rest for others to probe ... or maybe for future trips together.

## THE COMPASS

Now that we know what kind of path we're looking for, we're faced with another dilemma: In the heart of the woods, everything can start to look the same. It will be easy to get turned around. Especially with all of the side trails and parallel tracks that look like the main path. *Didn't we pass that stump already? Oh man, this fork looks familiar. I don't remember this place on the map?! Are we even moving in the right direction?!*

If our map consists of general principles but doesn't specifically tell us whether to go left or right at every fork in Revelation, how will we find our way? I'm glad you asked because I'm eager to introduce our next navigational tool: the compass! A compass will keep us from getting disoriented. A skillfully used compass can even help us locate contextual land features to deduce where we are when necessary.

Most compasses point to magnetic north, but ours is locked to the treasure at the heart of Revelation: Christ's Unveiling. And since our map was also built around His Unveiling, they are perfectly paired.

Our compass is the book of the Song of Solomon, or, as many refer to it, the Song of Songs. At first and second glance, the Song of Solomon has no obvious connection to the book of Revelation, but it won't take long to see how beautifully they synchronize.

The Song of Solomon contains deep truth on multiple levels. First and foremost, it is an intensely intimate love song between King Solomon and his betrothed Shulamite maiden through which we can derive godly principles for cultivating healthy romantic love, sexual desire, marriage, and faithfulness. While this is the most obvious and straightforward interpretation, it may also be the most important. After all, marriage is the centerpiece of God's plan for humanity, and it is under savage assault in today's culture.

At the same time, the Song of Solomon is also a metaphor for the spiritual relationship between Jesus Christ and His Bride. Marriage is a mysterious picture of the Church's mystical bond with Christ (see Ephesians 5:25-32). Many excellent books have been written from this perspective, particularly highlighting the value of the Song of Solomon as a devotional tool for understanding and growing our intimacy with Jesus.

However, to use the Song of Solomon as a compass, we're going to take a slightly different approach that honors and builds on both of those perspectives. We're not so much creating a new interpretation as applying those existing perspectives in a new way.

One quick side note: It is not always obvious who is talking in the Song of Solomon because the original Hebrew text doesn't directly identify the speaker. The context usually makes it obvious whether the singer is the Shulamite, Solomon, or some third party. However, the entire song is conveyed in a shifting first-person discourse, as if someone had watched a play with no narrator and only recorded the dialog, word-for-word, without noting the speaker.

Some Bible versions have attempted to decode the speaker based on the gender and tense of the surrounding Hebrew words, adding headings to each section whenever they think the speaker changes. But even that method isn't foolproof, and different translations vary with their conclusions in some key places.

I say all of that because, if you are familiar with the Song of Solomon from a particular translation, my conclusions about who is speaking may differ from your expectations in one or two places. I hope you will give me grace and recognize that the text affords some wiggle room in that regard.

Back to our compass. The first key to unlocking the alignment between Revelation and the Song of Solomon is to view Revelation as Christ's love letter to His Bride. In that frame, the Song of Solomon largely chronicles the Bride's response.

The second key to unlocking the benefits of our compass is understanding the legend on our map. Remember the legend? The one built from scriptural patterns (or fractals) that unlock deeper treasures from the numbers and symbols in Revelation? Our compass is marked with many of the same numbers and symbols. The same fractal approach we use to unpack the heart of Jesus in the book of Revelation can be used in the Song of Solomon. And when we do that, a larger pattern of events emerges between the two books. One of cause and effect, and of the divine dance of giving and receiving between Christ and His Bride. It's not just that the Song of Solomon illuminates the Book of Revelation. They illuminate each other.

The overlap between Revelation and the Song of Solomon won't always be obvious. Sometimes, we'll have to dig below the surface and think outside the boxes of our preexisting religious expectations. Sometimes, our compass will indicate we're facing one way, but based on where we think we are on the jour-

> The first key to unlocking the alignment between Revelation and the Song of Solomon is to view Revelation as Christ's love letter to His Bride. In that frame, the Song of Solomon largely chronicles the Bride's response.

ney, we won't immediately see the landmarks we expect. But always, if we trust our tools and remember to search for the principles of Christ's Unveiling, the connection will become clear, and the path will reveal itself.

## ALIGNING THE BOOKENDS

The first and last verses of Revelation and Song of Solomon provide examples of alignment so obvious they stand out like intentional bookends or signposts marking the beginning and end of a journey. The opening pair set the stage:

> The Song of Songs, which is Solomon's.
> —*SONG OF SOLOMON 1:1*

> The Revelation of Jesus Christ, which God gave Him to show to His bond-servants …
> —*REVELATION 1:1*

The Song of Songs. The Revelation of Jesus Christ. Solomon's greatest song. The ultimate Unveiling of Jesus. King Solomon revealing his most intimate desires to his betrothed. Christ revealing Himself to His bondservants. The parallels go deeper, but you get the point for now.

At the other end, the stories also close similarly:

> Hurry, my beloved, And be like a gazelle or a young stag on the mountains of spices.
> —*SONG OF SOLOMON 8:14*

> The Spirit and the bride say, "Come." And let the one who hears say, "Come." And let the one who is thirsty come; let the one who wishes take the water of life without cost.
> —*REVELATION 22:17*

> He who testifies to these things says, "Yes, I am coming quickly." Amen. Come, Lord Jesus. The grace of the Lord Jesus be with all. Amen.
> —*REVELATION 22:20-21*

In both books, the Bride's response to her Bridegroom's unveiling is an intense longing and expectation for everything promised to transpire soon.

In the case of the Song of Solomon, which is so obviously a song of betrothal, passion, courtship, desire, marriage, and consummation, the Shulamite bride's excitement at the end of the book ("hurry, my beloved") is easy to understand. Everything that transpires in her story is an integral part of the love song, and the entire process is beautiful. No surprise there.

But what about the Church's response at the end of the book of Revelation? Is her excitement equally logical, given the context of Revelation? Sure, we all yearn for Christ's return on some level, but do we truly know what we're thirsting for? Does our longing flow out of illumination? Do we understand how everything in the book of Revelation facilitates His Unveiling so that we can call for those events to unfold from a position of excitement born of sober wisdom and understanding? Are our eyes wide open like the Spirit and the Bride at the end of Revelation?

That is one of my goals in writing this series: to transform our general desire for the blessed hope of salvation into a raging passion to experience and participate in the fullness of the Unveiling of Jesus Christ. And that is why the Song of Solomon is the perfect compass to help us navigate the book of Revelation.

## OVERVIEW OF THE PATH

As we consult our compass going forward, we also need to keep our eyes open for the fingerprints of God—those fractal symbols described in our legend—to make sense of the landscape. After all, the ultimate goal may be the treasure at the end of the path, but the journey itself prepares us for the prize. If we are not absorbing everything that Christ is revealing about Himself along the way, then even if we make it to the end, we probably won't recognize the Treasure.

To that end, recall our discussion of the fractal of three in book 1. God's plan to move His people toward Christlikeness during the Unveiling generally follows the pattern of the tabernacle of Moses. The three sections of the tabernacle represent three phases of growth aligning with our threefold relationship with the Holy Trinity.

In the outer court, we lean into the Holy Spirit and learn to relate to Him as bondservants. In the inner court of the Holy Place, we lean into Jesus Christ and learn to relate to Him as a Bride. And in the most Holy Place (the holy of holies), we lean into the Father and learn to relate to Him as "sons" after the pattern of Christ.

Moreover, our growth through each of these three stages generally relies on the principles outlined in the fractal of seven, which we'll quickly review in the next chapter. In other words, there are seven general steps in our growth as bondservants, another seven in our growth as the Bride, and another seven in our growth in sonship.

Obviously, daily life rarely fits into such organized categories. Nevertheless, the book of Revelation follows this simple rubric to express the unfolding of Christ's Unveiling at the end of the age.

## THE MAIN LANDMARKS

Now, let's add a few more details to this general outline. I'm providing these barebones notes just to whet your appetite and provide enough structure for the overview to stick in your memory like peculiar landmarks in an otherwise busy landscape. These landmarks will make much more sense when we encounter them in context along the way.

Our journey through Revelation will be broken into four main sections following the four most prominent examples of the fractal of seven: the letters to the seven churches, the seven seals, the seven trumpets, and the seven bowls of wrath. Don't worry if these terms are unfamiliar at this point. We'll fill in the gaps when necessary. And chances are good that whatever you already know about the letters, seals, trumpets, and bowls of Revelation will be challenged, or at least significantly enhanced, by what's ahead.

Of these four landmarks, we will only talk in-depth about the letters to the seven churches in this book, but it is still important to know where the rest of the path will take us. For now, here is a high-level overview of the main sections of our journey. Think of it like drone footage taken fifty-thousand feet above the forest floor. Only, this drone uses night vision to cut through the darkness and hone in on the Bridegroom and Bride narrative. Yes, there are other things going on in the forest of Revelation as well, but they will make the most sense when viewed in light of the primary drama between Christ and His betrothed:

**The letters to the seven churches:** These are seven invitations—or proposals—to the seven portions of our spirit (on the micro level) and to the entire body of Christ (on the macro level) to leave behind our slave mindset and present ourselves as living sacrifices to God. You can compare it to the call given to Israel in Exodus 19 to present themselves before the Lord at the base of Mount Sinai.

In the Bride/Bridegroom paradigm, these seven letters can also be seen as the marriage proposal of the new covenant. This is the first stage of growth, and it precedes entry into the tabernacle. In this phase, Christ leads us from outside of the tabernacle into the outer court, where we can hear and accept His proposal.

**The seven seals:** These are the seven steps that seal those who have accepted the invitation of the seven letters. It's like the ceremony in Exodus 21 to seal those who chose to be bondservants forever. It includes the unfolding of astounding events on Earth and in heaven that God will use to seal His bondservants and engage His Bride.

Again, this is true on the micro and macro levels. In this phase, Christ leads us through the outer court, where we experience the full ministry of the Holy Spirit. It ends with us stepping into an innercourt level of spiritual maturity and Christlikeness.

**The seven trumpets:** These are the seven steps of the marriage ceremony. The trumpets are about Christ taking His betrothed bondservants into a marriage covenant and metaphorically consummating the marriage. In this phase, Christ leads us individually and as a corporate body through the inner court, where we experience Him completely as the Son and as our Bridegroom. It ends with us stepping into the holy of holies.

**The seven bowls of wrath:** These are the seven steps of the marriage feast, which is the celebration after the ceremony. In this phase, Christ leads us through the holy of holies, where we meet the Father and learn our full place in His plan and our full connectivity to His household. There, we take on the full nature of the Son and prepare to go back out to fulfill our true calling in creation. And trust me, creation will desperately need the intervention of Christ and His Bride at this point.

That was a ton of new information with very little supporting evidence. The evidence will come soon enough. At least now you know where we are headed, and you can prepare your heart and your questions while you start looking for signs along the path. Everything else in the book of Revelation will fit nicely into these four phases of our journey, and the Song of Solomon will help us see how. Even the darker aspects like the four horsemen, the great tribulation, the mark of the beast, the wrath of God, and everything in between will find its grandest purpose when viewed through this lens.

One more note: Remember everything we discussed in book 1 about Revelation chapter 12, or the Parable of the Unveiling? There will be three different types of Christians at the end of the age. That's because the Body of Christ will have three different responses to Christ's Unveiling, representing three different levels of maturity for God's people. And how we engage with Christ's Unveiling will largely be determined by how we engage with the preparatory wildernesses of life today.

Said another way, the three types of Christians will "enter the tabernacle" at different times and progress to maturity at different rates. But God's plan for the Unveiling is perfectly calibrated to handle this aspect of human free will while still ultimately accomplishing His own purposes.

It is important to keep these concepts in mind as we advance since each of the three types of Christians will have a different experience with the letters, seals, trumpets, and bowls.

---

In the Bride/Bridegroom paradigm, these seven letters can also be seen as the marriage proposal of the new covenant.

---

# CHAPTER 3

# THE SALUTATION: REVELATION CHAPTER 1

Without further ado, and with compass now in hand, we're ready to strike out upon the mysterious path stretching out before us like a mountain stream gilded in the sunlight, interwoven with the shadows of surrounding evergreens. The scenery is beautiful, though so much is still broken and unclear.

Our first step is a familiar one:

> The Revelation of Jesus Christ, which God gave Him to show to His bond-servants, the things which must soon take place; and He sent and communicated it by His angel to His bond-servant John, who testified to the word of God and to the testimony of Jesus Christ, even to all that he saw. Blessed is he who reads and those who hear the words of the prophecy, and heed the things which are written in it; for the time is near.
> —*REVELATION 1:1-3*

We won't linger here. We've seen this opening before, but the reminder is welcome: the Revelation is of Him, and He is the Revelation. Every footfall must land on ground illuminated by His countenance, lest we stumble and stray from our goal. Remember the words of Paul:

> Knowledge makes arrogant, but love edifies. If anyone supposes that he knows anything, he has not yet known as he ought to know; but if anyone loves God, he is known by Him.
> —*1 CORINTHIANS 8:1B-3*

> that their hearts may be encouraged, having been knit together in love, and attaining to all the wealth that comes from the full assurance of understanding, resulting in a true knowledge of God's mystery, that is, Christ Himself, in whom are hidden all the treasures of wisdom and knowledge.
> —*COLOSSIANS 2:2-3*

Our goal is not knowledge of events but rather the treasures of wisdom and knowledge hidden in Him. The value of that true knowledge is not information for legitimacy but love for intimacy. So if every step through Revelation is not enhancing our intimacy with Christ, then we have "not yet known as we ought to know." Let's carry that intention forward as we continue reading the salutation of Revelation:

> John to the seven churches that are in Asia: Grace to you and peace, from Him who is and who was and who is to come, and from the seven Spirits who are before His throne, and from Jesus Christ, the faithful witness, the firstborn of the dead, and the ruler of the kings of the earth. To Him who loves us and released us from our sins by His blood—and He has made us to be a kingdom, priests to His God and Father—to Him be the glory and the dominion forever and ever. Amen. BEHOLD, HE IS COMING WITH THE CLOUDS, and every eye will see Him, even those who pierced Him; and all the tribes of the earth will mourn over Him. So it is to be. Amen.

"I am the Alpha and the Omega," says the Lord God, "who is and who was and who is to come, the Almighty."

I, John, your brother and fellow partaker in the tribulation and kingdom and perseverance which are in Jesus, was on the island called Patmos because of the word of God and the testimony of Jesus. I was in the Spirit on the Lord's day, and I heard behind me a loud voice like the sound of a trumpet, saying, "Write in a book what you see, and send it to the seven churches: to Ephesus and to Smyrna and to Pergamum and to Thyatira and to Sardis and to Philadelphia and to Laodicea."
—*REVELATION 1:4-11*

The book of Revelation was recorded around 95 A.D. by the apostle John while exiled on the isle of Patmos. He was instructed (by Christ Himself, as we'll see in a moment) to write the vision in a book and send it to the seven churches. To be more precise, the Greek word (*biblion*) translated as *book* in this version of the New American Standard Bible is typically translated as scroll in other versions. Indeed, *biblion* often refers to a scroll of papyrus, which was the primary medium for written documents at that time. That detail doesn't matter much right now, but it will matter later in Revelation, so file it away.

Notice that, in verse 4, John personally addresses the scroll to "the seven churches that are in Asia," though, technically, the heavenly voice simply told him to send his scroll to "the seven churches: to Ephesus and to Smyrna and to Pergamum and to Thyatira and to Sardis and to Philadelphia and to Laodicea." In other words, Jesus did not mention Asia, and He gave no qualifier that He was only referring to the literal churches in Asia. John rightfully assumed that it should be sent to the actual churches in those Asian cities, but my point is that the identity of the seven churches had multi-

> Our goal is not knowledge of events but rather the treasures of wisdom and knowledge hidden in Him. The value of that true knowledge is not information for legitimacy but love for intimacy.

ple levels in God's mind beyond just the churches in Asia. More on that in a moment.

> Then I turned to see the voice that was speaking with me. And having turned I saw seven golden lampstands; and in the middle of the lampstands I saw one like a son of man, clothed in a robe reaching to the feet, and girded across His chest with a golden sash. His head and His hair were white like white wool, like snow; and His eyes were like a flame of fire. His feet were like burnished bronze, when it has been made to glow in a furnace, and His voice was like the sound of many waters. In His right hand He held seven stars, and out of His mouth came a sharp two-edged sword; and His face was like the sun shining in its strength.
> —*REVELATION 1:12-16*

Here, we see the subject and predicate of the Unveiling—the resurrected and glorified Jesus Christ. We're only going to focus on a few details of this description of Christ: His garment, the seven golden lampstands, and the seven stars in His right hand. The rest of it we'll skip over for now because we'll see the same attributes again later in our journey.

## HIS GARMENT

Jesus was clothed in a full-length robe that covered everything except His head, feet, and hands. It was both a kingly and priestly garment, indicating His office as High Priest forever according to the order of Melchizedek (see Hebrews 5). A golden sash was girded around His chest, likely speaking of two attributes: His royalty and His state of rest (since one involved in manual labor would be girded around the loins rather than the chest).

This is a picture of Christ in the middle of the seventieth week after His earthly ministry was complete. It's a similar scene to what we saw in the Book of Hebrews:

> Every priest stands daily ministering and offering time after time the same sacrifices, which can never take away sins; but He, having offered one sacrifice for sins for all time, SAT DOWN AT THE RIGHT HAND OF GOD, waiting from that

time onward UNTIL HIS ENEMIES BE MADE A FOOTSTOOL
FOR HIS FEET.
    —*HEBREWS 10:11-13*

So this is a vision of the gloried Christ waiting. His work is done, and now He intercedes for His Bride to reach maturity so that the Unveiling can begin. His face is unveiled, but His body is still fully covered, signifying that although the offer to see and experience His Unveiling is always available, His people—His Body on Earth—have not yet accepted that offer.

Remember Peter's admonishment that we ought to live with holy conduct and godliness, "looking for and hastening the coming of the day of God" (see 2 Peter 3:12)? I suggest this vision in Revelation chapter 1 is Jesus interceding for His Body to do exactly that, and offering the revelation of His unveiled face to aid us in the process. In a sense, everything that happens in Revelation will be the result of Christ's unveiled face drawing us deeper toward His full Unveiling.

## ABOUT THE CHURCH

Before we go any further, let's take a moment to consider a fundamental question that I danced around but never directly addressed in book 1: What is a church? Or better yet, what is *the Church*? Seems like an elementary question, right? But the word "church" carries enormous historical, cultural, and religious baggage for many people. More so than even the word apocalypse. Some of that baggage comes from toxic church experiences, and some of it is the byproduct of unbiblical teaching and religious misconceptions about Christ's plan for His Body.

To be clear, I have neither the inclination nor the wisdom to sort through and unload all of that baggage. I won't presume to define—or redefine—church for you. Even if I could, such a teaching would fill volumes. No, my goal here is to simply make a few clarifying statements about what I mean and what I don't mean when I talk about the Church. This is especially important to do now before we dive headlong into the letters to the seven churches.

Firstly, when I talk about the Church, I'm talking about the worldwide Body of Christ. Not a building. Not a denomination. Not a corporation or organization. Not a religious country club. Not a business.

Not a hierarchical system with a governing structure and creeds and rules and departments and membership lists. I'm simply referring to every single born-again follower of Jesus Christ throughout history—past, present, and future.

In some mysterious way, every Christian has been joined to the same Body of Christ, regardless of race, creed, or religious affiliation:

> There is one body and one Spirit, just as also you were called in one hope of your calling; one Lord, one faith, one baptism, one God and Father of all who is over all and through all and in all.
> —*EPHESIANS 4:4-6*

The Church is not a collection of multiple bodies each with their own smaller heads all reporting up to the main head. There is one body. There is one head. Christ is the Head, and we are all His members. Extending the body analogy to local expressions of the church or the headship analogy to local church leaders is a dangerous (and all too common) misappropriation of kingdom principles that only keeps us weak and immature.

Secondly, the Greek word translated in most English Bibles as church is *ekklesia*, and it literally means "called out". *Ekklesia* simply refers to an assembly or congregation of people that are "called out" of the general crowd for some shared purpose.

The Church—this called-out assembly—is described as many things in Scripture, including a Body, a Bride, a Tabernacle, a City, and more. Each of these metaphors, though closely related, highlights different aspects of what it truly means to be called out and separated from the fallen world systems and eternally joined to Christ.

The powers of darkness, the world, and even the people of God are forever trying to complicate Christ's original intention for His *ekklesia*. Over the centuries, we have piled on more and more systems and structures of control in the name of growth or protection or unity or some other ostensibly noble endeavor. More often than not, the results have been a further weakening, oppressing, and fracturing among the Body of Christ.

Obviously, I am painting with an overly broad brush. My perspective only extends to the modern institutional church systems I've experienced in America and observed in other Western nations. I can't speak to the health of the underground church in China, for instance. But what I'm describing is at least generally true, if not universally.

It is also generally true throughout Church history. It would be gross misconduct for me to summarize two thousand years of worldwide Church history in one paragraph, but I think it's fair to say this: Despite the risings and fallings, the periods of growth and atrophy, the dark ages and the great awakenings, the inquisitions and crusades and reformations and revivals—the modern Church still finds itself far from the purity and power of the first-century Church.

However, the problem goes further back than many realize. We tend to idolize the first-century Church as the perfect blueprint for the Body of Christ. True, they were a much clearer and brighter example than us, but as we'll see in Christ's letters to the seven churches, even they drifted pretty far from the mark. The apostle Paul warned about this in a statement that is often misconstrued:

> According to the grace of God which was given to me, like a wise master builder I laid a foundation, and another is building on it. But each man must be careful how he builds on it. For no man can lay a foundation other than the one which is laid, which is Jesus Christ.
> —1 CORINTHIANS 3:10-11

Many think of Paul's epistles as a New Testament instruction manual describing precisely how the structure of the Church must look and function. But that's not what Paul was referring to when he called himself a wise master builder. Notice that Paul said he laid a foundation but then clarified that Jesus Christ is the foundation. That's it. Only Jesus. He is the foundation, the blueprint, and the DNA of the Church. Paul laid a foundation for the expansion of the Church simply by preaching and demonstrating the reality of Jesus Christ.

Yes, Paul also communicated guidelines about church services. He described the proper use of spiritual gifts. He revealed the role of apostles, prophets, evangelists, shepherds, and teachers. He enumerated the qualifications for elders and deacons. He even outlined principles for church discipline. But we shouldn't look at these structures as part of the foundation of the *ekklesia* of Christ.

True, Paul's instructions came with great wisdom and through the inspiration of the Holy Spirit, but they were necessary responses to issues arising in the early Church. They weren't meant to be laws eternally etched in stone, and they certainly weren't meant to be worshiped in the way the Israelites worshiped the truth of the law of Moses while missing the principles of God's nature that it foreshadowed. In other words, they were guidelines to be observed with the freedom of sonship, not rules to be bound to like slaves. They were temporary examples of structures that could be built on the foundation, not the foundation itself.

Paul went on to describe the systems and structures that humanity would add to the foundation of Christ, perfectly foreshadowing the next two thousand years of Church history. And yes, Paul's own teachings beyond his preaching of Christ were included in this statement:

> Now if any man builds on the foundation with gold, silver, precious stones, wood, hay, straw, each man's work will become evident; for the day will show it because it is to be revealed with fire, and the fire itself will test the quality of each man's work. If any man's work which he has built on it remains, he will receive a reward. If any man's work is burned up, he will suffer loss; but he himself will be saved, yet so as through fire.
> —*1 CORINTHIANS 3:12-15*

So, as we approach Christ's letters to the seven churches as a prelude to His Unveiling, we need to recognize that He is preparing His Body for the fire that will test the quality of the structures we've built around His *ekklesia*. Some systems are made of hay and straw and are therefore unsuitable for even temporary purposes. Others are built from sturdy wood and have been useful for a season. But every system and structure will be purged, purified, or completely burned down before the end. That is a good thing. The process will reveal the true foundation, which is eternally unshakable:

> And His voice shook the earth then, but now He has promised, saying, "YET ONCE MORE I WILL SHAKE NOT ONLY THE EARTH, BUT ALSO THE HEAVEN." This expression, "Yet once more," denotes the removing of those things which can be shaken, as of created things, so that those things which cannot be shaken may remain. Therefore, since we receive a kingdom which cannot be

shaken, let us show gratitude, by which we may offer to God an acceptable service with reverence and awe; for our God is a consuming fire.
—*HEBREWS 12:26-29*

## SEVEN LAMPSTANDS

Okay, now back to the book of Revelation. Remember, John saw Jesus walking in the middle of seven golden lampstands, with seven stars in His right hand. What are these lampstands and stars?

Some symbols are left open to broad interpretation, but in this case, Jesus removed much of the ambiguity Himself:

> When I saw Him, I fell at His feet like a dead man. And He placed His right hand on me, saying, "Do not be afraid; I am the first and the last, and the living One; and I was dead, and behold, I am alive forevermore, and I have the keys of death and of Hades. Therefore write the things which you have seen, and the things which are, and the things which will take place after these things. As for the mystery of the seven stars which you saw in My right hand, and the seven golden lampstands: **the seven stars are the angels of the seven churches**, and **the seven lampstands are the seven churches**.
> —*REVELATION 1:17-20*

Before we talk about the lampstands, notice that, among other titles, Christ calls Himself "the living One." Remember the fractal of one and everything it suggests about God's aloneness? And His passionate disposition to fashion a Bride through whom He can share His divine nature so God can become all in all? All of that is wrapped up in the package of Jesus calling Himself the living One, and it is the perfect tone-setter for His letters to the seven churches. The other titles matter too, but we'll come back to them later.

As for the seven lampstands, they are the seven churches. In a later verse, Christ calls Himself, "the One who walks among the seven golden lampstands" (Revelation 2:1). So the picture is of Christ walking with an unveiled face amidst the seven churches while He orates customized letters of invitation—or marriage proposals—for each one to behold His glory in anticipation of becoming one with Him.

In light of everything I mentioned about there being one Body and one Head, you may be wondering why Christ would address His letters to *seven* churches? Doesn't that support the idea that He sees the Church as multiple organizations in the same way that we often do?

The short answer is "no," but to see why, we need to unpack the symbolism of lampstands and stars a bit more. I mentioned this in book 1, but consider that, with these lampstands, no mention is made of actual lamps or flames. The same Greek word (*lychnia*) used here for lampstands is also used throughout the gospels in a way that seems to accentuate the separateness of lamps from lampstands. For instance:

> You are the light of the world. A city set on a hill cannot be hidden; nor does anyone light a lamp and put it under a basket, but on the **lampstand**, and it gives light to all who are in the house. Let your light shine before men in such a way that they may see your good works, and glorify your Father who is in heaven.
> —*MATTHEW 5:14-16*

> And He was saying to them, "A lamp is not brought to be put under a basket, is it, or under a bed? Is it not brought to be put on the **lampstand**? For nothing is hidden, except to be revealed; nor has anything been secret, but that it would come to light. If anyone has ears to hear, let him hear." And He was saying to them, "Take care what you listen to. By your standard of measure it will be measured to you; and more will be given you besides. For whoever has, to him more shall be given; and whoever does not have, even what he has shall be taken away from him."
> —*MARK 4:21-25*

The best way to understand Revelation chapter 1 is in light of these passages. In both cases, Christ reveals that His Church (a corporate city on a hill) and His people (individual lamps in houses) are the vessels through which the light of God shines into the world. When He calls us the light of the world and a city set on a hill, He is speaking of the potential of our calling—in other words, what we are designed to be.

Lamps (the individual sources of light) must be on their lampstands to fill each house with light, and a city (a collection of individual houses full of individual lamps) must be on the hill to be seen by all. So here, as in Revelation, the lampstand isn't the light. It is merely a structure for elevating and displaying that light for maximum visibility.

Also notice the other elements that Christ mentions in these verses: revealing what is hidden, having an ear to hear, and the potential for receiving a reward or losing what we have been given. As we'll begin to see in the next chapter, all of these concepts are also found in Christ's letters to the seven churches. Keep that in mind as we move forward.

## SEVEN STARS

The separateness of the lamps and lampstands begs at least a couple of questions: Why are the seven churches seen as lampstands without lamps? And where are the lamps? After all, Jesus was seen walking among lampstands, not lamps.

That's where the seven stars in Christ's right hand come in. Remember, the seven stars are the angels of the seven churches. Nice, but what does that mean? In Revelation chapters 2 and 3, we'll read about Christ's unique exhortation for each of the seven churches, but for now, we'll focus on how each exhortation is specifically addressed to the *angel* of the church. The letter to Ephesus is written to the angel of the church in Ephesus, the letter to Smyrna is written to the angel of the church in Smyrna, and so on for each of the seven churches. Who or what is the meaning of these angels?

There are three common interpretations of the angels of the seven churches. First, and perhaps least likely, they could be literal angels, as in celestial beings who serve God and His people.

Even if we take it at face value that every church has a guardian or representative angel (or at least that these seven first-century churches did), what's the point? That seems like an odd and useless piece of information about an angelic middleman to feature so prominently in John's vision of Jesus. And why would letters containing exhortations to humans—letters meant to stir passion and cultivate intimacy with the Bride—be written to angelic beings rather than the Bride herself? I'm not a fan of this viewpoint.

The second common interpretation is that "angels" in this context refer to the human leaders of each church. The Greek word (*angelos*) translated as angels in these verses is also, on rare occasions, used by the New Testament writers to describe human messengers (see Luke 7:24 and James 2:25). This perspective also has problems.

First-century churches didn't have a hierarchical structure with a single human leader at the top presiding over every expression of Christ's Body in their city. The Church was far more organic and less organized at that point in history. And even if some did have pastors or bishops or elders over the city, the biggest issue with this perspective comes back to the incongruence between the headship of Christ and the idea of a middleman. This is Christ's Unveiling, directed toward His bondservants, curated for maximum intimacy to draw out a Bride. Why would Christ, the Head of His Body, speak to middlemen when He is directly connected to each member through the nervous system of the Holy Spirit? If you were sending a love letter to your fiancée, would you address it to her mother? You might use a middleman to *send* the letter. You might even use another to transcribe your words to paper, but the letter itself would be written in first person, speaking directly to your beloved. That's why I'm not a fan of this option either.

The third common interpretation is that angels in this verse symbolize the metaphorical "spirit" of each Church, as in the unique and specific manifestation of God's light in and through that particular expression of the Church. You could think of it as the personification of the heart and core of the Church, or the purest expression of the deepest motivations of that group of believers. In other words, the ideal essence of what they were designed to be, as seen through the spectrum of the seven redemptive gifts of Romans chapter 12.

I like this option because it honors the headship of Christ, eliminates the middleman, and leverages the fractal of seven to see seven aspects of the Body of Christ without splitting it into seven separate organizations. No human is the head of any part of Christ's Body, and His Body is not a mutated beast with many heads. Doesn't nature tell us that any creature with multiple heads is a monster? Again, there is only one Head and one Body and one Spirit expressed in seven flames.

This option is also consistent with the biblical truth that man looks at the outward appearance but God looks at the heart (see 1 Samuel 16:7). Deep calls to deep. Surely, Jesus, whose eyes are a flaming fire, would bypass the religious clergy-laity dynamic and speak directly to the deepest core identity of His people.

There is a fourth option that I'd like to present as a variation on the third. If the angels of the seven churches are the spiritual heart—the essence—of the seven churches at a macro level, then on a micro level wouldn't they also be the seven portions of the human spirit? You know, those seven "colors" of light within the human spirit reflecting the seven Spirits of God as described in Romans chapter 12?

Taking all of this together, the angels of the seven churches—the seven stars in Christ's right hand—have a dual role. They are the seven lamps of the Body of Christ, and they are the seven portions of the human spirit. They are self-sustaining balls of fire representing the light that Christ intends for His Body to shine into the world, and they are the lamps of God in our human spirit derived from the seven lights of the Spirit of God.

When Jesus addresses a letter to each of the seven angels, He is, in a corporate sense, calling out to the potential of that part of His Body. He is calling out to their futures and to the fullness of who they are called to be. You might say He is offering to place the star upon their lamp-stand if they will turn to Him and behold His Unveiling with eyes to see and ears to hear. Only then can they become the vessels of His Unveiling to the rest of the world.

In that light, the book of Daniel's description of the end-time resurrection after the great tribulation takes on deeper meaning:

> Many of those who sleep in the dust of the ground will awake, these to everlasting life, but the others to disgrace and everlasting contempt. **Those who have insight will shine brightly like the brightness of the expanse of heaven, and those who lead the many to righteousness, like the stars forever and ever.**
> —*DANIEL 12:2-3*

"Those who have insight" and "those who lead the many to righteousness" will be those who respond to the invitations in Christ's seven letters and therefore experience the full measure of His Unveiling on earth. That they will shine like the expanse of heaven and like the stars forever speaks of the progressively transformational impact of His Unveiling upon their spirit, soul, and body, enabling them to be effective witnesses of the gospel of the kingdom during the process—ultimately culminating in the resurrection and glorification of their bodies at the end.

Along those same lines, the lampstands speak of the potential place of prominence, visibility, and effectiveness that He offers to those who engage with His Unveiling. Related to that, the lampstands also represent the peculiar circumstances of the Unveiling that lead to our shining before the world: those wilderness trials that make us living epistles and spectacles of His grace.

A lamp should be placed on a stand rather than under a bushel. Likewise, the lampstands represent the structures and systems of our lives (the health of our soul and body) that support or hinder the shining of our human spirit. Remember, the seven Spirits of God are both eyes and lamps, and the corresponding seven portions of our human spirit are also eyes and lamps. If we learn to turn the eyes of our spirit to Christ and behold His unveiled glory, then the light inside of us grows strong and clear, becoming a lamp that first gives light to us and then through us to the world. But that requires the ongoing sanctification of our soul and body working together to form healthy lampstands that support the process.

So individually, when Christ inspects the lampstands, He is inspecting the quality of our lives compared to what we were designed to be. When He speaks to our lampstands, He is inviting, challenging, and correcting what we have built. He is also calling to the seven portions of our human spirit to behold a particular aspect of the glory emanating from His countenance so that we can engage in the process of transformation in that area and be prepared for the flames of the seven stars.

A city should be built on a hill rather than in a valley. Likewise, on the corporate level, the lampstands refer to the structures of *ekklesia* we have built upon the foundation of Christ that are meant to (but often don't) support the growing up of the entire Body of Christ:

> for the equipping of the saints for the work of service, to the building up of the body of Christ; until we all attain to the unity of the faith, and of the knowledge of the Son of God, to a mature man, to the measure of the stature which belongs to the fullness of Christ.
> —*EPHESIANS 4:12-13*

So corporately, when He inspects the lampstands, He is comparing the structures of the Church to Himself. When He speaks to those lampstands, He is addressing His Unveiling to seven fundamental aspects of the Church that together represent the full spectrum of who the Body of Christ is called to be—and He is calling us to become that *Ekklesia*. Again, not a building. Not a denomination. Not a corporation or organization. Not a religious country club. And not a business with a hierarchical system of governing structures, creeds, rules, departments, and membership lists. A universal Body, called out from the world's fallen systems, intimately connected to the Head and perfectly representing Him on earth.

## COMPASS CHECK

Let's take a quick peek at our compass. Everything we just read from Revelation chapter 1 is essentially the salutation of the Unveiling. It was Jesus saying, "My beloved, I have something immensely important and exciting to share with you about the deepest desires of My heart ...," and it is summarized in a single verse in the Song of Solomon:

> The Song of Songs, which is Solomon's.
> —*SONG OF SOLOMON 1:1*

"The Song of Songs, which is Solomon's." You can almost feel the words humming with all the promise and excitement befitting such a royal invitation. What is this Song of Songs? This greatest of all songs, which alone belongs to the King to sing?

The phrase is only a salutation—an appetizer for what's to come—but already, it establishes a longing tone and heightens our expectations for the future. So, with increasing anticipation, we lift our eyes up to the path ahead and find it newly illuminated. Now there's a golden-haloed light filtering through the trees—an expression of the hope growing in our hearts. Like sparkling honey for a longing soul, it draws us ever deeper. Let's keep moving forward!

# CHAPTER 4

# CHRIST'S SEVEN LETTERS: TO EPHESUS

Now we've come to the content of Christ's letters to the seven churches. Before rushing in, let's establish a rhythm and cadence for navigating this section since we'll be spending a lot of time with these letters. We'll leverage our understanding of the fractal of seven for this part of the path, but we'll also bounce back and forth between Revelation and Song of Solomon.

For each of the seven letters, we'll start by reading through the letter as recorded in Revelation. Each letter consists of an introduction, an encouragement, a correction, and a promised reward, so we'll touch on each element as we unpack what Christ was highlighting to His Bride in the letter. Then we'll end each letter by flipping over to the Bride's response in the Song of Solomon.

For the fractal of seven, recall our discussion of Romans chapter 12, where Paul introduced the names of the seven redemptive gifts in the context of the body:

> For just as **we have many members in one body** and all the members do not have the same function, **so we, who are many, are one body in Christ**, and individually members one of another.
> —ROMANS 12:4-5

Paul alluded to two applications of the body analogy as it relates to the seven redemptive gifts. The first is in an individual context where the redemptive gifts describe the "members" of our human spirit. In other words, the members are the seven "eyes" of our human spirit designed to receive the seven revelations of God's light from the face of Christ. They provide light to our inner temple. This ties in with Christ's analogy of the lamp that should be placed on the lampstand to give light to the house.

The second application, which is related and derived from the first, is in a corporate context where the general function of each member of the Body of Christ is described by one of the redemptive gifts. This ties in with Christ's analogy of the city set on a hill to give light to the world.

We will lean heavily on the individual application of the seven redemptive gifts throughout this book. That does not lessen the other interpretations of the lampstands and stars mentioned in the previous chapter. It's just that the individual application is most relevant to our personal experience of Christ's Unveiling. Even so, all of the principles we uncover can also be reapplied to the Church on a corporate level, and to the seven seasons of Church history, if you are so inclined.

So, as we dig into Christ's messages, our main focus will be viewing these seven letters as invitations to the seven portions of our human spirit to turn toward the face of Christ. That's ultimately how we position ourselves to experience His Unveiling.

To that end, we'll devote one chapter to each letter. It might be tempting to rush through the seven letters to get to the more exciting, action-packed parts of Revelation, but that would be a massive mistake. There's a reason Jesus started His Unveiling with these seven letters. They are essentially engagement proposals. To be clear, we are already engaged to Christ if we are born again and have received the gift of the Holy Spirit (see Ephesians 1:13-14), but you can think of these letters as clear declarations of that proposal sent to each portion of our spirit.

Each letter must be received with reverence and responded to wholeheartedly if we expect to experience His Unveiling. The only way we can be properly positioned for the rest of the book of Revelation is to learn everything He wants to show us about Himself through His proposal letters. Also, the issues He addresses in each letter follow the fractal of seven and establish a pattern that will be repeated throughout the rest of Revelation.

To refresh your memory on the fractal of seven before we begin, below is a table summarizing the main attributes discussed in book 1:

## FRACTAL OF SEVEN - QUICK REFERENCE GUIDE

| Redemptive Gifts (Romans 12) | Seven Spirits of God (Isaiah 11) | Days of Creation Summary (Genesis 1 & 2) | Fundamental Attributes |
|---|---|---|---|
| Prophet | Spirit of the Lord | Creation of physical and spiritual light, and all the physical, spiritual, and moral laws and principles that govern creation. Separation of light from darkness. | Design, initiation, illumination, discernment. |
| Servant | Spirit of Wisdom | Separation of the waters above from the waters below. Creation and separation of physical and spiritual matter. Creation of the atmosphere. | Safety, protection, cleansing, boundaries. Creates hospitable environments for life to thrive. |
| Teacher | Spirit of Understanding | Physical earth drawn out of the waters for foundation. Vegetation drawn out of the earth for food. | Takes the ethereal, raw, and conceptual and converts them to practical, substantive resources that support life. |
| Exhorter | Spirit of Counsel | Creation of sun, moon, and stars to shine light to earth and govern seasons and time. | Verbally expressive and outwardly focused. Like the shining of the sun, moon, and stars, takes heavenly wisdom and declares it to Earth so that things can be seen as they really are. |
| Giver | Spirit of Might | Creation of fish and birds. Commanded to be fruitful and multiply. | Effective stewardship of resources, especially the next generation, through nurture and sacrificial giving. |
| Ruler | Spirit of Knowledge | Creation of the other animals. Formation of mankind in God's image. Mankind commanded to be fruitful, multiply, fill the earth, and subdue it. | Pursues the knowledge of God's character and principles to build complex and free systems that help creation reach God's highest intention. |
| Mercy | Spirit of the Fear of the Lord | God rested. | God, alone in His holiness, savoring the fruit of His labor. Being instead of doing. |

## THE LETTER TO EPHESUS

Jesus begins His first letter in Revelation chapter 2:

> To the angel of the church in Ephesus write:
> The One who holds the seven stars in His right hand, the One who walks among the seven Golden Lampstands, says this:
> 'I know your deeds and your toil and perseverance, and that you cannot tolerate evil men, and you put to the test those who call themselves apostles, and they are not, and you found them to be false; and you have perseverance and have endured for My name's sake, and have not grown weary. But I have this against you, that you have left your first love. Therefore remember from where you have fallen, and repent and do the deeds you did at first; or else I am coming to you and will remove your lampstand out of its place—unless you repent. Yet this you do have, that you hate the deeds of the Nicolaitans, which I also hate. He who has an ear, let him hear what the Spirit says to the churches. To him who overcomes, I will grant to eat of the tree of life which is in the Paradise of God.'
> —REVELATION 2:1-7

The letter to the angel of the church in Ephesus is an exhortation to the prophet portion of the human spirit. In other words, it beckons to the part of our spirit that was made to align with the Spirit of the Lord. The letter is intended to help us receive from that aspect of God's character, shine that wavelength of God's light into our soul and body, and become more like Jesus in that area. Only then can we fully reflect that aspect of Christ out to the world.

On the corporate level, the letter to Ephesus also beckons to the "prophet" aspect of the larger *ekklesia* of Christ. And even though we'll stay largely focused on the individual applications of

> We are already engaged to Christ if we are born again and have received the gift of the Holy Spirit, but you can think of these letters as clear declarations of that proposal sent to each portion of our spirit.

the seven letters, it is important to note that the same principles apply without much tweaking to the corresponding parts of the corporate body as well.

In the fractal of seven, the Spirit of the Lord and the prophet redemptive gift are all about initiating God's plan and expressing His design. They sow the light of God's Word into a situation as a seed that contains the blueprint and raw material that will later be used by the other gifts to bring His purposes to pass.

So how did Christ introduce Himself to Ephesus? What did He want them to know about Himself before He encouraged and corrected their behavior to position them for His Unveiling? "The One who holds the seven stars in His right hand, the One who walks among the seven golden lampstands, says this ...."

In other words, Christ owns and has the singular ability to operate the very flames of God the seven aspects of the human spirit are designed to become. And He walks among the devices, or circumstances, intended to elevate and exercise those lights before the world. He understands His intention for our spirit and knows what is needed in our soul and body to bring each portion of our spirit to the fulfillment of its unique design. He knows what we need to experience to get us there.

To "walk among" is a statement of intimacy and empathy. He is not distant or indifferent. Our great High Priest has already walked the same road and embraced the trials, tribulations, and sacrifices necessary to inherit the promise and fulfill His purpose. As He walks among the lampstands, He fully empathizes with the struggles that the lampstands represent for His people, and He stays with us in the middle of them.

> To "walk among" is a statement of intimacy and empathy. He is not distant or indifferent. ... As He walks among the lampstands, He fully empathizes with the struggles that the lampstands represent for His people, and He stays with us in the middle of them.

That is how Christ frames His exhortation to the Ephesus part of our being (and of His Body). That is the aspect of His character that especially empowers the prophet portion of our spirit to overcome and shine His light into the darkness.

## EPHESUS ENCOURAGED AND CORRECTED

After that introduction, Jesus would go on to celebrate the ways that Ephesus already reflected the nature of the Spirit of the Lord before warning them about the areas where they fell short and still needed to overcome. As we look at some of those details, think about the strengths and weaknesses from multiple angles. On the corporate level, they represent the typical strengths and weaknesses of those members of the Body of Christ whose redemptive gift is prophet. On the individual level, they describe the attributes of Christ's nature that He wants to be reflected, at least in some measure, in the prophet portion of every Christian's spirit.

> I know your deeds and your toil and perseverance, and that you cannot tolerate evil men, and you put to the test those who call themselves apostles, and they are not, and you found them to be false; and you have perseverance and have endured for My name's sake, and have not grown weary.
> —*REVELATION 2:2-3*

Like the prophet gift naturally perceives God's intended design, a deep sense of righteousness (right alignment with God's character) drove Ephesus. And like the first day of creation, they especially cared about the foundations—or first things—being purely aligned with God's intention. That's why they worked tirelessly to expose false apostles.

True apostles don't just *call themselves* apostles. In other words, they don't assume the title of apostle to gain legitimacy or influence over others. True apostles are called as such by God, and they lay down their lives like a seed to establish the foundations of the corporate Body of Christ (we'll see how true that is when we get to Revelation chapter 21).

The redemptive gift of prophet (and the prophet portion of our spirit) is particularly adept at sniffing out the difference between righteous and evil leadership. It understands the principle of the seed and it knows that godly authority only grows out of selfless sacrifice.

> But I have this against you, that you have left your first love. Therefore remember from where you have fallen, and repent and do the deeds you did at first; or else I am coming to you and will remove your lampstand out of its place—unless you repent.
> —*REVELATION 2:4-5*

Christ's challenge to Ephesus? Return to your first love. In the prophet's zeal for righteousness, and in our spirit's drive to do what is right through selfless sacrifice, we sometimes leave behind the most important thing: the heart of the matter. Remember Mary and Martha?

> She had a sister called Mary, who was seated at the Lord's feet, listening to His word. But Martha was distracted with all her preparations; and she came up to Him and said, "Lord, do You not care that my sister has left me to do all the serving alone? Then tell her to help me." But the Lord answered and said to her, "Martha, Martha, you are worried and bothered about so many things; but only one thing is necessary, for Mary has chosen the good part, which shall not be taken away from her."
> —*LUKE 10:39-42*

Christ's tender adjustment to Martha's priorities is a gentler version of His rebuke to Ephesus. The prophet gift can be so focused on making sure everything aligns with the intention of God's Word (light) that it forgets the motivation of God's Word (love). Jesus warned Ephesus that if they didn't return to that primary motivation, He would remove their lampstand out of its place. We'll talk about what that means in a second, but first, notice again how this echoes the Mary and Martha story: "Mary has chosen the good part, which shall not be taken away from her" (Luke 10:42). In other words, Mary's lampstand will not be removed.

Mary wanted to sit at the feet of Jesus and listen to His Word. She was doing the right thing at the right time from the right motivation, and Jesus would not allow the blessing that was flowing to her from that alignment to be impacted by Martha's anxiety.

Martha was also doing the right thing—sacrificial service is right—but her timing and motivation were off. She was worried and bothered about everything except the one thing that was necessary in that particular moment. All of her sacrificial service, while an accurate reflection of Christ's nature as the seed of the Word of God, would amount to nothing if it flowed out of a sense of duty, or as a means to obtain legitimacy, rather than originating from a passionate love for Him.

Martha was also doing the right thing—sacrificial service is right—but her timing and motivation were off. She was worried and bothered about everything except the one thing that was necessary in that particular moment.

Jesus took on the form of a bondservant and endured a sacrificial lifestyle because His ultimate goal was to bring forth a Bride with whom He could share and multiply His glory. His motivation was love for His creation, so love MUST be the origin of everything we do.

When Christ called Ephesus to repent, "or else I am coming to you and will remove your lampstand out of its place" (Revelation 2:5), He wasn't threatening them with spiritual death, judgment, or apostasy. Removing their lampstand didn't mean removing them as part of His Body. He was warning Ephesus that they would miss the good part. If they didn't return to their first love, sit at His feet, and listen to His word like Mary, they would miss the transformational qualities of His Unveiling. They would miss the divine life hidden in the coming trials and wildernesses intended to elevate them to shine into the world's darkness.

## THE PROPHET REWARD

What reward did Jesus promise to the overcomers in Ephesus? Or what is the specific joy that Christ has set before the prophet portion of our spirit to help us endure the wilderness struggles of our transformation?

> He who has an ear, let him hear what the Spirit says to the churches. To him who overcomes, **I will grant to eat of the tree of life which is in the Paradise of God.**
> —*REVELATION 2:7*

The right to eat from the tree of life in the Paradise of God is a fitting reward for those who return to their first love. Consider what Paul said about Eve, who was a type of the Bride, just as Adam was a type of Christ:

> For I am jealous for you with a godly jealousy; for I betrothed you to one husband, so that to Christ I might present you as a pure virgin. But I am afraid that, as the serpent deceived Eve by his craftiness, your minds will be led astray from the simplicity and purity of devotion to Christ.
> —*2 CORINTHIANS 11:2-3*

Eve believed the serpent's lies that she was inadequate and that God was holding back what she needed for wholeness and fulfillment. She ate the fruit from the tree of the knowledge of good and evil because she thought it would give her the information necessary to fulfill her calling. In truth, God always intended for Adam and Eve to gain knowledge of good and evil. He just didn't want them gaining it instantly from the fruit of a tree. He wanted them to acquire it gradually, in intimate communion with Him, as they worked out their calling to bring the divine beauty and order of paradise into the rest of the untamed world. In other words, He wanted them to gain knowledge through a process that would also grow them in the wisdom of His character.

When Eve reached for the forbidden fruit, she was short-circuiting that process by reaching for an alternate source of legitimacy. In other words, she was associating her value and worth with her ability to be right and do the right things. Very much like the church in Ephesus. She was cutting God out of the process, not because she didn't love Him—after all, she was led astray from *the simplicity and purity* of devotion to God, not from devotion itself. In other words, she no longer fully trusted that

> God always intended for Adam and Eve to gain knowledge of good and evil. He just didn't want them gaining it instantly from the fruit of a tree. He wanted them to acquire it gradually, in intimate communion with Him, as they worked out their calling ...

the simplicity of His way would result in her wholeness and fulfillment. Again, very much like Ephesus ... and Martha ... who were more worried about getting the job done through hard work and cleverness than simply sitting at Christ's feet to learn the motivations of His heart. Which, ironically, would have made them more effective doers.

Because Adam and Eve reached for that shortcut, they were cast out of Eden and forced to toil on the untamed earth without having access to learn from God's template for paradise. And when they lost access to Eden, they also lost the best, simplest, purest place for intimacy with their Creator, where they were meant to learn of His heart without distraction. In other words, they were forced to rely on the supposed shortcut they had chosen. And, of course, they lost access to the tree of life:

> So He drove the man out; and at the east of the garden of Eden He stationed the cherubim and the flaming sword which turned every direction to guard the way to the tree of life.
> —GENESIS 3:24

We'll talk more about the tree of life in a later chapter. For now, let's just say that Ephesus's reward for returning to their first love will be the restoration of mankind's original birthright—to walk in the paradise of God where they have access to simple, pure, undistracted intimacy with Christ. There they will eat the fruit of His wisdom and learn the principles of His divine nature, like Mary rather than like Martha.

In a figurative sense, the principles of this promise are an ever-present reward available in smaller measure for us today. When the prophet portion of our spirit turns to the face of Christ in this area, we can receive pure, unadulterated revelation from God from a position of relationship, rather than the mixture we often get from the tree of knowledge of good and evil. But in the end, the ultimate, literal manifestation of this reward won't be fulfilled until the Church has walked through her final wilderness and entered the millennial reign of Christ.

## THE BRIDAL RESPONSE

This is a good time to check our compass and begin layering in the Bride's response as recorded in the Song of Solomon.

To set the stage and establish the appropriate atmosphere, imagine the corporate Body of Christ as a betrothed woman sitting alone in her bedroom at a vanity. You can also imagine yourself as the betrothed woman. She has just received a stunning letter from Her beloved—the King of the Universe—which now lies open on her desk. The King is coming soon to take her to the marriage banquet, and there are seven things He has asked her to do to renew her commitment and prepare for His arrival.

The implications are immense—she must make herself ready, not just for the splendor of His coming, but also for their eternity of life together. The insurmountable gap between the woman she sees in the mirror and the glorious Bride He expects is almost overwhelming. But the King's grace is more overwhelming, for He has pinpointed her every insecurity with tender empathy. His words reach beyond her self-imposed limits into the deepest desires of her heart, inviting her to become more than she thought possible in ways that excite and energize her imagination.

Caught up in the afterglow of His words, she stares into the mirror, imagining how she might greet Him when He arrives. Suddenly, a well of emotions bubbles up in response, and her heartsong breaks the silence with an audible chorus of anticipation:

> May he kiss me with the kisses of his mouth!
>
> For your love is better than wine.
>
> Your oils have a pleasing fragrance,
>
> Your name is like purified oil;
>
> Therefore the maidens love you.
>
> Draw me after you and let us run together!
>
> The king has brought me into his chambers.
> —*SONG OF SOLOMON 1:2-4*

Seven responses to match the seven letters. Seven statements from the Bride answering the Bridegroom's invitation to prepare. Seven ways

43

the Bride accepts the call. Seven times she looks into His eyes to accept the prerequisites of His Unveiling. All seven portions of her spirit saying yes to His proposal! We'll come back to each of these seven responses, looking at each one in turn as we move through Christ's seven letters.

## THE PROPHET RESPONSE

How did the Bride specifically respond to Christ's letter to Ephesus? You know, the letter that recognized her hard work and commitment to the righteousness of His Word while rebuking her for straying from the purest motivation of love?

> May he kiss me with the kisses of his mouth!
> —*SONG OF SOLOMON 1:2*

She has heard and accepted His rebuke so humbly and fully that her response is a desire to kiss the very mouth of Him who spoke such a direct, difficult, and challenging correction. And notice that she extolled the kisses *of his mouth*. It's a rather strange statement. What other kinds of kisses are there? This redundant description is more than just superfluous poetic language. She had previously focused on the truth of His words and the power of what came out of His mouth. But now her focus was the love that motivated those words, which she finally saw as kisses proceeding from His mouth. In other words, she was ready to return to her first love!

# CHAPTER 5

# CHRIST'S SEVEN LETTERS:
# TO SMYRNA

Jesus wasted no time moving from His letter to Ephesus straight into His letter to Smyrna. Let's do the same:

> And to the angel of the church in Smyrna write:
> The first and the last, who was dead, and has come to life, says this:
> 'I know your tribulation and your poverty (but you are rich), and the blasphemy by those who say they are Jews and are not, but are a synagogue of Satan. Do not fear what you are about to suffer. Behold, the devil is about to cast some of you into prison, so that you will be tested, and you will have tribulation for ten days. Be faithful until death, and I will give you the crown of life. He who has an ear, let him hear what the Spirit says to the churches. He who overcomes will not be hurt by the second death.'
> —*REVELATION 2:8-11*

The letter to the angel of the church in Smyrna is an exhortation to the servant portion of the human spirit. In other words, it beckons to the part of our spirit that was made to align with the Spirit of Wisdom so that our spirit can receive from that aspect of God's character. As our spirit reflects that color of God's light into our soul and body, we become more like Jesus in that area. And then we can shine that aspect of Christ back out to the world.

In the fractal of seven, the Spirit of Wisdom and the servant redemptive gift are all about creating hospitable environments for life to thrive. Just as God took the primordial waters (that He had previously embued with His life on day one) and separated them on day two into the spiritual realm (the waters above) and the physical realm (the waters below), so does the servant gift use the light and love of God to make safe spaces for others to fulfill their God-given purpose. And just as the atmosphere surrounding Earth is delicately tuned, and every variable of Earth's unique position within the solar system is perfectly calibrated, the servant has the divine wisdom to sense the details of what others need to thrive. And the servant finds their greatest fulfillment in filling that gap.

So how did Christ introduce Himself to Smyrna? What did He want them to know about Himself before encouraging and correcting their behavior to position them for His Unveiling? "The first and the last, who was dead, and has come to life, says this ...."

Jesus is the first and the last. He is the source and destination of the universe. The essence of what was and what will be. Everything came from Him, and everything will be summed up in Him:

> that in the dispensation of the fullness of the times He might gather together in one all things in Christ, both which are in heaven and which are on earth—in Him.
> —*Ephesians 1:10, NKJV*

During the Genesis creation, the waters were separated into heavenly and earthly realms by a middle layer called the expanse (or firmament in the KJV). This was a foreshadowing of Christ—the middle member of the Trinity—who currently bridges the gap between us and the throne room of God.

In the new creation Christ won't just bridge the gap; He will reverse it by gathering all of heaven and earth together *in Himself.* That means the entire universe will eventually conform to the character, nature, and essence of the resurrected Christ, in whose body the physical and spiritual have already merged. Christ's new creation body represents the pinnacle of God's intention for the universe.

Again, in the same sense that we are already seated with Christ in heavenly places (see Ephesians 2:6), the bringing together of all things in Christ is a present spiritual reality that we have the legal right to leverage through faith. At the same time, there remains an ultimate fulfillment that will transpire in us during the resurrection and then through us during His millennial reign.

> The entire universe will eventually conform to the character, nature, and essence of the resurrected Christ, in whose body the physical and spiritual have already merged.

We'll talk more about this later, but the millennial reign of Christ will unfold in a pattern that mirrors the Genesis creation story. Mirrors, as in, reverse order. During that season, Christ and His Bride will bring the principles of the new creation to bear on the universe in reverse order of the original creation story. The Kingdom age will commence with the principles of the seventh-day rest, and it will culminate when Christ, the Word of God, having summed everything up in Himself, hands the perfected universe back to His Father so that God can be all in all. Again, the mirror image of the first day when God sowed Himself into creation, planting His essence, His Son, into the universe. But I'm getting ahead of myself. Back to Smyrna …

Not only is Jesus the first and the last, but He also introduced himself to Smyrna as the One who was dead and has come to life. These two titles are related. It is only because Jesus died and rose again that He is the first and the last—the One who started it all and represents where it is all going. Remember the principle of the seed? He is the grain of wheat that went into the ground, so His essence will be present in every subsequent fruit. In other words, the power of His self-sacrificial love will bring all of creation together to reach the pinnacle of its purpose.

That is how Christ frames His exhortation to the Smyrna-part of our being (and of His Body) because that is the aspect of His character that especially empowers the servant portion of our spirit to overcome and shine His light into the darkness.

## SMYRNA ENCOURAGED

After the introduction, Jesus celebrated how Smyrna already reflected the nature of the Spirit of Wisdom. Unlike Ephesus, there was no direct rebuke or correction for Smyrna, but there was a warning:

> I know your tribulation and your poverty (but you are rich), and the blasphemy by those who say they are Jews and are not, but are a synagogue of Satan. Do not fear what you are about to suffer. Behold, the devil is about to cast some of you into prison, so that you will be tested, and you will have tribulation for ten days. Be faithful until death, and I will give you the crown of life.
> —*REVELATION 2:9-10*

Tribulation and poverty. Religious persecution and gaslighting by wolves in sheep's clothing. Christ mentions these things as though they are badges of honor to be commended. Indeed, this entire letter has similar themes to the opening of the book of James:

> Consider it all joy, my brethren, when you encounter various trials, knowing that the testing of your faith produces endurance. And let endurance have its perfect result, so that you may be perfect and complete, lacking in nothing.
> —*JAMES 1:2-4*

> But the brother of humble circumstances is to glory in his high position ...
> —*JAMES 1:9*

> Blessed is a man who perseveres under trial; for once he has been approved, **he will receive the crown of life** which the Lord has promised to those who love Him.
> —*JAMES 1:12*

One of the underlying themes of Christ's letter to Smyrna is endurance. They were already well acquainted with suffering. Indeed, the redemptive gift of servant often voluntarily places itself in positions of suffering to help others. They represent the aspect of Christ's nature that lays down its life to create hospitable environments for creation to encounter God. Their sacrifices soften, till, and enrich the soil of our hearts in advance so we can receive the seed of His Word when it comes.

In the servant's posture of selflessness, trials often come in earnest, especially from those who seek selfish gain. When speaking to Smyrna, Jesus called these opportunists "those who say they are Jews and are not, but are a synagogue of Satan" (Revelation 2:9). The inference was that Smyrna's present and future tribulations would be the direct antagonism of these blasphemers.

## A SATANIC SYNAGOGUE?

So who was this synagogue of Satan? Despite the ominous title, Jesus was likely not referencing satanists, pagans, or heathens. He was talking about those who claimed to worship God but inwardly were ravenous wolves who leveraged a pretense of godliness to enrich and aggrandize themselves at the cost of the sheep.

Let's review a few other passages to build a profile of these so-called Jews, and notice the common themes of their deception. They exemplify the opposite of the servant's heart, and that puts them in direct opposition to those who sacrificially serve out of a desire to connect others to God:

> [A group of Jews who had earlier believed Christ's words] answered and said to Him, "Abraham is our father."
>
> Jesus said to them, "If you are Abraham's children, do the deeds of Abraham. But as it is, you are seeking to kill Me, a man who has told you the truth, which I heard from God; this Abraham did not do. You are doing the deeds of your father."
>
> They said to Him, "We were not born of fornication; we have one Father: God."
>
> Jesus said to them, "If God were your Father, you would love Me, for I proceeded forth and have come from God, for I have not even come on My own initiative, but He sent Me. Why do you not understand what I am saying?

It is because you cannot hear My word. **You are of your father the devil, and you want to do the desires of your father.** He was a murderer from the beginning, and does not stand in the truth because there is no truth in him. Whenever he speaks a lie, he speaks from his own nature, for he is a liar and the father of lies."
—*JOHN 8:39-44*


Beware of the dogs, beware of the evil workers, **beware of the false circumcision**; for we are the true circumcision, who worship in the Spirit of God and glory in Christ Jesus and put no confidence in the flesh …

Brethren, join in following my example, and observe those who walk according to the pattern you have in us. For many walk, of whom I often told you, and now tell you even weeping, that they are enemies of the cross of Christ, whose end is destruction, **whose god is their appetite**, and whose glory is in their shame, **who set their minds on earthly things.**
—*PHILIPPIANS 3:2-3; 17-19*


If anyone advocates a different doctrine and does not agree with sound words, those of our Lord Jesus Christ, and with the doctrine conforming to godliness, he is conceited and understands nothing; but he has a morbid interest in controversial questions and disputes about words, out of which arise envy, strife, abusive language, evil suspicions, and constant friction between men of depraved mind and deprived of the truth, **who suppose that godliness is a means of gain**.

But godliness actually is a means of great gain when accompanied by contentment. For we have brought nothing into the world, so we cannot take anything out of it either. If we have food and covering, with these we shall be content. But those who want to get rich fall into temptation and a snare and many foolish and harmful desires which plunge men into ruin and destruction. For the love of money is a root of all sorts of evil, and some by longing for it have wandered away from the faith and pierced themselves with many griefs.
—*1 TIMOTHY 6:3-10*

Are you getting a clearer picture of what Jesus meant by those who say they are Jews and are not, but are a synagogue of Satan? It was the same spirit that caused the Jewish leaders to murder Christ to maintain their power and influence. It was the same spirit that fought against the servant nature of Christ in the early church. It was the same testing Jesus warned would come upon Smyrna in greater measure:

> Behold, the devil is about to cast some of you into prison, so that you will be tested, and you will have tribulation for ten days. Be faithful until death, and I will give you the crown of life.
> —*REVELATION 2:10*

Now take everything Christ mentioned to the servant church of Smyrna as a whole: tribulation, poverty, persecution, suffering, prison, testing, and even possible death. Ouch, that's some heavy stuff! But these things are a requirement for the greatest authority in the kingdom of God. And they stand in stark contrast to the "godliness is a means of gain" crowd from the synagogue of Satan. That is why Christ's promise to Smyrna, the suffering servant, was the crown of life. A crown speaks of authority, prestige, and position.

Think about the time when James and John asked Jesus, "Grant that we may sit, one on Your right and one on Your left, in Your glory" (Mark 10:37). They were seeking authority, prestige, and position. Basically, they were acting an awful lot like the "godliness is gain" crowd. What was Christ's response?

> But Jesus answered, "You do not know what you are asking. Are you able to drink the cup that I am about to drink?"
> —*MATTHEW 20:22*

"The cup that I am about to drink." In other words, the cup of His suffering. The cup of wine that represented His blood poured out as an offering. Jesus drank every last drop of that bitter torment because of the reward that awaited Him on the other side, which was to sit down at the right hand of the throne of God (see Hebrews 12:2). The cup of Christ speaks to the prerequisites for gaining authority, but it also defines the godly exercise of that authority, as He later expounded:

> Calling them to Himself, Jesus said to them, "You know
> that those who are recognized as rulers of the Gentiles lord
> it over them; and their great men exercise authority over
> them. But it is not this way among you, but whoever wishes
> to become great among you shall be your servant; and
> whoever wishes to be first among you shall be slave of all.
> For even the Son of Man did not come to be served, but to
> serve, and to give His life a ransom for many."
> —MARK 10:42-45

Only the servant who has laid down their life for others can be trusted with eternal authority, including authority over death itself—because the servant will not use that authority for selfish gain or subjugation of others. The servant will only use authority to continue serving and giving more life.

We don't selflessly serve in this life only to practice the lord-it-over-others kind of authority in the next. The exercise of authority in godly leadership always looks like service. That won't change in the kingdom age, and that is why only those who have selflessly suffered with perseverance—those who drink the cup that Christ drank—are entrusted with His authority.

Moreover, the true servant heart of Christ isn't just about filling every need. The servant portion of our spirit is meant to be enlightened by the Spirit of Wisdom. When we reflect that aspect of Jesus, we won't just haphazardly try to fill every external need around us. Instead, we'll perceive when a need should be filled to help connect someone to God and when a need should be left as an opportunity for personal growth.

Like those finely tuned variables that support life on earth, it takes wisdom to understand which specific environmental factors in a given situation or arena are necessary for life to thrive as God intends. That's another reason why the servant church of Smyrna is offered divine authority: their tribulations are meant to instill the wisdom of synchronizing their service with God's character and design.

> We don't selflessly serve in this life only to practice the lord-it-over-others kind of authority in the next. The exercise of authority in godly leadership always looks like service. That won't change in the kingdom age …

## THE SERVANT REWARD

What reward did Jesus promise to the overcomers in Smyrna who embraced the Unveiling of Him who is the first and the last, who was dead, and has come to life?

> He who has an ear, let him hear what the Spirit says to the churches. He who overcomes will not be hurt by the second death.
> —*REVELATION 2:11*

"He who overcomes will not be hurt by the second death." This promise is repeated later in Revelation, where it is associated with the first resurrection and the reward of authority with Christ during His millennial reign:

> Blessed and holy is the one who has a part in the first resurrection; over these the second death has no power, but they will be priests of God and of Christ and will reign with Him for a thousand years.
> —*REVELATION 20:6*

We'll talk more about the second death when we get to Revelation chapter 20. For now, just know that the second death is the lake of fire (see Revelation 20:14). The judgment of the second death happens after the one-thousand-year reign of Christ, and the last enemy to be thrown into the lake of fire will be death itself (see Revelation 20:14 and 1 Corinthians 15:26). But those who accept the invitation written to the angel of the church in Smyrna—those who turn the servant portion of their spirit to the face of Christ and embrace and overcome the trials and tribulations inherent in that aspect of His Unveiling—they will participate in the first resurrection and gain full authority over death.

## THE SERVANT'S RESPONSE

So what was the Bride's response to this bittersweet offer of tribulation and suffering? Gazing into the mirror with introspective reverie, she found but one reply to harmonize with her Bridegroom's harrowing invitation:

> For your love is better than wine.
> —SONG OF SOLOMON 1:2

Your love is better than wine! That is to say, "Yes, Lord Jesus, I will embrace the tribulation and testing of your cup if it means I can inherit the crown of life with You! For Your love is better than all of that! Your eternal affection is worth every sip of temporary bitterness infusing the wine of a sacrificial life."

We know she didn't say this lightly or from naiveté. Unlike James and John, the sons of thunder, who didn't understand the prerequisites for kingdom authority, let alone the godly exercise of it, the Bride had already suffered greatly and knew something of its cost. And so she turned her heart to the face of Christ in this area too, willing even to taste death in her pursuit of His Unveiling.

## CHAPTER 6

# CHRIST'S SEVEN LETTERS: TO PERGAMUM

B y now you know the steps, so let's keep the same rhythm going as we move quickly into Christ's third letter:

And to the angel of the church in Pergamum write:
The One who has the sharp two-edged sword says this:
'I know where you dwell, where Satan's throne is; and you hold fast My name, and did not deny My faith even in the days of Antipas, My witness, My faithful one, who was killed among you, where Satan dwells. But I have a few things against you, because you have there some who hold the teaching of Balaam, who kept teaching Balak to put a stumbling block before the sons of Israel, to eat things sacrificed to idols and to commit acts of immorality. So you also have some who in the same way hold the teaching of the Nicolaitans. Therefore repent; or else I am coming to you quickly, and I will make war against them with the sword of My mouth. He who has an ear, let him hear what

the Spirit says to the churches. To him who overcomes, to him I will give some of the hidden manna, and I will give him a white stone, and a new name written on the stone which no one knows but he who receives it.'
—*REVELATION 2:12-17*

The letter to the angel of the church in Pergamum is an exhortation to the teacher portion of the human spirit. It beckons to the part of our spirit that was made to align with the Spirit of Understanding. As our spirit reflects that color of God's light into our soul and body, we become more like Jesus in that area. And then we start to shine that aspect of Christ back out to the world.

In the fractal of seven, the Spirit of Understanding and the teacher redemptive gift are all about taking that which is ethereal, raw, and conceptual and converting them into practical, substantive resources that support life. As was demonstrated on the third day of creation, they use a deep understanding of God's character—and the principles that flow from that character—to bring the life of God to bear in new and exciting ways that are both the foundation (earth) and food (vegetation) for more complex and glorious forms of life.

## THE INTRODUCTION

So, how did Jesus introduce Himself to Pergamum? "The One who has the sharp two-edged sword says this ..."

The sharp two-edged sword. We saw this two-edged sword coming from the mouth of Christ back in Revelation 1:16 when He first appeared among the lampstands. In Revelation chapter 19 we'll see the same sword again when Christ returns to judge and wage war in righteousness. We need more context before unpacking that passage, so we'll save it for a future chapter. For now, we just need to know a few things about the sword to help us better understand Christ's letter to Pergamum.

Firstly, many Bible verses make it clear that the sword is the Word of God. No surprise there. Yet the Word of God is also called a seed, a light, a lamp, and a mirror, among other things. Why a sword here? Why introduce Himself to Pergamum as the wielder of an instrument of cutting, judgment, and war?

The writer of Hebrews sheds more light:

> For **the word of God is living and active and sharper than any two-edged sword**, and piercing as far as the division of soul and spirit, of both joints and marrow, and **able to judge the thoughts and intentions of the heart**. And there is no creature hidden from His sight, but all things are open and laid bare to the eyes of Him with whom we have to do.
> —*HEBREWS 4:12-13*

This entire passage revolves around the ability of the Word of God to judge righteously. He doesn't judge based on outward appearances. His Word exposes the deep things that are below the surface. It uncovers the heart of the matter. It reveals the root. Nothing is hidden from His sight.

Righteous judgment requires an unchanging righteous standard against which all things are consistently measured. Jesus is that righteous standard. The principles of His character were sewn (and sown) into the fabric of reality at the dawn of creation and then fully revealed and proven in the incarnated Christ. He will measure everything against Himself when He returns because everything was designed to come into alignment with Him. The sword of His Word will first expose and then judge the heart of all things against the principles of His character. We'll see exactly what that means and how He does that later in this series.

> The principles of His character were sewn (and sown) into the fabric of reality at the dawn of creation and then fully revealed and proven in the incarnated Christ. He will measure everything against Himself when He returns because everything was designed to come into alignment with Him.

For now, there is one more thing we need to see about the two-edged sword. We're not going to read it here, but the fuller context of Hebrews chapter 4 is an exhortation to enter the rest of God. It reminds us that a generation of Israelites failed to enter the rest of the promised land during the time of Moses. They escaped Egypt by God's miraculous hand, and they observed

His wonders time and again in the wilderness. Still, they mistrusted Him, so they misplaced their faith and rebelled against His command to enter Canaan when they heard that there were giants in the land (see Numbers 14). As a result of their cowardice and disobedience, God caused Israel to wander in the wilderness for forty years until that entire rebellious generation had died out. The writer of Hebrews described God's response to Israel's rebellion by quoting the Psalmist:

> Do not harden your hearts, as at Meribah,
> As in the day of Massah in the wilderness,
> When your fathers tested Me,
> They tried Me, though they had seen My work.
> For forty years I loathed that generation,
> And said they are a people who err in their heart,
> And they do not know My ways.
> Therefore I swore in My anger,
> Truly they shall not enter into My rest.
> —PSALM 95:8-11

The whole cautionary tale of Israel's rebellion is relevant to our journey through the Unveiling, but at this early stage, we just need to see it as the sober context into which Hebrews introduces the idea of the two-edged sword of the Word of God:

> So there remains a Sabbath rest for the people of God. For the one who has entered His rest has himself also rested from his works, as God did from His. Therefore let us be diligent to enter that rest, so that no one will fall, through following the same example of disobedience. For **the word of God is living and active and sharper than any two-edged sword** ...
> —HEBREWS 4:9-12

My point is this: When God swore in His anger that they would not enter into His rest, He was exercising the sword of His Word. The righteous judgments enacted by the sharp two-edged sword always separate between those who enter His rest and those who do not. Or they reveal how much we have entered His rest versus how much we are relying on our own works. In this particular case, God was judging a rebellious generation that saw His works yet refused to trust Him because they could not understand His ways.

Obviously, God's rest is no longer tied to the land of Canaan. Today we enter His rest in a spiritual sense by becoming one with Christ, not through the power of our own works but by the virtue of His. And God grades on a curve. The more we see His works, the more responsibility we have to understand and trust His heart, and then the deeper we can enter into His rest. Ultimately, the sabbath rest of God will be fulfilled in the millennial reign of Christ, but we'll discuss that aspect in later chapters, particularly in the context of the mercy portion of our spirit.

Still, God designed the teacher gift to play an important role in discerning and providing nourishment for the areas in our hearts where a misunderstanding of His character keeps us from His rest. The teacher gift works with the Spirit of Understanding to reveal the heart of God behind the works of God. And that is why Christ's introduction to Pergamum calls attention to the righteous judgments of His two-edged sword. Those judgments are designed to reveal the deepest secrets of our hearts so that we can align with His heart.

## PERGAMUM EXAMINED

After that incredible preface, Jesus says this about Pergamum:

> I know where you dwell, where Satan's throne is; and you hold fast My name, and did not deny My faith even in the days of Antipas, My witness, My faithful one, who was killed among you, where Satan dwells.
> —*REVELATION 2:13*

History records no specific mention of Satan's throne in the ancient city of Pergamum. Some scholars suggest it may have referenced a particular grove in Pergamum containing a cluster of Greek and Roman temples where idolatrous worship resulted in prolific abominations. Others point to the fact that Pergamum was a judicial center where judgments of persecution were often pronounced against Christians. Perhaps Satan's throne was some combination of both. We can only speculate about the exact source of the historical reference, but the spiritual significance is easier to discern from the context of Christ's Words.

Whatever else is meant, if you live in a city with Satan's throne, where Satan's authority is unencumbered, you can expect all of the city's systems to be twisted around Satan's desire to deceive, dominate, and oppress rather than to serve, protect, and empower. And you can expect those systems to coordinate attacks against anything that reflects the divine nature of Christ.

That's where the Pergamum church lived. And yet they still held fast to the name of Jesus and did not deny their faith, even after witnessing one of their brethren (Anitipas) being martyred for his faith. Again, history tells us nothing about Antipas, but the point is still clear: the enemy applied intense pressure against the believers in Pergamum to forsake their faith, and yet they stood strong.

Their courageous response to the very real threat of persecution stands in stark contrast to the Israelites in the wilderness who cowered at the mere report of giants and foreign armies in the land of Canaan. Those Israelites saw opposition as evidence that God could not be trusted. But like a well-planted oak, the redemptive gift of teacher has a more grounded understanding of God's character. And they are especially passionate about standing against injustice. Where others might be intimidated and dismayed after witnessing fierce persecution—especially the martyrdom of a friend (Antipas)—the teacher's reaction is often righteous indignation and holy defiance. And so Pergamum held fast and did not deny the faith.

That's a good response, but Christ was looking for more. He didn't place them near Satan's throne just so they could survive by the skin of their teeth, barely holding on to what they already knew of Him. He intended the adversity to drive their roots deeper. He wanted them to lean into the trials and learn more about His ways through the pressure. He wanted them to thrive and produce fruit that would strengthen the faith of others.

## PERGAMUM CORRECTED

> But I have a few things against you, because you have there some who hold the teaching of Balaam, who kept teaching Balak to put a stumbling block before the sons of Israel, to eat things sacrificed to idols and to commit acts of im-

> morality. So you also have some who in the same way hold
> the teaching of the Nicolaitans.
> —*REVELATION 2:14-15*

Christ's rebuke of Pergamum? Some of their members held to the teaching of Balaam, who, we are told, taught Balak how to bait the men of Israel into eating things sacrificed to idols and committing acts of immorality. There is also mention of some following the similar teaching of the Nicolaitans, which we'll discuss in a moment.

The story of Balaam is told in Numbers chapters 22 through 25, with a follow-up in Numbers 31. It happened at the end of Israel's forty-year wilderness wandering and shortly before they crossed the Jordan River to begin their conquest of the promised land. Israel was a vast host at that point, and they had just defeated the Amorites on their way to the plains of Moab where they would camp for a time before crossing the Jordan River. They were on the cusp of finally entering the promised land when Balak (king of Moab) hired Balaam (a pagan soothsayer) to curse Israel. Balak thought that by cursing Israel, his armies might defeat them in battle before they could overrun his land and continue into Canaan.

As the events unfolded, God warned Balaam not to curse Israel, but Balaam was more persuaded by Balak's offer of wealth and favor. As Balaam traveled to meet Balak, the Angel of the Lord appeared with a sword (yes, there's the sword again) and another warning. Balaam's donkey spoke, more shenanigans ensued, and in the end, every time Balaam attempted to curse Israel, the Lord turned his words into a blessing. Finally, Balaam gave up and returned home unsuccessful and empty-handed.

Where others might be intimidated and dismayed after witnessing fierce persecution—especially the martyrdom of a friend (Antipas)—the teacher's reaction is often righteous indignation and holy defiance.

It's a bizarre story, but unfortunately for Israel, that's not the last we hear of Balaam. He must have really wanted that payday, because after failing to curse Israel, Balaam concocted a more devious Plan B for Balak. If God wouldn't let him curse Israel, perhaps he could get Israel to sin so grievously that God would either remove His protective covering or destroy Israel Himself.

Balaam's plan was simple and effective. He instructed Balak to tempt the sons of Israel into sexual immorality with the daughters of Moab and Midian. Once the Israelites took the bait, the foreign woman convinced them to attend their pagan festivals, bow to their false gods, eat the food sacrificed to their idols, and participate in all manner of pagan debauchery.

The scheme almost worked. God was so furious at Israel's sin that He sent a plague that would have wiped out the sons of Israel, if not for a faithful priest named Phinehas, the grandson of Aaron. Phinehas appropriately expressed God's jealousy by thrusting a spear through one of Israel's chief idolaters who had brazenly trotted a Midianite princess through the middle of the camp while the rest of the congregation was crying out to God for mercy. The courage and zeal of Phinehas satisfied God's wrath and ended the plague.

## CONTEMPORARY BALAAM

Okay, that's the backstory. What does all of that have to do with the teacher church of Pergamum and the teacher portion of the human spirit? To get the full meaning, remember what we learned about the sharp two-edged sword: it reveals the deep things of the heart, and it determines who or what can enter the rest of God. It shows us the areas of our hearts that have yet to understand and trust in Christ.

Unlike the rebellious generation of Israelites who couldn't enter the promised land, Pergamum held fast to what they understood of Christ's nature. And like the new generation of Israelites standing on the cusp of the promised land after the older generation died out, Pergamum stood fast in the face of the enemy's bombastic threats. Every attempted curse only strengthened them. Even the power of the throne of Satan couldn't destroy them from without. So the enemy resorted to the underhanded trickery of Balaam to attack them from within.

We know this secondary attack was at least partially successful because some small subset of the Pergamum church began teaching others to embrace sexual immorality and idolatry. These false teachers and false prophets in their midst were motivated by greed, just as was Balaam (see 2 Peter 2:15), and we can assume that the promise of wealth and influence originated from the tangle of twisted systems built around Satan's throne.

As for the Nicolaitans, scholars say they were a heretical sect of gnostic Christians in the early church who believed that a Christian's freedom set them above the requirements of any moral law. The Nicolaitans viewed the profession of faith as everything and placed no significance on the acts of the body or the attitudes of the soul. They accepted the practice of all manner of moral and sexual debauchery because, to them, these things had no eternal significance. As a side note, this grievous error is alive and growing in the Body of Christ today, stoked by leaders who have embraced the teachings of Balaam in order to gain influence and wealth from world systems.

Some scholars point to the fact that the name Nicholas, from which Nicolaitans is derived, was merely the Greek equivalent of Balaam, both of which mean "destroyer of the people." In any case, the Nicolaitans were those who became entrapped in the false doctrines perpetuated by those who followed Balaam's way. Think of the Nicolaitan mindset as similar to the Israelite man who brazenly flaunted his adultery with the Midianite princess in front of the Israelite camp while the rest of the nation was crying out to God for mercy. In the context of Christ's letter to Pergamum, that means they were Christians who unapologetically ate food sacrificed to idols and committed brazen acts of immorality.

## ANCIENT EVIL REPACKAGED

The evil of such brazen immorality is self-explanatory, but what does it mean to eat food sacrificed to idols? First, consider that the ancient Levitical priests were required to eat food sacrificed to Yahweh as part of their duties under the Mosaic Law. The exact rules varied depending on the specific type of sacrifice, but, in many cases, a portion of the animal was burned on the altar as a pleasing fragrance to the Lord while another portion of the same sacrifice was given to the priest to be cooked and eaten—often in a celebration with his family—in the court of the tabernacle.

Now compare that to God's prohibition against eating foods sacrificed to idols. In ancient days, people sacrificed animals (and sometimes humans) on the altars of false gods in vain attempts to gain favor or avert wrath. They were offering something of value—a living thing that represented an investment of their time, energy, and money—in exchange for comfort, wealth, protection, or whatever else they thought they could get from their false god. After a portion of the sacrifice was burned on a pagan altar, some of the more radical devotees would then celebrate together by eating some of the remaining meat, often in vile ceremonies involving sexual abominations.

In God's eyes, for them to eat the food they had already consecrated to a pagan deity was to brazenly double down on their sin. Idol worship was bad enough, but to then openly celebrate that defilement, and to derive nourishment and strength from that wickedness by consuming the meat of the sacrifice? To essentially assume the role of a priest for the false god while encouraging others to defile themselves? That was an abomination requiring judgment from the sharp two-edged sword.

That's all quite terrible, but not many people still sacrifice animals to idols of wood and stone today. How does this apply to us in the twenty-first century?

Today, our culture worships idols of fame, wealth, comfort, entertainment, and just about anything else we think can bring us fulfillment. We may not build physical idols of wood and stone, and we may not slaughter animals, but we often sacrifice more valuable things like time and energy and morality and marriages and children and our god-given birthrights on the altar in pursuit of blessing from these false gods.

Sometimes we follow after our idols in ignorance or to fit in with the culture simply because we haven't yet seen the aspect of the nature of Christ that truly fulfills that desire in our hearts. In that case, God is patient to offer us a better way. But to brazenly celebrate our idolatry as good? To embrace immorality in pursuit of our idols and to twist God's nature by proselytizing others to do the same? That kind of rebellion leads to God's wrath.

> We may not build physical idols of wood and stone, and we may not slaughter animals, but we often sacrifice more valuable things like time and energy and morality and marriages and children and our god-given birthrights …

## PERGAMUM'S CHALLENGE

So what was Christ's requirement of Pergamum in light of the deception they had allowed to fester in their camp? How did He call them to overcome the darkness in their midst?

> Therefore repent; or else I am coming to you quickly, and I will make war against them with the sword of My mouth.
> —*REVELATION 2:16*

Do you see how this again ties back to Israel in the wilderness? Jesus was basically calling for Pergamum to respond with the courage and zeal of Phinehas, who ruthlessly killed a pair of brazen adulterers to avert God's wrath in the wilderness. Obviously, I'm not saying Jesus was calling for physical violence against the human offenders in Pergamum. Remember the apostle Paul's exhortation:

> For our struggle is not against flesh and blood, but against the rulers, against the powers, against the world forces of this darkness, against the spiritual forces of wickedness in the heavenly places.
> —*EPHESIANS 6:12*

Likewise, Jesus was calling Pergamum to war against the spiritual forces that were holding their brothers and sisters in bondage using the principles of new covenant spiritual warfare:

> We are destroying speculations and every lofty thing raised up against the knowledge of God, and we are taking every thought captive to the obedience of Christ ...
> —*2 CORINTHIANS 10:5*

This can be a difficult challenge for the teacher portion of our spirit, because the teacher is, by nature, understanding. It sees the deep things, the pain, and the injustices that drive people into the embrace of false gods. And since the teacher gift is also grounded in God's nature, it has the patience to minister to the wounded and to help them see Christ more clearly. But if the teacher's understanding and patience become an inappropriate toleration of the teachings of Balaam or the Nicolaitans, then divine rebuke is needed to avoid the wrath of God.

Just in case there is any doubt about God's perspective on the Nicolaitans, remember how He commended the church in Ephesus:

> Yet this you do have, that you hate the deeds of the Nicolaitans, which I also hate.
> —REVELATION 2:6

God hates *the deeds* of the Nicolaitans, not the Nicolaitans themselves. The prophet portion of our spirit (based on the letter to the church in Ephesus) has no problem boldly calling good, good, and evil, evil. That is a legitimate expression of God's heart, though the challenge for the prophet is to be centered in love when speaking the truth. On the other hand, the teacher gift adds a balancing perspective of reconciliation, though their challenge is to maintain the courage and zeal of Phinehas even when it risks offending others.

Notice that Christ told Pergamum to repent or "I will make war against them." War against *them*, not work against *you*. The majority of Pergamum did not participate in the teachings of Balaam nor the deeds of the Nicolaitans, but the silence of the many enabled the sin of the few. It only takes a little leaven to leaven the whole loaf (see Galatians 5:9). So Jesus called the whole group to repent for not confronting the error, but the judgment of the sword was reserved for the smaller portion of idolaters if they didn't repent.

The teacher's deep empathy born from understanding and patience gave Pergamum a divine authority to correct and heal the twisting of God's nature, but only if they were courageous enough to confront the sin. If they failed to do so, they would leave the idolaters at risk of being forever excluded from God's rest when Christ returned with the two-edged sword in His mouth to judge the nations. Like a priest who stands in the gap between God and man, the teacher gift plays an im-

> The teacher's deep empathy born from understanding and patience gave Pergamum a divine authority to correct and heal the twisting of God's nature, but only if they were courageous enough to confront the sin.

portant role in reconciling all things to Christ, but they must fully embrace both sides of His sword to do so—the side that reveals to us the deep things of His nature and the side that judges that which does not align with Him. They must embrace both the kindness and the severity of God.

## THE TEACHER'S REWARD

What reward did Jesus promise to those in Pergamum who overcame the throne of Satan and the defilements they had tolerated in the Church by embracing the Unveiling of the One who has the sharp two-edged sword?

> He who has an ear, let him hear what the Spirit says to the churches. To him who overcomes, to him I will give some of the hidden manna, and I will give him a white stone, and a new name written on the stone which no one knows but he who receives it.
> —*REVELATION 2:17*

"Hidden manna" and a "white stone." So there were two rewards for the teacher church of Pergamum because there were two different parties with different issues to overcome. One reward was for the faithful of Pergamum who needed to repent for not confronting the defilement in their midst, and another reward was for the defilers if they turned from their wicked ways. More on that in a moment.

Commentators have long speculated about the exact meaning of these two rewards. Some suggest that the hidden manna and the white stone referred to two ancient Jewish temple artifacts. From that perspective, the hidden manna could be a reference to the golden jar of manna that was placed either inside or next to the ark of the covenant (see Exodus 16:33-34 and Hebrews 9:4), and the white stone could be a reference to the Urim and Thummim stones worn in a pouch at the breast of the Jewish high priest. These viewpoints have merit. However, the Bible doesn't provide much detail on the mysterious Urim and Thummim, and the testimony of Jewish tradition and historical accounts are complex and leave too much open to speculation, so we'll save that rabbit trail for another time.

Instead, I think we can approach a reasonable interpretation simply by looking at the context of everything else Jesus said to Pergamum.

## THE HIDDEN MANNA

Manna was bread from heaven. We know the original manna was a divine gift to sustain the Israelites during their forty-year wilderness wanderings. We know that fresh manna appeared every morning (except on the sabbath) and it needed to be gathered and used daily or it would spoil. The Israelites literally lived hand-to-mouth, dependent every day on God's Word:

> He humbled you and let you be hungry, and fed you with manna which you did not know, nor did your fathers know, that He might make you understand that man does not live by bread alone, but man lives by everything that proceeds out of the mouth of the LORD.
> —*DEUTERONOMY 8:3*

We also know that Jesus called Himself the living bread that comes out of heaven and gives life to the world (see John 6:32-35). So when He offers some of the hidden manna, He is offering to show us things about Himself that have never before been understood. Things that were always true but never illuminated. Such a promise is particularly poignant for the teacher portion of our spirit, which thrives on extracting the nutrients hidden deep in the soil to produce life-giving fruit for themselves and others.

It is fascinating that in the same passage where Jesus revealed Himself to be the fulfillment of the Old Testament sign of the manna, He went on to extend the metaphor in a very challenging and controversial way. This also happens to be a counterpoint to the sin of eating food sacrificed to idols:

> So Jesus said to them, "Truly, truly, I say to you, unless you eat the flesh of the Son of Man and drink His blood, you have no life in yourselves. He who eats My flesh and drinks My blood has eternal life, and I will raise him up on the last day. For My flesh is true food, and My blood is true drink.

> He who eats My flesh and drinks My blood abides in Me,
> and I in him. As the living Father sent Me, and I live be-
> cause of the Father, so he who eats Me, he also will live be-
> cause of Me. This is the bread which came down out of
> heaven; not as the fathers ate and died; he who eats this
> bread will live forever."
> —*JOHN 6:53-58*

This is an example of Jesus revealing some hidden manna about Himself to His disciples, and doing so with unapologetic boldness, knowing exactly how it would be perceived by those with worldly minds who couldn't perceive the things of the spirit. In other words, He was using the sharp two-edged sword of His mouth. Indeed, many of His disciples were so offended that they stopped following Him at that point. His words cut them to the quick and exposed those who were only there for selfish gain. The hidden manna isn't meant for the lazy and self-centered. It is meant for those who desire to produce life-giving fruit from the deepest principles of the Word.

## THE WHITE STONE

What about the white stone with a new and secret name written on it? Again, it's hard to say for sure what this means, and commentators have offered many viable options over the centuries. In the interest of time, I'll just expound on one that fits well into the overall context of Pergamum and leave the rest for you to investigate on your own, if you so desire.

In ancient Roman courts of law, a white stone was sometimes presented to a defendant when they received a verdict of innocence. The white stone represented the absolution of their guilt. Considering that Pergamum was a center for judicial proceedings, it's possible that this custom was well-known to the Christians in that city.

In the same way, when Jesus offered them a white stone with a new name written on it, perhaps He was offering complete pardon and newness of life to those who had practiced the abominations of Balaam and the Nicolaitans. Their destiny would no longer be tied to those defiled names. The stone was His righteousness imputed to them.

The new name written on the stone could represent the wiping out of their old reputation, the receiving of a new way of life, and the new destiny that would bring them complete fulfillment. Or, the new name could refer to Christ's new name, which He would reveal only to them, similar to the hidden manna. Either way, a secret new name is, again, a most appropriate reward for the teacher gift.

## DO NOT JUDGE?

It is important to recognize what all of this means for those in the Body of Christ who teach or intentionally practice immorality, because there are many in that precarious position in the Church today. All manner of twisted perversions are belching out of the mouth of Satan's throne into the world today. God's original intention for the pure beauty and blessing of sexual intimacy between one man and one woman united in marriage is under savage attack from every angle. We are called to stand firm against such overt outward attack against Christ's nature.

Unfortunately, some Christians have begun to embrace and even preach acceptance of these abominations. Whether they do this out of pressure to avoid persecution, a desire to gain influence and wealth from the world systems, or simply because the injustices of life have twisted their view of God's nature, the letter to Pergamum is clear about the responsibility of the Church.

Notice that Jesus didn't rebuke the idolaters in Pergamum directly. He rebuked the rest of the faithful whose silence had enabled the sin to perpetuate among their fellow believers. If the silent enablers would embrace the two-edged sword of the Word, then they would learn what they were missing about Christ's nature, and then they could effectively confront, correct, and heal the others. Or at least they could present the truth in love, whether or not it was received. But the point is, the silent faithful hadn't done that yet, so Christ was withholding judgment, even against the followers of Balaam and the Nicolaitans.

This same thing is happening in the Church today, empowered by a foolish and ignorant doctrine claiming that Jesus commanded us not to judge. This "do not judge" idea, which was the very attitude Christ was rebuking in Pergamum, is derived from one Bible verse taken out of context:

**Do not judge so that you will not be judged**. For in the way you judge, you will be judged; and by your standard of measure, it will be measured to you. Why do you look at the speck that is in your brother's eye, but do not notice the log that is in your own eye? Or how can you say to your brother, 'Let me take the speck out of your eye,' and behold, the log is in your own eye?
—*MATTHEW 7:1-4*

Jesus wasn't commanding us not to judge in this passage. It is not Christ-like love to blindly accept everyone as they are and leave the judging to God. He was commanding us to be careful *how* we judge. If our judgments are unrighteous, *then* we should not judge, because we will also be judged for judging unrighteously. But the full intent of Christ's words is revealed in the next verse:

You hypocrite, first take the log out of your own eye, and then you will see clearly to take the speck out of your brother's eye.
—*MATTHEW 7:5*

The whole point is that we are supposed to remove the log from own eye so that we can help our brother remove his speck. In other words, we need to embrace the two-edged sword in our own hearts, because then we can see Jesus more clearly, and only then can we help others do the same.

That also means we must understand the kindness and severity of God before we can judge righteously. And make no mistake, it is more akin to cowardice than compassion when we know the Truth but refuse to mention the speck in our brother's eye because we don't want to offend.

> This "do not judge" idea, which was the very attitude Christ was rebuking in Pergamum, is derived from one Bible verse taken out of context.

Jesus did not judge the idolaters of Pergamum. He commanded the faithful to do the judging, but only with compassion and understanding, so He wouldn't have to strike them down with the eternal judgment of His sword. If the teacher portion of our spirit doesn't take up that responsibility now before Christ returns, how can we be trusted to judge righteously in the age to come:

> Do you not know that we will judge angels? How much
> more matters of this life?
> —*1 CORINTHIANS 6:3*

Judging righteously is not the same as being judgmental. Neither does it give us license to be intolerant and argumentative about non-essential doctrines. We should always look to preserve the unity of the Spirit in the bonds of peace (see Ephesians 4:3), and a gentle and humble heart are core characteristics of Christ (see Matthew 11:29). But the kinds of brazen wickedness and twisting of God's nature described in the letter to Pergamum cannot be ignored. That's why the teacher portion of our spirit, in partnership with the Spirit of Understanding, is tasked with confronting wickedness inside the Body.

## THE TEACHER'S RESPONSE

So what was the Bride's response to the challenge of her Bridegroom's rebuke? How would she answer the One who had allowed her to bear the temporary injustices issuing from Satan's throne while asking her to dig deeper for courage and understanding to push back against its defiling influences?

Would she rise to the occasion, taking responsibility for confronting the immorality and, if possible, save her brethren from judgment? Would she see the deeper reason behind her trials? Would she unpack from them a deeper understanding of Christ's nature to heal the wounded and defiled among her? Would she embrace the sharp two-edged sword?

As she weighed all these things in her heart, she found herself empathizing with those disciples who walked away after Jesus' difficult words about the bread of His body. But then a more powerful emotion reverberated in her soul as she remembered Peter's response:

> So Jesus said to the twelve, "You do not want to go away
> also, do you?"

> Simon Peter answered Him, "Lord, to whom shall we
> go? You have words of eternal life. We have believed and
> have come to know that You are the Holy One of God."
> —*JOHN 6:67-69*

"You have words of eternal life," she repeated to herself, and, somewhere in the utterance, a deeper response was unlocked in her spirit. Timid and soft at first, hiding in the corners and shadows of her thoughts, an esoteric phrase of poetry and passion grew as it navigated a labyrinth of emotions to find its escape from her lips:

> Your oils have a pleasing fragrance …
> —*SONG OF SOLOMON 1:2*

"A pleasing fragrance." It's a phrase used dozens of times throughout the Old Testament to describe offerings that God received as holy and acceptable. It's not that He enjoyed the smell of burning animal flesh or charred grains, but He loved the heart of worship and the humble spirit behind these symbolic acts. In truth, every acceptable offering in the Old Testament was merely a foreshadowing of Christ's perfect sacrifice, and that's why they were pleasing fragrances to God. Jesus is the pleasing fragrance, and when we reflect His character—particularly His sacrificial love—we smell just like Him:

> Therefore be imitators of God, as beloved children; and
> walk in love, just as Christ also loved you and gave Himself
> up for us, an offering and a sacrifice to God as a fragrant
> aroma.
> —*EPHESIANS 5:1-2*

So why did the Bride respond with, "Your oils have a pleasing fragrance?" Because, she was beginning to see a deeper beauty in Christ's sacrificial lifestyle, and she recognized that her circumstances were opportunities to act like her Beloved and fellowship with Him in His sufferings. And she finally saw that the selfish idolatry and immorality that she had tolerated for so long was the opposite of Christ's pleasing fragrance. It was a stench to her Beloved. She was ready to apply her newfound understanding of His nature as a sword to bring illumination, correction, and hopefully healing to those who were standing on the precipice of judgment:

> But thanks be to God, who always leads us in triumph in Christ, and manifests through us the sweet aroma of the knowledge of Him in every place. For we are a fragrance of Christ to God among those who are being saved and among those who are perishing; to the one an aroma from death to death, to the other an aroma from life to life. And who is adequate for these things?
> —2 CORINTHIANS 2:14-16

To manifest His sweet aroma, regardless of how it would be received, would be no easy mission. To risk scorn and rejection by presenting both edges of the sword of His Word would be its own kind of sacrifice. Would they smell the fragrance of life that draws them toward Christ into greater life? Or the stench of death that repels them away from Him into greater death?

And what if she got the presentation wrong? What if she did not relay His Words perfectly, or somehow misrepresented His heart? Was she really adequate to brandish the sharp edges upon which others must chose life or death? No, she knew that she was not. But her Beloved was a pleasing fragrance! He was adequate! And He would give her the Spirit of Understanding when it was needed for the task!

## CHAPTER 7

# CHRIST'S SEVEN LETTERS:
# TO THYATIRA, PART 1 - SHE NEEDS TIME

If the letter to Pergamum was heavy, Christ's message to Thyatira only increases the intensity. This one will take extra time to navigate, so we'll break it into two chapters. The slower pace will help us fully savor its ramifications and absorb what the Bridegroom is saying:

> And to the angel of the church in Thyatira write:
> The Son of God, who has eyes like a flame of fire, and His feet are like burnished bronze, says this:
> 'I know your deeds, and your love and faith and service and perseverance, and that your deeds of late are greater than at first. But I have this against you, that you tolerate the woman Jezebel, who calls herself a prophetess, and she teaches and leads My bond-servants astray so that they commit acts of immorality and eat things sacrificed to idols. I gave her time to repent, and she does not want to repent of her immorality.

'Behold, I will throw her on a bed of sickness, and those who commit adultery with her into great tribulation, unless they repent of her deeds. And I will kill her children with pestilence, and all the churches will know that I am He who searches the minds and hearts; and I will give to each one of you according to your deeds.

'But I say to you, the rest who are in Thyatira, who do not hold this teaching, who have not known the deep things of Satan, as they call them—I place no other burden on you. Nevertheless what you have, hold fast until I come. He who overcomes, and he who keeps My deeds until the end, TO HIM I WILL GIVE AUTHORITY OVER THE NATIONS; AND HE SHALL RULE THEM WITH A ROD OF IRON, AS THE VESSELS OF THE POTTER ARE BROKEN TO PIECES, as I also have received authority from My Father; and I will give him the morning star. He who has an ear, let him hear what the Spirit says to the churches.'
—*REVELATION 2:18-29*

The letter to the angel of the church in Thyatira is an exhortation to the exhorter portion of the human spirit. It beckons to the part of our spirit that was made to align with the Spirit of Counsel. As our spirit reflects that color of God's light into our soul and body, we become more like Jesus in that area. And then we start to shine that aspect of Christ back out to the world.

In the fractal of seven, the Spirit of Counsel and the exhorter redemptive gift are all about making known the invisible attributes and purposes of God. In other words, declaring the divine nature to creation. Shining heaven to earth.

Whereas the teacher gift is more inwardly focused on unpacking the nature of God from physical creation, the exhorter gift is more outwardly focused on helping creation see aspects of God's divine nature, purposes, and timing that we couldn't otherwise decipher from the physical realm. It shows us how to see the divine nature in the face of Christ, to understand reality through that light, and to declare that reality into the world around us.

## THE INTRODUCTION

How did Jesus introduce Himself to Thyatira? "The Son of God, who has eyes like a flame of fire, and His feet are like burnished bronze, says this …."

So, it starts with Christ pointing to His own Sonship. Remember, a son does the will of the Father. Not just as an immature child being led around by the hand, but as one who has submitted to the Father's discipline through the trials of life. He understands the Father's heart and is therefore trusted to exercise creative initiative wherever specific instructions are not given.

There are two aspects of His Sonship that Jesus wanted Thyatira to focus on. First, His eyes. Christ's eyes are a flame of fire because His Spirit was fully illuminated when the Spirit descended on Him like a dove and He heard the Father's love and pleasure after His baptism. As a result, His eyes receive and give light, just like the seven lamps and eyes of the seven Spirits of God. He sees all reality, and He helps all see reality through Him. He is the source of the light of God, and He provides that light to us.

Likewise, if we stare into Christ's eyes and come to understand the depth of God's love for us through Him, we'll also begin to receive our identity and legitimacy from the Father's love. Our spirit will become entrained with His over time, and we'll begin to see reality through His eyes.

As the Son of God, Jesus also has feet like burnished bronze. Earlier, John described it this way:

> His feet were like burnished bronze, **when it has been made to glow in a furnace** …
> —*REVELATION 1:15*

Some translations describe it as bronze refined in a furnace. Others say polished brass. Both bronze and brass are copper alloys with different secondary metals. Either way, the idea is a spotless metal refined in the fire, strengthened through forging, and still glowing brightly. Again, this attribute is tied to His earthly Sonship and harmonizes with other Scriptures:

> So then, brethren, we are under obligation, not to the flesh, to live according to the flesh—for if you are living according to the flesh, you must die; but if by the Spirit you are putting to death the deeds of the body, you will live. For all who are being led by the Spirit of God, these are sons of God.
> —*ROMANS 8:12-14*

To have feet refined in the fire speaks of the purified walk of Sonship and the earned authority that the Son takes with Him because He has submitted to the refining process and proven that He knows the Father's heart. Feet become refined in the fire by walking through the wilderness. This was true of Jesus, and it is true for us. Maybe that's why God chose a pillar of fire to guide the children of Israel through their wilderness at night during their forty-year wandering, signifying that He was walking before them.

Notice that no sandals are mentioned on the burnished feet of Christ. This suggests that He was barefoot in the presence of God, like Moses at the burning bush and the High Priest in the holy of holies. Only, in this case, Christ's feet are the holiness that brings the presence of God and the message of His authority wherever He goes:

> To have feet refined in the fire speaks of the purified walk of Sonship and the earned authority that the Son takes with Him because He has submitted to the refining process ...

> How lovely on the mountains are the feet of him who brings good news, who announces peace and brings good news of happiness, who announces salvation, and says to Zion, "Your God reigns!"
> —*ISAIAH 52:7*

## THYATIRA EXAMINED

So what did the Son of God see when He examined the exhorter church of Thyatira?

> I know your deeds, and your love and faith and service and
> perseverance, and that your deeds of late are greater than
> at first. But I have this against you, that you tolerate the
> woman Jezebel ...
> —*REVELATION 2:19-20*

> But I say to you, the rest who are in Thyatira, who do not
> hold this teaching, who have not known the deep things of
> Satan, as they call them—I place no other burden on you.
> Nevertheless what you have, hold fast until I come.
> —*REVELATION 2:24-25*

We'll talk about Jezebel in a moment. First, notice the positive
points: Thyatira performed good deeds, exercised love and faith, and
they served. They also responded to difficulty with perseverance and
even greater deeds. Similar in some ways to Pergamum, their only issue
was tolerance of a particular evil. But unlike Pergamum, Jesus did not
hold the rest of the church in Thyatira accountable for the sins of those
who followed the teachings of Jezebel. Why the difference? Why hold
the teacher church responsible for the few who followed the teachings of
Balaam and the Nicolaitans but not hold the exhorter church responsible for those who followed the teachings of Jezebel? Hold on to that
question, and we'll come back to it shortly.

## TIME TO REPENT

I'd prefer not to talk about Jezebel at all because the subject has been
overdone and misappropriated in many Christian circles. But Jezebel is
a major component of the letter to Thyatira, so we'd be foolish to ignore
it. More importantly, the subject provides a good contrast to help highlight certain attributes of Christ. So as we move through this section of
the path let's try to be like those faithful Thyatirans who Jesus commended for not knowing "the deep things of Satan."

Before we go there, I want to make it abundantly clear that although the original Jezebel in the Old Testament was a woman, when
we talk about Jezebel now, as Christ did in Revelation, the spiritual application does not favor one physical gender over the other. Yes, Jesus
did refer to "the woman Jezebel," but I suggest that is because the influence of Jezebel attacks our ability to receive from God directly, and re-

ceiving from God is a spiritually female function. Personally, the most destructive expressions of Jezebel I've seen in the church were perpetrated by male leaders. But I digress.

Also, I am going to resist the temptation to refer to this as the Jezebel spirit. Some streams of Christianity use that term aggressively, but I don't care for how it dehumanizes those who are under its influence and obfuscates the process they need to embrace for freedom. Is Jezebel a spirit? Maybe. Was the original Jezebel (whom we'll talk about in a moment) influenced by evil spirits? Definitely. But saying someone has a Jezebel spirit conjures images of possession, or at least of demons sitting on people's shoulders—as if it's something we can cast out or vanquish like Ghostbusters.

I see Jezebel as more of a pattern of behavior and a mindset, born out of deep-seated, often generational legitimacy issues and misconceptions about God's nature. Dark spiritual forces may be involved in orchestrating the circumstances and feeding the lies that foster the misconceptions, but Jezebel isn't removed without the revelation of the true nature of Christ first invading and rebuilding the mind:

> For the weapons of our warfare are not carnal but mighty in God for pulling down strongholds, casting down arguments and every high thing that exalts itself against the knowledge of God, bringing every thought into captivity to the obedience of Christ ...
> —2 CORINTHIANS 10:4-5, NKJV

> For we wrestle not against flesh and blood, but against principalities, against powers, against the rulers of the darkness of this world, against spiritual wickedness in high places.
> —EPHESIANS 6:12, KJV

Some enemies need to be wrestled with, not just cast out with a word. The arguments and misconceptions and lofty philosophies that empower their evil must be systematically dismantled and replaced with the Truth before the stronghold can be overthrown. And that means more than mere words. That means our words must match our reality. If we want our words to carry the authority to dislodge Jezebel, they must flow from an authentic, experiential knowledge of Christ in the specific area of His character that the stronghold has twisted.

Nothing about the process is instant. That's why Jesus gave Jezebel "time to repent" (Revelation 2:21). And that's why we're going to spend some time talking about Jezebel. Our goal is to see what aspect of Christ is being twisted so we can lean into Jesus in that area. As a byproduct, we'll also gain the authority to dislodge Jezebel whenever Christ leads us into contact with her mindset—if we're willing to wrestle.

## TEACHINGS OF JEZEBEL

Any discussion of Jezebel should probably start with Ahab. Ahab was king of the northern ten tribes of Israel about fifty-five years after the reign of Solomon. In those days, the twelve tribes of Israel were already divided into two kingdoms as divine judgment for Solomon's idolatry. The ten northern tribes were ruled from Jezreel by the King of Israel, and the two southern tribes of Judah and Benjamin were ruled from Jerusalem by the King of Judah.

It is important to note that when God first divided the nation into two kingdoms after Solomon's death, King Jeroboam, the very first king of the northern tribes, committed a heinous sin (see 1 Kings 12). Even though God had established his Kingship, Jeroboam worried that the people would forsake him for the King of Judah if they continued worshiping at the illustrious temple in Jerusalem. So, out of fear of losing his kingdom (and probably his life), he established an alternative form of worship for the northern tribes. He set up golden calves and counterfeit altars in two different cities under the false pretense of providing a closer location and more easily accessible form of Jehovah-worship. As a result of this great sin, Jeroboam and his entire lineage inherited God's wrath.

When Ahab became king of northern Israel many years later, he continued these practices of Jeroboam, likely for the same cowardly reasons. So Ahab was already a bad dude before he married Jezebel. It was Ahab's cowardice, his fear of losing his wealth and influence, and his willingness to compromise morally to avoid those things that opened the door to Jezebel.

Now enter Jezebel. The original Jezebel was the daughter of Ethbaal, king of the Sidonians (see 1 Kings 16:31). According to extra-biblical history, Ethbaal was a priest of Ashtoreth (the ancient Phoenician goddess of fertility, sexual love, and war) who murdered his brother to become king. Ethbaal clearly passed the same demonic fanaticism on to his daughter, Jezebel.

Jezebel means *without cohabitation*, and she was appropriately named. Her soul was utterly twisted around a perverse generational devotion to false ideologies supporting a false reality, and she used a combination of overt violence, blustery threats, and underhanded deception to force everyone around her to embrace her perspective or die. She was the ultimate bully. There was no compromise with Jezebel. No room for anything else. No cohabitation.

Under her influence, Ahab built graven images of Ashtoreth (a female false diety) for worship, and also built temples to Baal (a male false deity), defiling Israel's ability to receive from and give to Jehovah. Jezebel also directly oversaw the hunting and slaughtering of the true prophets of God, and she established an order of false prophets through whom she could control the narrative of truth and further twist Israel's perception of reality.

In every way, Jezebel was an illustration of the spiritual warning spoken by Christ:

> But if your eye is bad, your whole body will be full of darkness. If then the light that is in you is darkness, how great is the darkness!
> —MATTHEW 6:23

I've seen some Christian leaders hurl the name of Jezebel around like an axe against strong-willed people (often against women) who don't quickly fall in line with their leadership. But so-called resistance to leadership was not Jezebel's thing. Jezebel was *in* leadership. She used her position to consolidate power and conform everyone to her version of truth, not because she was greedy or even power-hungry, but because she was rabidly convinced she was right, and she needed to be right to feel legitimate. She left no room for differences or

So-called resistance to leadership was not Jezebel's thing. Jezebel was *in* leadership. She used her position to consolidate power and conform everyone to her version of truth ...

uniqueness. That's why she called herself a prophetess and silenced all other voices she couldn't control.

## SAME SONG, DIFFERENT SIREN, DIFFERENT AUDIENCE

Compare the way Christ described Balaam's teachings with how He described Jezebel's teachings:

> who kept teaching Balak to put a stumbling block before the sons of Israel, to eat things sacrificed to idols and to commit acts of immorality.
> —*REVELATION 2:14*

> and she teaches and leads My bond-servants astray so that they commit acts of immorality and eat things sacrificed to idols.
> —*REVELATION 2:20*

So Balaam and Jezebel were similar but not exactly the same. Both of their teachings revolved around eating things sacrificed to idols and committing acts of immorality, but there are some key differences.

Balaam taught Balak, a heathen king, how to tempt the people of God. And, as we know, Balaam was just a pagan soothsayer for hire, motivated only by selfish gain. Neither he nor Balak directly infiltrated Israel, nor did they claim to be anything they weren't. Balak simply used his resources to put obvious stumbling blocks in front of the people of God, and the people willingly stumbled.

Remember, that same principle was at work in Pergamum through Satan's throne. The people weren't forced or even tricked into the deeds of the Nicolaitans—they freely chose to follow that twisted ideology because they wanted to. They were immature Christians who hadn't yet learned a better way. That's why Christ challenged the rest of the church of Pergamum to stand in the gap for their brethren, to teach them the truth of God's character, and to help them overcome the darkness.

Jezebel, on the other hand, was queen of Israel. She was in a position of authority over the people of God and had direct influence with the king. She forced her will upon others. She didn't just place passive stumbling blocks in front of God's people; she threatened them with death if they didn't obey. Moreover, she not only passed her abusive philosophies off as righteous leadership but, in that place of authority, claimed the office of prophetess, giving her words greater influence in the minds of those who leaned on her for legitimacy.

Notice that in Thyatira, Jezebel directly pursued the bondservants of God. Unlike Balaam, whose teachings indirectly targeted the spiritually weak (outer court Christians), Jezebel sought to corrupt the sincere of heart who had wholly committed themselves to Christ and His house (inner court Christians). She probably leveraged the promise of learning the deep things of God, though they were actually the deep things of Satan. Or perhaps she simply bullied well-meaning, sincere believers who had not yet grown strong in their identity as sons of God through the wildernesses of life. In either case, it says, "she teaches and leads My bond-servants astray so that they commit acts of immorality and eat things sacrificed to idols" (Revelation 2:20). First, the bondservants submit to Jezebel's authority, and only then, under her tutelage, are they corrupted morally, becoming adulterers with her.

Jezebel's moral corruption is the natural result of staring at an idol that doesn't reflect the true nature of Christ. When we submit to leaders who use any form of fear, gaslighting, or intimidation to manipulate, bully, or control, we are submitting to Jezebel and opening ourselves up to her corruption. When we live for the approval of another person, or derive our legitimacy from leaders who stand between us and hearing directly from God ourselves, we are submitting to Jezebel and are no longer receiving from Christ. And in that place, our perception of reality gets twisted around Jezebel's worldview.

So Jezebel's initial attack is against our ability to receive (our female role as the Bride), but her ultimate goal was to keep the people of God from walking in sonship. Again, sonship has nothing to do with physical gender—it's all about the freedom of an individual to be led by the Spirit in doing the will of the Father. Sonship looks like creative and industrious initiative from

> When we live for the approval of another person, or derive our legitimacy from leaders who stand between us and hearing directly from God ourselves, we are submitting to Jezebel and are no longer receiving from Christ.

men, women, and children who know the Father's heart and are prepared to embrace the pain of the wilderness—that is, the Father's discipline—as they use their gifts to increase the influence of Christ's authority.

In other words, sonship looks like Christ's feet of burnished bronze, as alluded to in Isaiah 52:7: "How lovely on the mountains are the feet of him who brings good news ...." It's not about increasing the authority of the institutional Church, or the size and influence of its leadership system; that's more in line with what Jezebel tries to do.

Sonship and the institutional Church system are not mutually exclusive, but sonship rarely expresses itself in religiously predictable or acceptable frames. It is simply God's children intentionally advancing the impact of the kingdom of God by reflecting the nature of Christ in whatever arena of life they are in.

Jezebel is threatened by sonship because it challenges her sense of legitimacy, which she derives from being the only one who hears from God for others. That's why she calls herself a prophetess and demands that everything be done her way. But Christians who walk in sonship like Jesus don't need permission or activation from anyone else. Instead, they are energized by the reality that they are beloved and pleasing to the Father.

That's not to say that they are rebels who cannot learn from, partner with, or work within established authority structures, but they don't derive their legitimacy from any human system. They are free to do as they feel led and unafraid of messing up or getting it wrong (which are common accusations from Jezebel) because they know the Father's heart.

## WHO IS CULPABLE?

Christ's letter to Thyatira doesn't explicitly state that Jezebel had a place of leadership in the church. However, it does say that she "teaches and leads My bond-servants astray" (Revelation 2:20). Teaching and leading are typically functions of church leadership, and based on the biblical pattern of the original Jezebel, I think it is a safe assumption. It also explains Jesus' challenge to Thyatira:

> But I say to you, the rest who are in Thyatira, who do not
> hold this teaching, who have not known the deep things of
> Satan, as they call them— I place no other burden on you.
> —REVELATION 2:24

Like Ahab, Thyatira's leaders had tolerated Jezebel. They had succumbed to the same cowardice and misdirected sense of legitimacy, allowing her philosophy to gain some level of influence over them. Not every leader was squashing sonship like Jezebel, but some were, and the others were either afraid to confront it or happy to benefit from its strength. That's why, on the one hand, Christ said, "I have this against you, that you tolerate the woman Jezebel," while on the other hand, He said, "the rest ... who do not hold this teaching ... I place no other burden on you." The leaders who tolerated needed to repent, as did those who submitted to her authority and followed her perverse philosophy. But the rest of the church simply needed to hold fast to the Truth.

## JUSTICE FOR THE BULLY

> Behold, I will throw her on a bed of sickness, and those
> who commit adultery with her into great tribulation, unless
> they repent of her deeds. And I will kill her children with
> pestilence, and all the churches will know that I am He who
> searches the minds and hearts; and I will give to each one
> of you according to your deeds.
> —REVELATION 2:22-23

Jezebel's judgment is appropriate for her crimes. The one who tried to keep God's people from freely receiving from Christ and acting like Him would become bedridden and ineffective, dependent on others for the necessities of life. On the bed of sickness, she also inherited the natural consequences of her sexual immorality and perversion.

Notice that she did not receive eternal punishment but rather pain and reduced quality of life, which made her a public spectacle and a lesson to the rest of the church. There is mercy in that judgment because it gives her even more time to repent. However, given the pattern of her life, future repentance would be difficult.

Those who committed adultery with Jezebel—that is, those who tolerated her influence and benefited from her control— will experience "great tribulation." If you recall our discussion in book 1 about how the three parts of the Body of Christ will experience the great tribulation in different ways, this is a reference to the leaders in the institutional church who keep their people spiritually immature and disempowered:

> But woe to those who are pregnant and to those who are nursing babies in those days! But pray that your flight will not be in the winter, or on a Sabbath. For then there will be a great tribulation, such as has not occurred since the beginning of the world until now, nor ever will.
> —*MATTHEW 24:19-21*

In one sense the discipline of tribulation is true throughout history for those who tolerate Jezebel. Whenever the inevitable tragedies of life come—the natural disasters, the wars, the famines, and the diseases—they experience the full brunt of these things outside of the grace of God because they have not submitted to His preparatory disciplines in the wilderness.

But there is also an ultimate fulfillment of this judgment at the end of the age during the actual great tribulation. When the worldwide movement of the sons of God comes forth and the second half of the seventieth week begins, those in the Church who opposed the growth of sonship will have a much more difficult experience of the great tribulation. And because of their choices, they will risk missing out on the most transformational aspects of Christ's Unveiling during that time.

Do you see why Jesus introduced Himself to Thyatira as the Son of God? It's the specific aspect of Christ's nature that most effectively counters the influence of Jezebel. Especially the flaming eyes that receive and give the light of God directly, and the refined feet that boldly and effectively walk through the wilderness like a Son who knows His Father's heart. These attributes are particularly important for the exhorter portion of our human spirit and those members of the Body of Christ who are exhorters. The exhorter gift is designed to be an outwardly focused, verbally expressive, influential leader and light bearer—all things that Jezebel savagely opposes in others because they have been perversely distorted in her life.

Okay, that's enough about Jezebel. Hopefully, I've given you some general principles for recognizing her influence. At the same time, I've intentionally avoided over-explaining with explicit real-world examples or directives. I want you to have the freedom to figure out if and how this applies to you. If I tried to provide every little step and detailed characteristic according to my narrow understanding of how to overcome Jezebel, I'd only be infringing on the wonder and diversity of your journey. And I'd be teaching more like Jezebel than Christ. Notice that Jesus didn't provide step-by-step instructions for overcoming Jezebel. He simply pointed to attributes of His character that we should lean on, and then He challenged us to work it out. Exercising the perseverance and courage required to unpack those principles in our own lives is part of the refining process that produces authority over Jezebel.

The exhorter gift is designed to be an outwardly focused, verbally expressive, influential leader and light bearer—all things that Jezebel savagely opposes in others because they have been perversely distorted in her life.

# CHAPTER 8

# CHRIST'S SEVEN LETTERS:
# TO THYATIRA, PART 2 - WHAT'S IN A NAME?

W hat reward did Jesus promise for those who embraced the Unveiling of Christ as the Son of God and overcame the influence of Jezebel?

> He who overcomes, and he who keeps My deeds until the end, TO HIM I WILL GIVE AUTHORITY OVER THE NATIONS; AND HE SHALL RULE THEM WITH A ROD OF IRON, AS THE VESSELS OF THE POTTER ARE BROKEN TO PIECES, as I also have received authority from My Father; and I will give him the morning star.
> —*REVELATION 2:26-28*

First, notice the reward is for those who overcome and keep His deeds until the end. Yes, waiting on God and receiving from Him are necessities. Communing with Him and with His people in intimate worship is also beautiful. Resting in His finished work is the glorious goal. But the reward of Thyatira is for those who walk in sonship. It is for those who persevere in doing His deeds.

Sonship looks different for different people, and each redemptive gift manifests their sonship in slightly different ways. As we'll see in a moment, Thyatira's reward is especially poignant for the exhorter's expression of sonship. It is meant for the creative initiators, the light shiners, and the extroverted expressives who actively bring the message of kingdom peace and salvation to bear on Earth. Their sonship doesn't necessarily look like evangelism or religious proselytizing, but it is always an unashamed expression of Christ's character in word or action that illuminates the surrounding darkness.

## ROD OF IRON

To those overcoming exhorters, there are two rewards. The first is "authority over the nations," which includes a "rod of iron" for ruling and smashing. This promise comes directly from a famous messianic Psalm in which said authority was given to Christ. It was one of the clearest Old Testament articulations that the Messiah is also the Son of God:

> But as for Me, I have installed My King
> Upon Zion, My holy mountain.
> I will surely tell of the decree of the LORD:
> He said to Me, 'You are My Son,
> Today I have begotten You.
> Ask of Me, and I will surely give
> the nations as Your inheritance,
> And the very ends of the earth as Your possession.
> **You shall break them with a rod of iron,**
> **You shall shatter them like earthenware.**
> —PSALM 2:6-9

The context of Psalm 2 is all about the nations and their governments boasting of their intention to rebel against God and to redefine reality around something other than the divine principles of Christ's character. It was a very Jezebelian attitude.

God simply laughed in their faces. Their efforts are doomed to fail because Christ has already proven His character as the perfect Son reflecting the Father's heart. He has overcome every other lofty idea raised up against the knowledge of God.

For those who reflect Christ's Sonship—who overcome the defiling and overbearing leadership style of Jezebel, who submit to the refinement of the wilderness and learn to express the Father's heart in their actions—to those, Jesus will share His authority over the nations. As with many of these promises, there is a token measure of this authority available today and a mature expression available during the Unveiling. And then there will be an ultimate fulfillment during Christ's millennial reign.

> Sonship looks different for different people, and each redemptive gift manifests their sonship in slightly different ways.

Notice that the authority God promises is a breaking authority: "As the vessels of the potter are broken to pieces …" (Revelation 2:27). The authority is for shattering the nations like pottery. To get a better idea of what that means, consider this verse from Jeremiah:

> and say to them, 'Thus says the LORD of hosts, "Just so will I break this people and this city, even as one breaks a potter's vessel, **which cannot again be repaired** …"'
> —JEREMIAH 19:11

This passage is part of a larger prophecy where God announced His intention to judge Jerusalem and Judah for their idolatries and abominations. It is similar in purpose to the prophecy we discussed in book 1 about the seventy-year Babylonian captivity to give the land rest after 490 years of defilement. In the case of Jeremiah 19:11, God likened the destruction of the people and the city to the breaking of a potter's vessel. The implication was that Israel was His vessel, but in their formation process they had resisted the Potter's hands and become misshapen. And it was too late to simply add water and reform the clay. They were set in their ways, already fired through time and adversity and continual rebellion. As a result, He was about to smash the hardened vessel because it was useless and unsalvageable. And as God pointed out to Israel, when you smash pottery, it cannot be remade. There is no putting it back together.

The prophecy in Jeremiah 19:11 didn't mean He was severing His covenant with Israel. Their messianic promises remained, and God would eventually draw them back to their land. However, He was promising to destroy every ungodly thing the nation had built their society around, along with many godly things they had defiled in the process. Yes, some humans would die in the judgment, but many would not.

That is exactly what Christ will do with the nations when He returns. The Greek word for nations is *ethnos*, which can refer to tribes, ethnicities, cultures, countries, etc. *Ethnos* is as much about the common attributes that bind people groups together as it is about the physical boundaries of a country.

The point is that Christ will inspect the fabric of every nation and destroy every cultural bond built on principles that do not reflect His character. This has nothing to do with the level or type of religious observation in the nation. This is all about what aspects of their culture actually reflect the unshakable principles of Christ's character, whether it professes to be a Christian nation or not. At that time, how a culture has treated the poor, the orphan, the widow, and the needy will determine if and how their nation enters the millennial reign of Christ (see Matthew 25:31-46). In other words, did their society reflect the sacrificial love of God? Against that standard, some nations will be utterly broken to pieces, never to be reformed. Others will need less severe destruction. And some will be rewarded for their faithfulness.

We'll look at the details of that process later in this series. For now, we just need to see that those who embrace the refining journey of sonship will participate with Jesus in that breaking. They will be trusted with such authority because they are proven builders who have courageously invested their lives in spreading His light. They applied the leadership and influence of their exhorter gift in beautifully bold acts of sacrificial service like Christ, not to manipulate, control, or coerce like Jezebel. Not in pursuit of their own kingdoms but in support of His.

## THE MORNING STAR

There is a second reward for the overcomers in Thyatira:

> and I will give him the morning star.
> —*REVELATION 2:28*

Some scholars note that the planet Venus was known in the ancient world as the morning star because its seasonal shining was so beautiful and bright that it was still visible even in the waning moments of the night sky, like a herald of the coming dawn. Whatever the celestial identity of the morning star, the point remains: it was a harbinger of the day. When the morning star was the only light still shining in the sky, observers knew the night was almost over and the dawn was imminent. It was a sure thing. As reliable as the path of the stars.

Let's look at a few other references to the morning star in Scripture to help decode why this matters:

> I, Jesus, have sent My angel to testify to you these things for the churches. I am the root and the descendant of David, the bright morning star.
> —*REVELATION 22:16*

Jesus is the bright morning star, and He claims that title in the context of being the Messiah and the rightful heir to David's throne. So the morning star also has something to do with authority. Hold onto that idea, because we'll revisit it in a moment.

Here's another reference to the morning star with a similar messianic context:

> For when He received honor and glory from God the Father, such an utterance as this was made to Him by the Majestic Glory, "This is My beloved Son with whom I am well-pleased"—and we ourselves heard this utterance made from heaven when we were with Him on the holy mountain.
>
> So we have the prophetic word made more sure, to which you do well to pay attention as to a lamp shining in a dark place, **until the day dawns and the morning star arises in your hearts.**
> —*2 PETER 1:17-19*

Peter's words are fascinating here. The entire passage is placed in the context of his experience of the transfiguration of Christ. The book of Mark describes the whole event:

Six days later, Jesus took with Him Peter and James and John, and brought them up on a high mountain by themselves. And He was transfigured before them; and His garments became radiant and exceedingly white, as no launderer on earth can whiten them. Elijah appeared to them along with Moses; and they were talking with Jesus.

Peter said to Jesus, "Rabbi, it is good for us to be here; let us make three tabernacles, one for You, and one for Moses, and one for Elijah." For he did not know what to answer; for they became terrified.

Then a cloud formed, overshadowing them, and a voice came out of the cloud, "This is My beloved Son, listen to Him!" All at once they looked around and saw no one with them anymore, except Jesus alone.
—MARK 9:2-8

During the transfiguration, Christ's closest disciples beheld Him in a glorious form that represented the purest and fullest expression of His Sonship. This was before Jesus had completed His work, before His resurrection, and before His flesh had put on the immortality of His new creation body. The privileged disciples saw a token example—an earnest deposit on the promise of the new creation. Peter summarized the event as "the prophetic word made more sure." The law and the prophets had prophesied about the coming King and His coming kingdom, but at the transfiguration that prophetic word was made more sure with an undeniable preview of coming attractions.

Peter continued referencing the transfiguration when he said, "to which you do well to pay attention as to a lamp shining in a dark place, until the day dawns and the morning star arises in your hearts." Like a morning star, the transfiguration was a lamp shining in a dark place, heralding the coming of the dawn.

In one sense, you could say that Christ's transfiguration was the morning star of His resurrection body. It was a bright shining pointing to the coming fullness of glory that His body would eventually inherit. In that way, it is also the pattern for understanding how the morning star applies to His people at the end of the age.

"Until the day dawns and the morning star arises in your hearts." As we discussed in book 1, the day dawning refers to the process of Christ's Unveiling during the second half of the seventieth week, and it leads to the Day of the Lord and the millennial reign of Christ. Christ's Unveiling will cause the morning star to arise in our hearts *before* that full day. In other words, before the Day of the Lord. And it will cause His people alive on earth to look like Christ and act like Him as effective witnesses of the coming kingdom during the season immediately preceding the resurrection—before the rapture, if you are so inclined to use that term—when we finally put on immortality.

So part of Christ's promise to the overcomers in Thyatira about the morning star was that they would behold His Unveiling so clearly (like Peter, James, and John beheld the transfiguration) that they too would shine like stars in the darkness. Then the brightness of their shining as they reflected Christ's nature would herald the soon-coming kingdom of Christ in its fullness. Said another way, they would be part of the mature man-child of Revelation chapter 12—those sons of God who participate with Him in the Unveiling.

> Part of Christ's promise to the overcomers in Thyatira about the morning star was that they would behold His Unveiling so clearly (like Peter, James, and John beheld the transfiguration) that they too would shine like stars in darkness.

## AUTHORITY OVER WHAT?

There's another layer to the symbol of the morning star. It also speaks of authority because Christ called Himself the bright morning star in the context of being the root and descendent of David, which means the original purpose (root) for and the rightful heir (descendant) of David's throne. So what kind of authority are we talking about?

The morning star has a kind of authority over time. It is the herald of a new season. It appears right before the dawn and declares the dawn is coming. It is a faithful witness of what is to come. As the descendent of David who came many generations later in the fullness of time to do the Father's will and not His own, Christ is the bright morning star who takes the mystery of the Father's will for the times and seasons and shines it to earth.

Authority over the times and seasons is an appropriate reward for the exhorter gift. It was, after all, on the fourth day that God set the lights in the heavens to govern the day and the night, to separate light from darkness, and to "be for signs and for seasons and for days and years" (see Genesis 1:14-19).

## OTHER MORNING STARS?

I would be remiss not to mention another occurrence of morning stars in Scripture. This one appears as part of a breathtaking challenge God spoke to Job. Dripping with divine sarcasm and esoteric knowledge, this epic attitude adjustment effectively brought Job back from the brink of despair and defiance:

> Where were you when I laid the foundation of the earth?
> Tell Me, if you have understanding,
> Who set its measurements? Since you know.
> Or who stretched the line on it?
> On what were its bases sunk?
> Or who laid its cornerstone,
> When **the morning stars** sang together
> And all the sons of God shouted for joy?
> —Job 38:4-7

The morning stars singing together? All the sons of God shouting for joy?! Needless to say, there are a wide range of opinions about the identity and role of these morning stars and these sons of God. In this particular scene, God describes their reaction to the third day of creation when He drew the physical earth out of the physical waters (the waters that had been separated by the expanse on the second day). Some scholars connect them to other Old Testament passages that allude to the existence of a divine council of heavenly beings created by God to rule over different aspects of the spiritual realm. For example, they may also be referred to as "the council of the holy ones" in Psalm 89:7, "the host of heaven" in 1 Kings 22:19, and again "the sons of God" in Job 1:6. Moreover, the physical appearance of the sun, moon, and stars on the fourth day of creation may reflect the spiritual reality and governmental roles of these heavenly beings.

There are even multiple references in the Old Testament to members of this divine council rebelling against their Creator and bringing severe wickedness and trouble to earth as they ruled over the nations from behind the scenes in the heavenly realm. (See Genesis 6:1-6, Deuteronomy 32:7-9, Job 1:6-12, Psalm 82, and Daniel 10 for a few examples.)

I generally agree with this perspective, though a thorough exposition of its theology is beyond the scope and purpose of this book. You might be wondering how the existence of such spiritual beings—particularly the mention of "sons of God" outside the context of the Body of Christ —meshes with everything else we've discussed about the end-time sons of God. Rest assured, we'll touch on some of that in a later chapter, and a fuller answer will come into focus as we progress deeper into the book of Revelation later in this series.

For now, let's connect these ideas in our minds with how the apostle Paul spoke of "the rulers and authorities in heavenly places" (Ephesians 3:10). In book 1 we hypothesized that these evil beings (under the auspices of the prince of the power of the air) ruled in the darkness from the second heaven. It's also possible that Paul had both good *and* evil spiritual powers in mind in this passage, in which case "heavenly places" may include both the second and third heavens. In either case, Paul also revealed that the Father seated the resurrected Jesus Christ "at His right hand in the heavenly places, far above all rule and authority and power and dominion ..." (Ephesians 1:20-21), and then "He raised us up with Him, and seated us with Him in the heavenly places in Christ Jesus" (Ephesians 2:6). For that reason, regardless of how the specifics of our theology about the divine council of heavenly beings shakes out, we know for sure that the Body of Christ is destined to judge and rule at Christ's side over the earth *and* all the heavenly host in the age to come. More on that later in this series.

## COUNTERFEIT AUTHORITY

Now let's carry that knowledge into one more biblical reference to the morning star. It is no accident that the enemy covets the title of the morning star:

> How you have fallen from heaven,
> **O star of the morning, son of the dawn!**

You have been cut down to the earth,
You who have weakened the nations!
—*ISAIAH 14:12*

"Star of the morning" comes from the Hebrew word *helel*, which literally means *shining one* or *light-bringer*. Some translations replace it with the Latin name "Lucifer," which means *light-bearer*. Combined with the proceeding title "son of the dawn," the idea is similar (though not exactly the same) in concept to the ancient understanding of Venus as the astrological morning star discussed above. This is fitting given that Isaiah's prophecy started as a taunt against "the king of Babylon" (Isaiah 14:4), and the fact that ancient Babylon was renowned for deriving wisdom and knowledge from occultic astrology. They even boasted of their interaction with supernatural beings.

Many scholars consider "star of the morning, son of the dawn" to be a reference to Satan's role in heaven before his rebellion (and before he was called Satan). That is possible, though certainly not required. It is also possible that Isaiah wasn't describing the devil's original legitimate title, but rather alluding to that which he coveted most. Again, I want to avoid sidetracking us into a deeply technical (yet still highly subjective) discussion about different kinds of spiritual beings in Scripture. An exhaustive study, while fascinating and beneficial, is beyond the scope of this series and mostly outside of our main focus to see and experience the Unveiling of Jesus Christ. If you are interested in further research, I recommend the scholarly work of Dr. Michael S. Heiser and his seminal book on the subject: *The Unseen Realm: Recovering the Supernatural Worldview of the Bible.*

For now, I brought all of that up as context for comparing the way Isaiah mocks our great adversary with "O star of the morning, son of the dawn" and how Christ definitively claims the title of "the bright morning star" in Revelation 22:16. How do we synthesize the two titles? And what is the message to us, considering that Christ also promised to give the overcomers in Thyatira "the morning star"?

Now is a good time to remember the larger context of Isaiah 14 discussed in book 1. There we saw it as part of a jubilant taunt spoken over Satan by God's covenant people as they enter the millennial reign of Christ. It aligns with Revelation chapter 12 when the dragon is cast out of heaven after failing to abort the birth of the male child. In both cases (Isaiah and Revelation), we see the enemy trying to assume power and authority that he does not possess. And in both cases, he fails spectacularly.

So was "O star of the morning, son of the dawn" actually Satan's original function as designed by God? Maybe in some limited and lesser way that didn't satisfy his ambition. Or maybe it was someone else's title that he coveted, reflecting his desire to govern times and seasons in a way that infringed on God's ultimate plan for humanity through the resurrected Body of Christ. In that case, it only appears in Isaiah 14:12 as an ironic celebratory insult pronounced by the people of God after the day has dawned through Christ's Unveiling, and the true, ultimate expression of the morning star has arisen in their hearts. At that time, I imagine the people of God will declare incredulously: "*This* is the one who fancied himself a morning star?! *This* is the one who boasted of his ability to reveal divine light when and how he pleased?! *This* is the one who thought he could change the times and the law to forestall his day of judgement?! Truly, God's patience is worthy of praise, His judgments wholly appropriate, and His wrath entirely just!"

Either way, it is fair to say that everything Satan does in Revelation chapter 12 reflects his desire to control time and to bend it to his agenda. He spent millennia trying (and failing) to abort the birth of Christ to delay the hourglass of Daniel's seventy-week prophecy because he knows the Son of God is the true morning star around which the seasons flow. Jesus is the harbinger of the Day of the Lord, which will utterly destroy Satan's kingdom.

Satan didn't fully understand Daniel's prophecy, and he couldn't comprehend the purpose of Christ's first coming, so all of his machinations only played into God's plan. Even so, when he realized his failure, he shifted attention to aborting the birth of the sons of God who are destined to arise in Christ's likeness at the end of the age, hoping to delay the full manifestation of Christ's kingdom. That too will fail (for similar reasons). And when it does fail, the end-time sons of God will

> Or maybe it was someone else's title that he coveted, reflecting his desire to govern times and seasons in a way that infringed on God's ultimate plan for humanity through the resurrected Body of Christ.

come forth as heralds of the coming dawn, like morning stars exercising godly authority over the times and seasons, casting the enemy down to earth and initiating the second half of the seventieth week.

Even then, Satan will attempt one final, desperate gambit to change the times and the laws in his favor (see Daniel 7:25) to prolong his short earthly reign and delay the return of Christ. But his plan is hopeless, and the people of God will celebrate his foolish failure in the end because all of his attempts to play the role of morning star will only play into the hands of Christ, "the bright morning star," who will arrive right on time and without delay (Revelation 22:16).

## THE BRIDE'S RESPONSE

Compass check time! We've taken a very slow and meticulous stroll through Christ's letter to Thyatira, so it's been a while since we last checked in on the Song of Solomon. Where are we now? How will the faithful Bride respond to Christ's exhortation to overcome Jezebel's influence? Will she receive her legitimacy directly from His flaming eyes? Will she boldly embrace the wilderness trials that will refine her walk of sonship and produce authority over times and seasons? We return now to the context of the first few verses of the Song of Solomon to find our answer:

> May he kiss me with the kisses of his mouth!
> For your love is better than wine.
> Your oils have a pleasing fragrance,
> **Your name is like purified oil** …
> —SONG OF SOLOMON 1:2-3

Her fourth response? "Your name is like purified oil!"

Shakespeare famously wrote in Romeo and Juliet: "What's in a name? That which we call a rose by any other word would smell as sweet!" With all due respect to the Bard, sometimes *everything* is in a name! Names can represent essence, as well as reputation and renown derived from one's actions. And for the exhorter church of Thyatira, that was everything!

Remember, Jesus had one thing against Thyatira, and He didn't shy away from calling it by name: Jezebel. It was, perhaps, the most vile and hated epithet in Jewish history. Jezebel. A curse of a name, synonymous with witchcraft, sexual immorality, aggressive control, and persecution. That kind of rebuke could leave a traumatic mark, or arouse a bitter defense, if not received from One whose heart you fully trusted.

But the Bride did know something of her Lover's intention. She had listened to His introduction. She knew true sonship would require the eyes of her heart to be fixed on His and not the darkness. The defilement of Jezebel was nothing compared to the passion burning in His molten eyes. The rebuke was merely an invitation to stare into those eyes and be overcome by Him alone. Even now she felt them speaking dignity and life into her spirit, calling her "beloved" and "pleasing to the Father." Encouraging her to courageously embrace the walk of sonship as He had so long ago.

"But how?" She thought. "How do I boldly stand,
And shine the beauty of this light He's given me
Into the ugly darkness, without fear of falling easily
Into the same old trap of Jezebel's seduction
That so many others use to gain authority
So they can make their voices heard
And build their kingdoms in the sand?"

"The sand," she mused aloud, as the poetry replayed inside her mind. "No amount of pressure or coercion will shape it to your will in any lasting fashion. I'm glad His kingdom isn't made of sand. It's sturdier than that, and easier to build with."

And then she remembered the other aspect of His Sonship that He so wonderfully described: His feet of polished bronze, refined in the fire! Those steady, perfect feet, forged in a wilderness of weakness and temptation. Now they carried unblemished and unshakable authority into the darkest places!

"How lovely are those feet," she recited the verse. "How they announce peace and bring good news of happiness and salvation! And they remind me that He reigns! With every step He takes, and everywhere He goes, He brings His kingdom!"

She knew His letter was calling her to walk the same walk with Him. To build with kingdom principles and not with shifting sand. To become the beacon and the herald of His coming reign. But how?!

And that's when it hit her! The attitude that He was seeking in response to His rebuke was the very attitude that had refined His authority, and it would surely forge hers:

> Have this attitude in yourselves which was also in Christ Jesus, who, although He existed in the form of God, did not regard equality with God a thing to be grasped, but emptied Himself, taking the form of a bond-servant, and being made in the likeness of men. Being found in appearance as a man, He humbled Himself by becoming obedient to the point of death, even death on a cross. **For this reason also, God highly exalted Him, and bestowed on Him the name which is above every name, so that at the name of Jesus EVERY KNEE WILL BOW**, of those who are in heaven and on earth and under the earth, and that every tongue will confess that Jesus Christ is Lord, to the glory of God the Father.
> —*PHILIPPIANS 2:5-11*

"What's in a name?!" She pondered as a smile flashed across her eyes. "Everything! Everything is in His name! He didn't coerce obedience or force worship from this fallen universe. He freely gave Himself instead. And one way or another EVERYONE will eventually recognize the beauty of His name because His example of sacrificial love is the only way that overcomes the darkness and builds an everlasting kingdom!"

Finally, she was ready to unleash her response to Him:

> Your name is like purified oil!
> —*SONG OF SOLOMON 1:3*

"You, even YOU, submitted to the process. Your beauty, Your renown, and Your authority in the coming kingdom flowed from Your willingness to embrace Your wilderness trials. And You did so with full confidence in the Father's heart. And now I want to learn to do the same!"

## CHAPTER 9

# CHRIST'S SEVEN LETTERS: TO SARDIS

We took the long path through the letter to Thyatira, weaving in and out of many different Scriptures and going out of our way to gain a deeper understanding of Christ's message. It was a large, but worthy, expenditure of energy. Thankfully the letter to Sardis has a shorter, more direct path to glean what is necessary for this leg of the journey. After Thyatira, a chapter with fewer side quests will be refreshing. Most of what we need will be found in a single section of the book of Matthew and, of course, the letter to Sardis itself. Let's start there:

> To the angel of the church in Sardis write:
> He who has the seven Spirits of God and the seven stars, says this:
> 'I know your deeds, that you have a name that you are alive, but you are dead. Wake up, and strengthen the things that remain, which were about to die; for I have not found

your deeds completed in the sight of My God. So remember what you have received and heard; and keep it, and repent. Therefore if you do not wake up, I will come like a thief, and you will not know at what hour I will come to you. But you have a few people in Sardis who have not soiled their garments; and they will walk with Me in white, for they are worthy. He who overcomes will thus be clothed in white garments; and I will not erase his name from the book of life, and I will confess his name before My Father and before His angels. He who has an ear, let him hear what the Spirit says to the churches.'
—*REVELATION 3:1-6*

You know the drill. The letter to the angel of the church in Sardis is an exhortation to the giver portion of the human spirit. It beckons to the part of our spirit that was made to align with the Spirit of Might. As our spirit reflects that color of God's light into our soul and body, we become more like Jesus in that area. And then we start to shine that aspect of Christ back out to the world.

In the fractal of seven, the essence of the Spirit of Might and the giver redemptive gift are summed up in God's command to the birds and fish on the fifth day of creation: "Be fruitful and multiply" (Genesis 1:22). This command reflects God's heart to effectively steward resources, especially the next generation, by taking the life of God in embryo form, nurturing it through the early difficulties of life, and then releasing it back to God in maturity at the correct time.

## THE INTRODUCTION

So, how did Jesus introduce Himself to Sardis? "He who has the seven Spirits of God and the seven stars, says this ...."

The seven Spirits of God *and* the seven stars. This verse is one of the reasons why, early on, I suggested we think of the seven stars (which are the seven angels of the seven churches) as the seven portions of the human spirit and the seven redemptive gifts of the Body of Christ, rather than as the seven Spirits of God. Here we see them as two separate but related things. Jesus has the seven Spirits of God (which, perhaps, are reflected in His flaming eyes), and He also has the seven stars in His right hand.

Why would Christ introduce Himself in this way, pairing these two things together by mentioning them in the same breath? It's almost like He is inviting comparison. The seven Spirits of God are the original pattern—the perfect, unadulterated shining of the spectrum of God's character into the world. The seven stars are meant to take on the same likeness as they experience Christ's Unveiling. But until then, there remains a gap between the two.

Perhaps Jesus was drawing Sardis's attention to the reality that He has the fullness of God's provision—every resource they could possibly need—to effectively steward the rest of the Body. This is important for Sardis because the giver gift is designed to help nurture the entire human spirit (on an individual level), and the whole Body of Christ (on a corporate level), through the early stages of development to help them reach maturity.

> The seven Spirits of God are the original pattern—the perfect, unadulterated shining of the spectrum of God's character into the world. The seven stars are meant to take on the same likeness as they experience Christ's Unveiling. But until then, there remains a gap between the two.

## SARDIS EXAMINED

It is in that context that Jesus says to Sardis:

> I know your deeds, that you have a name that you are alive, but you are dead. Wake up, and strengthen the things that remain, which were about to die; for I have not found your deeds completed in the sight of My God. So remember what you have received and heard; and keep it, and repent. Therefore if you do not wake up, I will come like a thief, and you will not know at what hour I will come to you.
> —*REVELATION 3:1-3*

Jesus went straight to the rebuke phase with Sardis, bypassing the encouraging buildup He used in the previous letters. There would be an encouragement later in the letter, but that would have to wait. Their failure was impacting the rest of the Body, and it needed to be addressed immediately.

Sardis had a name—that is, they had a reputation amongst the other churches. It was a reputation for being alive. Perhaps they were renowned for their deeds, and were, at one time, respected and celebrated by the rest of the Body of Christ as an example to be followed. Even so, when Christ inspected Sardis, He found their actual deeds did not match their reputation. They were, as Christ described it, asleep, and whatever remained of their original vigor was almost dead. They may have started strong but they had grown complacent, and now they lacked the might to finish the work for which they were designed.

Christ's challenge to them was simple: "Wake up, and strengthen the things that remain, which are about to die!" And again, "If you do not wake up, I will come like a thief, and you will not know at what hour I will come to you."

Does this admonishment sound familiar? Remember the analogy that both Jesus and Paul used to describe the coming of the Day of the Lord? Here it is again:

> Therefore be on the alert, for you do not know which day your Lord is coming. But be sure of this, that if the head of the house had known at what time of the night **the thief was coming**, he would have been on the alert and would not have allowed his house to be broken into. For this reason you also must be ready; for the Son of Man is coming **at an hour when you do not think He will**.
> —*MATTHEW 24:42-44*

Some Christians interpret this passage to mean that Jesus will rapture His Church away from the earth unexpectedly, like a thief in the night. They consider these verses, and a few other passages surrounding them, to be evidence of a pre-tribulation rapture that is imminent and that will happen without warning before the great tribulation begins. For them, the timing of the rapture is the centerpiece of their eschatology.

If you've stuck with me for this long, you probably understand why I find that perspective so shortsighted and dangerous. Besides, there are so many greater treasures available to us in Christ's Unveiling. I only bring this up now because I want you to know that we will, eventually, discuss the rapture when we get deeper into the book of Revelation. But not yet. For now, we're just looking for the larger context of this verse to help us understand Christ's letter to Sardis.

To that end, remember what we learned about the thief analogy in book 1. According to Paul in 1 Thessalonians 5, only those who are in darkness—those who sleep and get drunk at night—will perceive the coming of the Day of the Lord as a thief in the night. But we (the sons of day) are called to stay awake and sober, watching for the signs of the coming day.

## AWAKE OR ASLEEP?

So what does it mean to stay awake? And how did Sardis fall asleep? Let's look at some of the surrounding context of Christ's original "thief in the night" analogy to find the answers. We'll start with the passage immediately preceding Christ's statement about coming like a thief:

> But of that day and hour no one knows, not even the an-gels of heaven, nor the Son, but the Father alone. For the coming of the Son of Man will be just like the days of Noah. For as in those days before the flood they were eating and drinking, marrying and giving in marriage, until the day that Noah entered the ark, and they did not under-stand until the flood came and took them all away; so will the coming of the Son of Man be. Then there will be two men in the field; one will be taken and one will be left. Two women will be grinding at the mill; one will be taken and one will be left.
> —*MATTHEW 24:36-41*

There are three things we need to glean from this passage. First, al-though no one knows the day or the hour of Christ's return, it doesn't say no one knows the year, the month, or the season. In other words, we can't know the precise time down to the day and hour, but we can and must discern when the time is close.

Second, Jesus compared His coming to the coming of the world-wide flood in the days of Noah. Noah was a preacher of righteousness (see 2 Peter 2:5), but while he was building the ark the world continued on with their normal lives, rebelliously ignoring Noah's warnings, deliriously oblivious to the cataclysm hanging over their heads like the Sword of Damocles.

I say normal lives, but their lives were not exactly normal. Yes, they continued eating and drinking and marrying as if nothing was wrong, but according to Genesis 6:5, wickedness had become so ubiquitous that every motivation of their hearts was continually evil. That means even their eating, drinking, and marrying were defiled. The light of their spirit had become utter darkness, and they were asleep in the false reality of their own deception right up until the moment the flood waters swept them away.

In this analogy, the flood waters represent the wrath of God that is connected to the Day of the Lord, as well as the sword that proceeds from Christ's mouth when He physically returns to earth. The wrath of God begins with the seven bowls of wrath, and it is separate from and subsequent to the great tribulation, but we'll get into all of that later in this series.

Third, notice that after comparing His coming to the time of Noah, Jesus drew a distinct contrast. During the flood, everyone died except for Noah and his family. Eight people on the ark were saved while the entire population of the earth was destroyed. That will not be the case when Christ returns. The analogy suggests something more like a fifty-fifty split: "Then there will be two men in the field; one will be taken and one will be left. Two women will be grinding at the mill; one will be taken and one will be left."

I don't know if the ratio is meant literally, but the point is that many, but certainly not all, will be spiritually asleep and so consumed by the darkness of the times that they won't perceive the light of Christ being demonstrated by the sons of day. And those who rebelliously remain asleep during that loudest, clearest, boldest clarion call of the ages will be taken (swept away) by God's wrath.

There are multiple ways to interpret those "taken" and those "left." Some say that to be taken means to be raptured and to be left means to miss the rapture. I don't think that fits very well with the context, but as long as we understand the flood to be synonymous with the wrath of God during the Day of the Lord after the great tribulation, then I'm fine with that perspective as one possibility. Again, we'll talk about all of that in more detail later.

Another possibility is that being taken and being left has nothing to do with the rapture. Perhaps Jesus wasn't drawing a parallel between the Church and the world, but rather between those who survive the wrath of the Day of the Lord and those who don't.

In Noah's time, everyone else was killed. At the end of the age, the judgment of the sword of the Lord will be more surgical. Those who walk in darkness, whose every imagination is continually wicked, will reap a harvest of destruction. But not every unbeliever will fully embrace the darkness at the end, and not everyone on the earth will die from God's wrath. Many will, but many people and nations will survive, as through fire, to enter the season of Christ's millennial reign. They will be the nations Christ and His Bride will rule over as they work to bring healing to the earth. But I'm getting ahead of myself again.

## SENSIBLE GIVER?

Where does Sardis fit into all of this? Remember, Christ told them that if they didn't repent and wake up, He would come like a thief. But how could they be in danger of being swept away by God's wrath? Would Jesus do that to a part of His Body? If so, wouldn't that mean that they were in danger of losing their salvation? Is that even possible? We're getting close to the answers, but we still need more context. Let's keep reading in the book of Matthew. After comparing His coming to the days of Noah, and then elaborating that He would come like a thief in the night for the unaware, Jesus told three parables that drove home the very principles He would later use to discipline Sardis:

> Who then is the faithful and sensible slave whom his master put in charge of his household to give them their food at the proper time? Blessed is that slave whom his master finds so doing when he comes. Truly I say to you that he will put him in charge of all his possessions. But if that evil slave says in his heart, "My master is not coming for a long time," and begins to beat his fellow slaves and eat and drink with drunkards; the master of that slave will come on a day when he does not expect him and at an hour which he does not know, and will cut him in pieces and assign him a place

with the hypocrites; in that place there will be weeping and
gnashing of teeth.
—*MATTHEW 24:45-51*

The giver church of Sardis was like the slave put in charge of the
master's household to give them their food at the proper time. They had
a special dispensation of grace and responsibility to provide for the rest
of the Body of Christ. That's one of the main roles of the giver gift. As
we'll see in a moment, some in Sardis were like the faithful and sensible
slave. But many others had shirked that responsibility, instead using
their gift for selfish indulgence. And those selfish slaves were the members of Sardis to whom Christ said:

> for I have not found your deeds completed in the sight of
> My God. So remember what you have received and heard;
> and keep it, and repent. Therefore if you do not wake up, I
> will come like a thief ...
> —*REVELATION 3:2-3*

But what if they didn't repent? According to the parable, what was their
punishment when the master returned
and found their deeds incomplete while
they were misappropriating his resources?

First, the master would cut them
into pieces. This is likely a reference to
the sword coming from the mouth of
Christ when He returns to strike the
nations. It may include physical death,
though not necessarily. The main point,
though, is that the sharp two-edged
sword of Christ reveals the heart and
judges the deepest things. And these
members of Sardis would be found, in

> The giver church of
> Sardis was like the
> slave put in charge of
> the master's household
> to give them their food
> at the proper time. They
> had a special dispensa-
> tion of grace and re-
> sponsibility to provide
> for the rest of the Body
> of Christ.

the end, to be evil slaves. Though they had been in the Master's household, they were not actually born again and they were never truly alive,
which is why they would experience Him coming as a thief, and they
would inherit wrath.

Another way to think of those evil slaves is in light of Christ's parable of the wheat and the tares in Matthew 13:24-30. We won't read it here, but in that parable an enemy sows tares into a farmer's newly planted wheat field. The field is "the world," the wheat are "the sons of the kingdom," and the tares are "the sons of the evil one" (Matthew 13:38).

In the parable, rather than uprooting the tares early on and endangering the health of the wheat, the farmer allows both wheat and tares to grow to maturity together. The difference between the two will be most obvious at harvest time (the end of the age) because the tares will still stand tall while the wheat bows low from the weight of its fruit. And that's when the farmer will send workers to gather up the tares and throw them into the fire. So too will the evil slaves be cast out of the Master's household during the season of His Unveiling. Their true nature will be revealed and they will be assigned a place with the hypocrites where there will be weeping and gnashing of teeth. More on that later.

## WISE GIVER?

Right after the parable about the faithful and the wicked slaves, Jesus launched into another parable that even more directly relates to Sardis:

> Then the kingdom of heaven will be comparable to ten virgins, who took their lamps and went out to meet the bridegroom. Five of them were foolish, and five were prudent. For when the foolish took their lamps, they took no oil with them, but the prudent took oil in flasks along with their lamps.
>
> Now while the bridegroom was delaying, they all got drowsy and began to sleep. But at midnight there was a shout, 'Behold, the bridegroom! Come out to meet him.'
>
> Then all those virgins rose and trimmed their lamps. The foolish said to the prudent, 'Give us some of your oil, for our lamps are going out.' But the prudent answered, 'No, there will not be enough for us and you too; go instead to the dealers and buy some for yourselves.'
>
> And while they were going away to make the purchase, the bridegroom came, and those who were ready went in

with him to the wedding feast; and the door was shut. Later
the other virgins also came, saying, 'Lord, lord, open up for
us.' But he answered, 'Truly I say to you, I do not know
you.' Be on the alert then, for you do not know the day nor
the hour.
—*MATTHEW 25:1-13*

In this analogy the faithful members of Sardis are the five wise virgins while the rest are the five foolish virgins. I don't know if Jesus intentionally chose the number five with future Sardis in mind, but it certainly is fitting, considering Sardis is the fifth church and giver is the
fifth redemptive gift. Also notice the fifty-fifty split, which is a recurring
theme in the parables about His return.

The central theme of this parable is, again, stewardship. The wise
virgins brought extra flasks of lamp oil. They understood their Bridegroom might take longer than expected. They knew it was possible He
might even come at the darkest time of night, and so they made sure
they had enough resources to be ready and faithful when He appeared.
As a result, they were welcomed into the wedding feast.

Notice how this aligns with what Jesus said about the wise in
Sardis:

But you have a few people in Sardis who have not soiled
their garments; and they will walk with Me in white, for
they are worthy. He who overcomes will thus be clothed in
white garments; and I will not erase his name from the
book of life, and I will confess his name before My Father
and before His angels.
—*REVELATION 3:4-5*

To be clothed in white garments is to be prepared for the wedding
feast. As we'll see when we get to Revelation chapter 19, the white garments also represent the righteous acts of the saints. Sardis was meant to
steward resources that would nurture the rest of the Church rather than
caring only for their own selfish, temporary interests. The wise in Sardis
did this, but the foolish left the work undone.

So how, exactly, were the wise givers in Sardis meant to steward
Christ's resources? And why did many fail to do so? The answers are
found in Christ's third parable about His coming.

## TALENTS FOR THE GIVER

The parable of the talents is well-known, and also quite lengthy, so we won't read the whole thing now. But here is the setup:

> For it is just like a man about to go on a journey, who called his own slaves and entrusted his possessions to them. To one he gave five talents, to another, two, and to another, one, each according to his own ability; and he went on his journey
> —*MATTHEW 25:14-15*

You're probably familiar with the rest: When the master returned and called the slaves to give an account of his money, the one who received the five talents had invested wisely and turned them into ten talents. He received a great reward from the appreciative master. The one with three talents had also invested and turned them into six talents. He, too, received a great reward. But the one who received one talent did nothing with it. He simply buried it in the ground and then gave it back when his master returned. This slave was harshly rebuked and cast into outer darkness.

What can we learn from this? First, notice the reason the third slave gave for burying his single talent:

> And the one also who had received the one talent came up and said, 'Master, I knew you to be a hard man, reaping where you did not sow and gathering where you scattered no seed. And I was afraid, and went away and hid your talent in the ground. See, you have what is yours.'
> —*MATTHEW 24:24-25*

"Reaping where you did not sow and gathering where you scattered no seed." In other words, the slave was accusing the master of being a thief. He didn't want to invest his own time and energy sowing and watering the seed of the master's initial investment, just to turn a profit that the master would reap for himself. So the lazy slave buried the talent to keep from having to put the work in.

The slave didn't understand the principle of stewardship or his master's heart. Yes, the initial talent belonged to the master. Yes, the proceeds from the slave's labor would go back to the master's household. But the master wasn't only seeking his own enrichment. He set the entire scenario up to help the slave learn how to steward a small amount of resources so that he could be trusted with much greater resources and increased authority in the master's kingdom.

Again, this is precisely what happened in Sardis. The faithful slaves understood the stewardship with which they were entrusted. They took the task seriously. They trusted their Bridegroom's heart. They worked with all of their strength, in concert with the Spirit of Might, to make the most out of what they had been given. As a reward, they were promised entry into the marriage supper of the Lamb to join the Bride at the Lord's side, inheriting great authority for their good stewardship.

> The master wasn't only seeking his own enrichment. He set the entire scenario up to help the slave learn how to steward a small amount of resources so that he could be trusted with much greater resources and increased authority in the master's kingdom.

But the lazy members of Sardis despised the talents they had been given, choosing, instead, to spend their time on temporary pursuits for their own pleasure. If they didn't wake up and repent, they were in danger of being judged as spiritually dead. As such, they risked being kicked out of the Master's house, excluded from the wedding feast, cast into outer darkness, and having their names erased from the Book of Life (see Revelation 3:5).

## POWER TO OVERCOME

How does all of this connect back to "He who has the seven Spirits of God and the seven stars"? Remember, in Revelation 3:1 that's how Jesus introduced Himself to Sardis. How does that aspect of Christ help the giver overcome a tendency to misinterpret the Master's heart and to misunderstand the principle of stewardship?

The fact that Jesus possesses the seven Spirits of God means that He already has all provision for every good work. He doesn't need the giver's work. He owns the cattle on a thousand hills. He owns everything. He doesn't need the giver to invest their resources or their energy or their time. Instead, He gives His resources to the giver and asks them to invest wisely because they are designed to thrive in that position and to find their greatest fulfillment engaging in the process of stewardship.

Consider that Jesus emptied Himself of His innate divine power and authority when He came to earth as a bondservant. But then the Dove came down from the Father during His baptism and He received the full abiding presence of the seven Spirits of God. In other words, in that moment, Jesus became a steward of the Father's resources, and He remained a wise and faithful steward for His entire ministry, only ever using those resources to accomplish the Father's will. He fully trusted the Father's heart, and He gave every last ounce of His life to accomplish the work He was entrusted to perform. And we know that because of His faithful stewardship, He was given the name above every other name and exalted high above all other authority.

On the other hand, the fact that Jesus also possesses the seven stars means that He knows exactly what each part of His Body was designed to do, and He knows what provision they need and what difficulties they need to experience to reach maturity. He knows the mixture of darkness and light in each of us, and He knows exactly what aspect of Himself will help us overcome. And that is why He challenges each of the churches, including Sardis. After all, He is a good steward of the Bride, because we were given to Him by the Father.

As for the giver, Jesus doesn't need them to nurture the rest of the Church. He already knows what is needed, and He could derive that provision from anywhere, or from any one of the other gifts. But, again, He offers that role to the giver church of Sardis (and to the giver part of our spirit) because the giver loves to give wisely in ways that help others mature (like the sensible slave who provides food at the proper time). And the giver recognizes what is needed to get a job done (like the wise virgins who knew to bring extra oil). And the giver knows how to turn a little into a lot (like the faithful slave with five talents).

## THE BRIDE'S RESPONSE

So what was the Bride's response to Christ's letter to Sardis? Would she receive the rebuke exposing her work as incomplete? Could she recognize the Bridegroom's heart inviting her to walk side-by-side with Him in stewardship and thus receive her full reward? Or would she shrink away from the job ahead, opting for a life of luxury and entertainment?

For just a moment she held the stinging letter in her fingers, turning every word around inside her mind so she could count the cost of trusting Him again. The parables He once had told now tumbled through her halls of recollection, like many voices asking all at once for her attention. She tried her best to filter through the memories and find the one that spoke most dearly to this part of her heart, hoping somewhere in His words she'd find her faith …

*The sensible servant, knowing what food to give and when?* "I love that one," she thought, "but I think I need something else right now …."

*The trusted money manager, wisely investing the master's wealth?* "Inspiring and relevant, but somehow not the sparkle I'm looking for …."

*The prudent maidens taking extra oil so they wouldn't miss their bridegroom's late arrival?* "Yes, of course! That's the one!" she almost shouted to herself. "That's the parable that hums the melody of wedding bells and promises forever at His side! For a vow like that, I'll wait as long as He desires! And should He tarry until midnight, I won't waste my oil on trivial pursuits or temporary selfish pleasures. Has He not done the same for me? And if He's running late, I know it's not because He has forgotten! He merely bides His time so I can grow."

She warmed to this new faith growing so quickly in her heart. In the past, the very idea of the Bridegroom tarrying turned her stomach. It always hit too close to her insecurities. But after reading His letter to Sardis, she was beginning to see it differently.

When He spoke to her of Pergamum, He had asked her to seek the deeper treasures of her trials so she could speak the truth to the wounded and defiled. She told him, "Your oils have a pleasing fragrance!"

When He spoke to her of Thyatira and challenged her to overcome that cursed Jezebel, she replied, "Your name is like purified oil!"

And now He spoke to her of Sardis, asking her to keep working until the very end, to use her oil to keep her lamp burning brightly into the night, even as He tarried and she grew tired. But this, too, revealed His goodness!

"Yes, yes, a thousand times yes!" She thought. "I'll steward everything You give me, even if the cost seems great, because it's not really my time or energy that You require. Everything I have is Yours! You are my provision. You are everything I need. The oil in my lamp comes from You. My strength and time are Yours. And my reward for investing what You have given me? You are my reward! You and all of You for all eternity! Has there ever been a better deal? A more glorious trade-off? It's no wonder the five wise virgins loved you so!"

And then she couldn't stop from blurting it out loud into the empty room:

> Therefore the maidens love you!
> —*SONG OF SOLOMON 1:3*

# CHAPTER 10

# CHRIST'S SEVEN LETTERS:
# TO PHILADELPHIA, PART 1 - THE KEY OF DAVID

O ur journey through Sardis was relatively laid-back and straightforward. It was a nice change of pace after the heaviness of
Thyatira. But if you're anything like me, you may be itching
for a more challenging stretch. Something with a bit more complexity.
Tighten your laces because our path through Philadelphia involves multiple side trails with enough twists and turns to keep us engaged for four
whole chapters. In the middle, we'll brave an epic detour through the
book of Acts that may recontextualize first-century Church history in
ways you've never considered, illuminating some ancient wounds in the
body of Christ that only Jesus' promise to Philadelphia can heal.

Don't fear the length of this one—every step will be full of mysteries
that draw us toward the immense reward of Philadelphia. And since this
reward is often misunderstood and desperately needed for the days
ahead, we're going to change our approach by starting with a review of
the principles of the sixth day of creation before jumping into the meat

of Christ's letter. That way, we can hit the ground running with the right mindset when we get into the letter itself. Off we go …

## THE SIXTH DAY

As you've probably come to expect, the letter to the angel of the church in Philadelphia is an exhortation to the ruler portion of the human spirit. It beckons to the part of our spirit that was made to align with the Spirit of Knowledge. As our spirit reflects that color of God's light into our soul and body, we become more like Jesus in that area until we shine that aspect of Christ back out to the world.

In the fractal of seven, the essence of both the Spirit of Knowledge and of the ruler redemptive gift can be seen by contrasting mankind with everything else God created on the sixth day. There are many differences, from the intimate way God created humans in His own image, to the special commission Adam and Eve were given to rule over the earth, and so on. But at a functional level, I like to boil it all down to one phrase: the pursuit of knowledge.

No other species was designed with the self-awareness, drive, and capacity to learn and grow in an endless pursuit of knowledge. And this capacity was central to humanity's original dominion mandate as described in Genesis:

> God blessed them; and God said to them, "Be fruitful and multiply, and fill the earth, and subdue it; and rule over the fish of the sea and over the birds of the sky and over every living thing that moves on the earth."
> —GENESIS 1:28

Knowledge is meant to increase our capacity for fellowship with God, which, in turn, releases wisdom and true creativity. That's why God originally gave mankind a wide-open sandbox—a wild earth full of untamed, untapped potential that required them to learn. Mankind was called to study the fingerprints of God in the Garden of Eden, identify the specific divine attributes embedded in those fingerprints, and then derive principles that they could apply in creative ways to extend God's life, love, and order throughout the rest of the earth.

They weren't given a coloring book to measure how well they stayed within the lines, or a paint-by-numbers to replicate a specific color scheme. The garden was their example, and the rest of the earth was a blank canvas waiting for them to paint a picture of divinity through the filter of their own creativity.

Now think about the relationship between knowledge and creativity. Even God's creativity flows out of His wisdom and knowledge. He knows all things and understands all things, so He is able to weave together the principles of His own nature in endlessly creative ways. Of course it helps that He also has all power and authority to make it happen, but that's part of the point. He chose to exercise His omnipotent sovereign rule by sacrificially expressing creative freedom to create free things. What does that tell us about how God intends knowledge and authority to be used? What does that tell us about the ruler gift?

Likewise, Adam and Eve were meant to extend that same ethos of creative freedom into every system and structure they built in pursuit of their calling. They were to use creativity to release creativity. God didn't intend them to bend everything to their own will, nor to use heavy-handed coercion to subdue the earth. They were meant to follow a God-ordained process for gaining the knowledge and wisdom necessary to help every aspect of creation find freedom, harmony, and fulfillment congruent with its design. That's what godly dominion looks like. It is a servant kind of leadership that requires self-sacrifice.

> Knowledge is meant to increase our capacity for fellowship with God, which, in turn, releases wisdom and true creativity. That's why God originally gave mankind a wide-open sandbox—a wild earth full of untamed, untapped potential that required them to learn.

Unfortunately, Adam and Eve fell when they reached for a shortcut to knowledge that offered to bypass the uncertainty and sacrifice of God's intended process. Of course, they got more (and less) than they bargained for when they ate the forbidden fruit, ingesting with it the defilements of selfishness, self-reliance, and shame. But the fall didn't change the principles of God's original intention for rulership. Neither did it change the process by which we are invited to learn knowledge with God's wisdom so that we can become like Him.

## THE LETTER TO PHILADELPHIA

With all of that in mind, now we can read Christ's letter to Philadelphia:

> And to the angel of the church in Philadelphia write:
>
> He who is holy, who is true, who has the key of David, who opens and no one will shut, and who shuts and no one opens, says this:
>
> 'I know your deeds. Behold, I have put before you an open door which no one can shut, because you have a little power, and have kept My word, and have not denied My name. Behold, I will cause those of the synagogue of Satan, who say that they are Jews and are not, but lie—I will make them come and bow down at your feet, and make them know that I have loved you. Because you have kept the word of My perseverance, I also will keep you from the hour of testing, that hour which is about to come upon the whole world, to test those who dwell on the earth. I am coming quickly; hold fast what you have, so that no one will take your crown.
>
> He who overcomes, I will make him a pillar in the temple of My God, and he will not go out from it anymore; and I will write on him the name of My God, and the name of the city of My God, the new Jerusalem, which comes down out of heaven from My God, and My new name. He who has an ear, let him hear what the Spirit says to the churches.'
>
> —*REVELATION 3:7-13*

We'll start from the top. How did Jesus introduce Himself to Philadelphia? "He who is holy, who is true, who has the key of David, who opens and no one will shut, and who shuts and no one opens, says this ...."

This intro is a bit more complex than the previous ones because the attributes mentioned don't come from John's earlier vision of Christ among the lampstands. At first glance, they may seem random and unrelated, so let's unpack them individually and then tie them together:

"**He who is holy.**" As we saw in book 1, holiness means to be consecrated or set apart. For a created thing to be holy means that it is given to God and not used for anything else.

On the other hand, God, the uncreated Creator, is holy in and of Himself. He is set apart and completely "other than" His creation.

Christ, who is the Word made flesh, is both kinds of holy. He is consecrated and set apart to God, and He is wholly other because He is God. And in that way He is the bridge that allows us to be holy, connecting our consecration with God's otherness.

"**He who is true.**" This statement has multiple layers. First, Jesus doesn't lie. Everything He says is accurate. That's obvious. But more than that, He is true because He is the Word of I AM. What He says *is* reality. He is also the perfect expression of divinity. All true knowledge has its source and destination in Christ. That means every Old Testament type and shadow has its truest expression in Christ. He is the point.

"**Who has the key of David.**" This one's a bit of a puzzle requiring assembly. I've heard many theories about the key of David but nothing approaching a concrete biblical description. The best we can do is hypothesize from the little that Scripture does say. First, we know that whatever the key opens no one else can shut, and whatever it shuts no one else can open. Second, it's called the key of David, so there must be something David did to earn the authority of the key. Third, we know that Christ now has the key, so it was either passed down to Him generationally as the heir of David's throne, or He earned the key in the same way that David did. Or, more likely, both: it was passed to Him generationally, *and* He earned the right to use it by His actions during His ministry.

## SHEBNA AND ELIAKIM

The term "key of David" only appears one other time in Scripture—in a prophecy from the book of Isaiah. The prophecy was spoken against a man named Shebna, who was an unfaithful steward of the royal household of Hezekiah, the King of Judah. Shebna apparently leaned on his own understanding and abused his position for his own enrichment rather than serving the king's interests. For example, speaking to the inhabitants of Jerusalem who were operating under Shebna's direction,

Isaiah prophesied a judgement that would eventually implicate Shebna directly:

> And you saw that the breaches in the wall of the city of David were many; and you collected the waters of the lower pool.
>
> Then you counted the houses of Jerusalem and tore down houses to fortify the wall. And you made a reservoir between the two walls for the waters of the old pool.
>
> But you did not depend on Him who made it, nor did you take into consideration Him who planned it long ago.
> —ISAIAH 22:9-11

Shebna authorized changes to the structures surrounding Jerusalem in an attempt to streamline and fortify the city against enemy siege. These decisions were well within the purview of the steward of the royal household. Unfortunately, he was relying on human strength and ingenuity to protect Jerusalem rather than seeking God's wisdom. Moreover, these changes didn't take God's original long-term design for the city or its people into account.

By demolishing people's homes to build the city wall, Shebna was also subjugating the rights of the individual in ways that violated God's intention for leadership. In other words, he used his authority to bend things to his will rather than helping others find the freedom of alignment with God's intention. Basically, Shebna was not exercising servant-rulership in the Spirit of Knowledge to align all things with God's design. He didn't understand God's ways or His purposes. Largely as a result of these offenses, God decided to remove Shebna's authority and give it to a man named Eliakim:

> I will depose you [Shebna] from your office, and I will pull you down from your station.
>
> Then it will come about in that day, that I will summon My servant Eliakim the son of Hilkiah, and I will clothe him with your tunic and tie your sash securely about him.
>
> I will entrust him with your authority, and he will become a father to the inhabitants of Jerusalem and to the house of Judah.

> Then I will set the key of the house of David on his shoulder, when he opens no one will shut, when he shuts no one will open.
> I will drive him like a peg in a firm place, and he will become a throne of glory to his father's house.
> —ISAIAH 22:19-23

Later, in Isaiah chapter 36, we find that Eliakim did indeed replace Shebna as steward over King Hezekiah's household. So this was a fast-acting prophecy with literal ramifications. But just as Jesus called Himself "the One who is true," this prophecy is also a type and a shadow of a larger reality that is most true in Christ.

To that end, think about "the key to the house of David" in Isaiah's prophecy. The key metaphorically represented the authority and responsibility that came with being steward of the royal palace in Jerusalem. The steward was trusted to govern the affairs of the king's household, so he could freely use the key as the final authority to open and shut. Within his sphere of responsibility, the steward could make impactful decisions and even build systems and structures to support the king's household—all without consulting the king. That's the whole point of having a steward with delegated authority.

Notice to whom this authority was given: "*My servant* Eliakim." In contrast to Shebna, the king could trust Eliakim to wield such authority because Eliakim already knew how to serve selflessly. He was holy, consecrated to God, and set apart for God's work, so his decisions would naturally reflect the heart of the king and flow from God's wisdom.

Do you see how Shebna and Eliakim are an object lesson in the ruler gift's expression of sonship? Shebna didn't have the character or wisdom to lead effectively, and therefore couldn't be trusted to be creative and make his own decisions. Eliakim was a type of Christ, who had learned obedience through the things he suffered as a servant. That's why he was trusted with the freedom offered by the key of David.

## DAVID'S AUDACITY

Now let's take it a step further. It's not called the key of Eliakim; it's the key of David. David was the one who established a pattern of leadership that produces carte blanche authority with God. How did David do that? David was famously called a man after God's heart, but what does that mean?

Consider that David was first anointed king only after King Saul had disobeyed a prophetic word from Samuel. The story is told in 1 Samuel chapter 13. Saul was preparing the people of Israel for war with the Philistines. Samuel had previously instructed Saul to wait seven days for him in Gilgal, where, when he arrived, Samuel said he would offer burnt offerings before instructing Saul on the next steps for battle. When the seventh day came and Samuel was still not there, Saul observed the people growing restless and fearful of the Philistines, so he felt compelled to offer the burnt offerings himself. Immediately after the illicit sacrifice, Samuel arrived and rebuked Saul:

> Samuel said to Saul, "You have acted foolishly; you have not kept the commandment of the LORD your God, which He commanded you, for now the LORD would have established your kingdom over Israel forever. But now your kingdom shall not endure. **The LORD has sought out for Himself a man after His own heart**, and the LORD has appointed him as ruler over His people, because you have not kept what the LORD commanded you."
> —*1 SAMUEL 13:13-14*

Ouch. Notice that the transfer of authority described here is similar to the Shebna and Eliakim situation that would come hundreds of years later. It's also fascinating that Saul was removed for presuming to act without first consulting God's prophet for specific instructions. How does that fit with the type of creative and free exercise of sonship we've been talking about? Doesn't that suggest that God really does want His people to remain like little children that have to be led around by the hand, or slaves that require explicit instruction for every decision? No, and that's where David comes in.

On the surface, it almost sounds like God chose David to replace Saul merely because David would do everything he was commanded to do. But that's not what it means to be a man after God's own heart. Yes, David would do the will of the Lord, but he would do so because he had come to know the Lord's heart as a shepherd in the wilderness. David had learned the bridal position of waiting and receiving from

God, which is a prerequisite to sonship. And before he could actually inherit the kingdom, he would have to spend many more years learning about the free, creative, and wise exercise of leadership while he fled Saul's murderous rampage.

The clearest example of David being a man after God's own heart is found in 2 Samuel chapter 7. It was shortly after David had become king of Israel. He had already established Jerusalem as his capital city and moved the Ark of the Covenant into a tent in his backyard:

> Now it came about when the king lived in his house, and the LORD had given him rest on every side from all his enemies, that the king said to Nathan the prophet, "See now, I dwell in a house of cedar, but the ark of God dwells within tent curtains." Nathan said to the king, "Go, do all that is in your mind, for the LORD is with you."
> —2 SAMUEL 7:1-3

Do you see the contrast with Saul? On the one hand, Saul lost his authority merely because he presumed to make a sacrifice without permission. On the other hand, David took the initiative to move the Ark of the Covenant out of the holy of holies, out of the tabernacle of Moses (which was in Gibeon at that time), into a tent of his own making in a city that he chose for his home. God

**D**avid had learned the bridal position of waiting and receiving from God, which is a prerequisite to sonship.

didn't tell David to do these things. Yes, David did his best to execute his plans within the guidelines of God's revealed will (the law of Moses), and he sought divine counsel when appropriate (mostly), but at the end of the day, he just followed his heart. And when he audaciously followed up those bold decisions by seeking to build a permanent temple for God in Jerusalem, the Lord's response was epic:

> But in the same night the word of the LORD came to Nathan, saying, "Go and say to My servant David, 'Thus says the LORD, "Are you the one who should build Me a house to dwell in? For I have not dwelt in a house since the day I brought up the sons of Israel from Egypt, even to this

day; but I have been moving about in a tent, even in a tabernacle. **Wherever I have gone with all the sons of Israel, did I speak a word with one of the tribes of Israel, which I commanded to shepherd My people Israel, saying, 'Why have you not built Me a house of cedar?'"**

—2 SAMUEL 7:4-7

I used to think that God was somewhat annoyed at David in this response, but then I heard a friend describing Christ's parable of the unprofitable servant in a new light, and it changed my perspective:

And which of you, having a servant plowing or tending sheep, will say to him when he has come in from the field, 'Come at once and sit down to eat'? But will he not rather say to him, 'Prepare something for my supper, and gird yourself and serve me till I have eaten and drunk, and afterward you will eat and drink'? Does he thank that servant because he did the things that were commanded him? I think not. So likewise you, when you have done all those things which you are commanded, say, 'We are unprofitable servants. We have done what was our duty to do'.

—LUKE 17:7-10, NKJV

This parable hints at the reality that obedience is not God's end goal for human free will. Obedience requires that an explicit command is first given. But God's ultimate intention is that we will share His heart and freely act out of the same motivation.

So think of King Saul as the unprofitable servant who only sought to do the bare minimum he was commanded (and even that, he failed to do correctly). David, on the other hand, knowing the master's heart, sought to bless God above and beyond his duty. As a result, God wanted David (and everyone, everywhere, for all eternity) to understand that He had never, ever so much as hinted to anyone that He wanted a permanent home. Yet David, the man after God's own heart, wanted to bless Him with one. Was God upset? Did He rebuke David's presumptuous initiative? Did He at least slap David's wrist for daring to move the Ark into his backyard before getting permission for such a project? Quite the opposite:

The LORD also declares to you that the LORD **will make a house for you**. When your days are complete and you lie down with your fathers, I will raise up your descendant after you, who will come forth from you, and I will establish his kingdom. **He shall build a house for My name, and I will establish the throne of his kingdom forever. I will be a father to him and he will be a son to Me**; when he commits iniquity, I will correct him with the rod of men and the strokes of the sons of men, but My lovingkindness shall not depart from him, as I took it away from Saul, whom I removed from before you. **Your house and your kingdom shall endure before Me forever; your throne shall be established forever**.
—2 SAMUEL 7:11-16

God was so pleased with David's heart that He promised to build David a house and establish his kingdom forever! David's initiative was outside the Lord's explicit command but directly in line with the Father's heart, and it was the key that opened an everlasting door for God's life to flow to humanity in a new way. It produced a generational blessing that would flow through David's descendants all the way down to Jesus Christ.

Despite many future centuries of wicked kings that would descend from David's family line and commit abominable acts leading to God's judgment, God always ensured that David's bloodline persisted. Nobody could shut the door that David had opened, nor open a different door through which Christ would come. Jesus would come from the line of David and rule on David's throne because David's initiative to build a house for God had perfectly captured the essence of sonship.

> Obedience is not God's end goal for human free will. Obedience requires that an explicit command is first given. But God's ultimate intention is that we will share His heart and freely act out of the same motivation.

In the end, David wasn't allowed to build the temple himself because he was a man of war with much blood on his hands (see 1 Chronicles 28:2-3). Instead, as God promised, He chose David's son Solomon to build the physical temple in Jerusalem. But Jesus, the One who is holy and the One who is true, is the ultimate fulfillment of this prophecy.

Don't get me wrong, obedience is important. It's a good place to start but it's not the destination. Obedience requires knowledge about God's commands, but if we don't learn what that information reveals about God's heart from the Spirit of Knowledge, we will remain unprofitable servants only ever doing the least amount required. Moreover, the Spirit of Knowledge doesn't typically drop information into our minds. He often leads us through a liberating process of gathering knowledge that grows us in wisdom and makes us more like Christ, the source and destination of all knowledge.

Ultimately, we are not called to be like Saul, who required hyper-specific step-by-step instructions to keep him out of trouble. We are called to be like David, who could be trusted to initiate brand-new ideas beyond God's explicit instruction because he understood the Father's heart.

That's why Christ introduced Himself to the ruler church of Philadelphia as "He who is holy, who is true, who has the key of David, who opens and no one will shut, and who shuts and no one opens" (Revelation 3:7). Everything He was about to say would be about the kind of sonship that leads to bold and beautiful expressions of creativity that move the Father's heart and build the kingdom of Jesus. And that is how God desires the ruler portion of our spirit to lead. True godly leadership reproduces courageous freedom and innovation, not timid rule-followers.

---

Ultimately, we are not called to be like Saul, who required hyper-specific step-by-step instructions to keep him out of trouble. We are called to be like David, who could be trusted to initiate brand-new ideas beyond God's explicit instruction because he understood the Father's heart.

---

# CHAPTER 11

# CHRIST'S SEVEN LETTERS:
# TO PHILADELPHIA, PART 2 - WISDOM OR FOLLY?

W ith the echos of David's audacity still reverberating in the atmosphere, and the idea of opening and shutting offering tantalizing clues about where this is going, Jesus continued His letter to Philadelphia:

> I know your deeds. Behold, I have put before you an open
> door which no one can shut, because you have a little pow-
> er, and have kept My word, and have not denied My name.
> Behold, I will cause those of the synagogue of Satan, who
> say that they are Jews and are not, but lie—I will make
> them come and bow down at your feet, and make them
> know that I have loved you. Because you have kept the
> word of My perseverance, I also will keep you from the
> hour of testing, that hour which is about to come upon the
> whole world, to test those who dwell on the earth. I am
> coming quickly; hold fast what you have, so that no one will
> take your crown.
> —*REVELATION 3:8-11*

Like the servant church of Smyrna, Jesus had no rebuke for Philadelphia. In fact, many of Smyrna's themes are also present in Philadelphia, though from a different angle. That's not surprising, considering there is a very close, almost balancing relationship between the servant gift and the ruler gift.

Smyrna suffered through blasphemy and persecution at the hands of the synagogue of Satan, while Philadelphia was promised that the synagogue of Satan would bow down at their feet and recognize the truth of Christ's love through them. Smyrna would be imprisoned, while Philadelphia was given an open door. Smyrna would suffer "ten days" of tribulation, while Philadelphia would be kept from the hour of testing coming upon the whole world. Smyrna was promised the crown of life if they were faithful to the point of death, while Philadelphia was told to maintain their devotion to the end so that their crown would not be taken. If we look at these letters as a progression, it's as if Philadelphia benefited from the authority earned from Smyrna's perseverance.

Notice that both letters largely revolve around the synagogue of Satan who falsely called themselves Jews. Again, we're not talking about literal Satanists worshipping in occult temples. We previously identified these masqueraders as people who claimed to worship God but inwardly were ravenous wolves using a pretense of godliness to enrich themselves at the cost of the sheep.

It's not that they weren't Jews by ancestry, but they leveraged the legitimacy of the label of Jew while, in their hearts, they lacked faith in the Child of Promise:

> A man is not a Jew because he is one outwardly, nor is circumcision only outward and physical. No, a man is a Jew because he is one inwardly, and circumcision is a matter of the heart, by the Spirit, not by the written code. Such a man's praise does not come from men, but from God.
> —ROMANS 2:28-29, BSB

> But it is not as though the word of God has failed. For they are not all Israel who are descended from Israel; nor are they all children because they are Abraham's descendants, but: "THROUGH ISAAC YOUR DESCENDANTS WILL BE NAMED." That is, it is not the children of the flesh who are

children of God, but the children of the promise are re-
garded as descendants.
—*ROMANS 9:6-8*

To be clear, I'm not saying this "synagogue of Satan" is exclusively
linked to the Jewish race. The label has to do with heart attitude and
action, not ethnicity. Some Pharisees actually supported Christ, as did
many Jewish laypeople, so this has nothing to do with physical race or
creed.

Think of those Pharisees and Sadducees who opposed Christ because they were afraid to lose their positions of influence and wealth.
They closed their ears and eyes to the truth and used their authority
only for personal gain. The servant church of Smyrna was especially
equipped to counteract such abuse.

All of that applies here too, but with Philadelphia there is an additional characteristic of these false Jews that we need to understand to
grasp the full weight of Christ's letter. As we'll see in a moment, the
book of Acts contains a secondary story thread—an often-missed subtext—that deals with the false Jews and many of the same themes that
run through the letters to Smyrna and Philadelphia. By examining that
thread, we can gain a much deeper understanding of Christ's exhortation to Philadelphia (and Smyrna, for that matter).

This is the start of that epic detour I mentioned earlier. As we move
forward, just remember that it will all tie together wonderfully in the end.

## THE JERUSALEM COUNCIL

Our side quest revolves around the council at Jerusalem that occurred
around 48 A.D. The story is told in Acts chapter 15, though it requires
some knowledge of the surrounding events to get the whole picture.
We'll jump right into the main narrative and add additional context as
necessary:

> Some men came down from Judea and began teaching the
> brethren, "Unless you are circumcised according to the
> custom of Moses, you cannot be saved." And when Paul
> and Barnabas had great dissension and debate with them,
> the brethren determined that Paul and Barnabas and some

others of them should go up to Jerusalem to the apostles and elders concerning this issue. Therefore, being sent on their way by the church, they were passing through both Phoenicia and Samaria, describing in detail the conversion of the Gentiles, and were bringing great joy to all the brethren.

When they arrived at Jerusalem, they were received by the church and the apostles and the elders, and they reported all that God had done with them. But some of the sect of the Pharisees who had believed stood up, saying, "It is necessary to circumcise them and to direct them to observe the Law of Moses."

*—ACTS 15:1-5*

The conflict described in these verses centers around the teachings of a sect of Christian Pharisees who contended that salvation required observing the law of Moses. This was a difficult question for the young Church. After all, Jesus Himself had observed the spirit and the heart of the law of Moses, while living a life that fulfilled the letter of its requirements. At that time in Church history, many Jewish converts, including some of the disciples themselves, wrestled with whether or not they were still bound to the law.

Observing the law was the only form of righteousness the Jewish people had known for thousands of years, and their new Messiah never explicitly instructed them to throw it away. It wasn't a pressing issue as long as the Church consisted entirely of Jewish believers. Jewish converts to Christianity could continue following the law as a good and moral way of life while also knowing they were loved by the Father and redeemed through Christ's sacrifice.

However, by the time of the Jerusalem Council, the Holy Spirit was growing the Church beyond the boundaries of Israel. Once God extended salvation to Gentile nations who didn't know or observe the law, the early Church leadership was finally forced to confront some fundamental questions about their relationship with the law of Moses.

These questions were vital, not just for the Gentile branches, but for the future of the entire olive tree of Christ's Body. They were questions of legitimacy more than cultural traditions. If the natural branches continued clinging to the law of Moses for legitimacy, they would never grow strong enough to support the fruit they were intended to bear.

## WHAT KIND OF FRUIT?

Along those lines, as we unpack this debate about the law of Moses during the Jerusalem Council, think of the law as an expression of the fruit from the tree of the knowledge of good and evil. The law is not evil, just as the knowledge of good and evil isn't evil. The law is a righteous and accurate expression of God's principles, as was the fruit of the forbidden tree. But God commanded Adam and Eve not to eat that fruit because it represented a shortcut to knowledge that bypassed His intended process of sonship. It gave them knowledge of His truth without the wisdom to see or understand the principles of their life-giving application. It made them like Shebna instead of Eliakim, or Saul instead of David.

The same is true of the law of Moses, which was originally given at Mount Sinai to an immature group of rebellious slaves who refused to submit to the wilderness of God's growth plan. Since they were unwilling to learn His heart and walk in a manner congruent with His principles, God bound them like children to a strict set of instructions that would keep them out of trouble but could never bring them to maturity. The law was still beautiful—if Israel could learn to discern what it intimated about God's character—but it was only meant as a temporary tutor until Christ, the tree of life, was presented to them.

> The law was still beautiful—if Israel could learn to discern what it intimated about God's character—but it was only meant as a temporary tutor until Christ, the tree of life, was presented to them.

## AN OUTSIDE PERSPECTIVE

Before we go back to the Acts chapter 15 narrative, let's quickly jump over to the Apostle Paul's account of an earlier trip to Jerusalem in the book of Galatians. In this account, Paul describes a private meeting with a small group of apostles and elders in Jerusalem. There is some debate among scholars about when this meeting took place in the timeline of the book of Acts. I lean toward the view that the book of Galatians was written before the Jerusalem Council, which means this private meeting happened sometime before the big council. But either way works for the point I'm building toward:

> Then after an interval of fourteen years I went up again to Jerusalem with Barnabas, taking Titus along also. It was because of a revelation that I went up; and I submitted to them the gospel which I preach among the Gentiles, but I did so in private to those who were of reputation, for fear that I might be running, or had run, in vain.
> —*GALATIANS 2:1-2*

So Paul went to Jerusalem to present the gospel of righteousness by faith alone, which he had received by divine revelation and had been preaching among the Gentiles for some time. He did this not to seek the apostles' opinion on his doctrine, but to seek unity among the brethren and, as we'll soon see, to obtain their help in pushing back against those in the church who taught that righteousness still depended on adherence to the law of Moses. What he encountered on that trip is telling:

> But not even Titus, who was with me, though he was a Greek, was compelled to be circumcised. But it was because of the **false brethren secretly brought in**, who had sneaked in **to spy out our liberty** which we have in Christ Jesus, in order **to bring us into bondage**. But we did not yield in subjection to them for even an hour, so that the truth of the gospel would remain with you.
> —*GALATIANS 2:3-5*

These false brethren who were secretly brought in to spy on Paul's company are the same group that Acts 15 later describes as "some men who came down from Judea." In Acts 15 we saw them teaching "unless you are circumcised … you cannot be saved," and that's what led Paul to travel to Jerusalem for the council. It's hard to know for sure if they were also linked to the sect of believing Pharisees mentioned in Acts 15 who taught the same heresies, but the connection is likely. Their purpose was twofold: observe if the Gentile believers obeyed the law of Moses, and then instruct them on how to follow it. In reality, these false brethren were leveraging religion and accusation to bully new believers into bondage.

In case it's not obvious yet, these false brethren are of the same ilk as the "synagogue of Satan" described in Christ's letters to Smyrna and Philadelphia. They were continuing the same tactics employed by the Jewish Sanhedrin during Christ's ministry, who often sent members to follow Christ around, gather intel for false accusations, combat Christ's teachings in real-time, and generally work to undermine His support among the people. Their main weapons were accusations of unrighteousness based on their misunderstanding of the intention and spirit of the law. They also threatened to use the Jewish religious system to alienate the followers of Christ from family, friends, and society. It is no wonder that Jesus later referred to their type as a synagogue of Satan. Satan literally means *the accuser*. They were an organized group of accusers wrongly weaponizing the law of Moses.

Some commentators refer to these false brethren—and the related sect of believing Pharisees—as *the Judaizers*. If you are wondering who brought them into the Body of Christ, and whether they were brought in intentionally or naively, the answer is impossible to know for sure. However, some potential clues will surface as we go. For now, let's keep reading Paul's account of his private meeting with the apostles in Jerusalem some years before the larger council meeting:

> But from those who were of high reputation (what they were makes no difference to me; God shows no partiality) —well, those who were of reputation contributed nothing to me. But on the contrary, seeing that I had been entrusted with the gospel to the uncircumcised, just as Peter had been to the circumcised (for He who effectually worked for Peter in his apostleship to the circumcised effectually worked for me also to the Gentiles), and recognizing the grace that had been given to me, James and Cephas and John, who were reputed to be pillars, gave to me and Barnabas the right hand of fellowship, so that we might go to the Gentiles and they to the circumcised.
> —*GALATIANS 2:6-9*

"Those who were of reputation contributed nothing to me." Can you hear Paul's disappointment? Surely there was some sarcasm when he said, "Those who were reputed to be pillars." It seems Paul viewed his meeting with James, Cephas (Peter), and John as a partial disappointment yielding mixed results. Yes, they recognized the legitimacy of his apostleship and extended to him the right hand of fellowship. That was immense because it meant his work with the Gentile churches shouldn't cause a schism with the natural branches of the Body of Christ. But what about the influence of the false brethren? Was that issue adequately addressed?

I don't think so, which leads us to the subsequent public council meeting in Acts chapter 15 that was called to address that very topic. As we'll see in a moment, Peter (unsurprisingly) was the first leader "of reputation" to speak up in that meeting, and he came out strongly against applying the requirements of the law to the Gentiles. After Peter's comments, Paul and Barnabas described the signs and wonders that God had performed among the Gentiles. And then, after everyone else had spoken, James offered his final judgment on the matter.

## JAMES WHO?

Before we look at the context of the Jerusalem Council comments, let's clarify which James we're talking about. The James speaking here is thought, at least by many scholars, to have been the bishop of the Jerusalem Church at that time. Whether or not that was his actual title, he clearly held a position of respect and authority during the council, as he presided over the meeting and got the last word.

His exact identity is the subject of much debate. Paul refers to him as "the Lord's brother" in Galatians 1:19 and 1 Corinthians 9:5, but there is some disagreement about what that means.

We know for certain it wasn't James the son of Zebedee and Salome, the brother of John the Beloved, because that James was martyred in Acts chapter 12.

Many believe that because he was called "the Lord's brother," and because Scripture mentions Jesus' "mother and brothers" on multiple occasions, this James was the son of Joseph and Mary, which would make him a younger half-brother of Jesus and not one of the original twelve apostles.

Others believe he was James the son of Alphaeus (also called Clopus), who was married to Mary's sister (also named Mary), and therefore a cousin of Jesus and one of the original twelve apostles (see John 19:25).

Either way, my point is that James almost certainly had some kind of familial relationship with Jesus. That much is clear, and it raises important questions. This might be a controversial perspective, and I could be wrong, but I find it odd that this James, whether he was the half-brother of Jesus or a half-cousin/original apostle, would have such a pre-eminent leadership position over the early church. More than just a man reputed to be a pillar in the Church, James's name is typically mentioned first, and it seems his word carried the most weight. More weight than even Peter and John.

I could understand Peter having such influence. He was never shy to take the lead. His declaration of faith became the rock upon which Christ said he would build His Church. Jesus also directly commissioned Peter to shepherd His sheep (see John 21:16). And he, along with John, was part of Jesus' innermost circle of trust. So Peter would make sense. But why this James?

I'm not suggesting that it was absolutely wrong for James to rise to such prominence in leading the early church. He had the respect and trust of the apostles, and his speech at the Jerusalem Council demonstrated wisdom. I just find it interesting that a relative of Jesus was running things at that point. From the outside looking in, it is hard not to see at least a tiny hint of church politics and nepotism at work here, especially considering the words of Christ:

> While He was still speaking to the crowds, behold, His mother and brothers were standing outside, seeking to speak to Him. Someone said to Him, "Behold, Your mother and Your brothers are standing outside seeking to speak to You." But Jesus answered the one who was telling Him and said, "Who is My mother and who are My brothers?" And stretching out His hand toward His disciples, He said, "Behold My mother and My brothers! "For whoever does the will of My Father who is in heaven, he is My brother and sister and mother."
> —*MATTHEW 12:46-50*

Scripture gives no explanation for James's leadership, so we are left to reason from the evidence (which is a sophisticated way of describing an educated guess). Perhaps the Holy Spirit made it abundantly clear to the other apostles that James's authority should be elevated, which is why his words carried more weight at that time in Church history. But that is not necessarily the case.

There is no reason to think the apostles became perfectly wise and unified after receiving the Holy Spirit in the upper room. The book of Acts and many of the Epistles contain ample testimonies of the early Church's mistakes, including some of the same personality clashes, power struggles, and doctrinal arguments that plagued the disciples before the resurrection. Also, instant maturity certainly hasn't been my Christian experience, and I'm sure it hasn't been yours either. All of that to say this: James's appointment didn't necessarily come through divine guidance. I'm not saying the size of his leadership role was definitely a mistake, but it's fair to weigh the question as we study the surrounding events.

Jesus never gave the apostles a clear blueprint for how to build the Church. There were no divinely dictated instructions for growth, Church government structures, or mediation strategies for doctrinal disputes. Like Adam and Eve's original commission in the garden, Jesus simply demonstrated the principles of the kingdom in front of his disciples and then sent them into the rest of the world to replicate the results, expecting them to act like sons (in the spiritual sense) while leaning on the Holy Spirit to unpack the life of God that was now inside of them. He wasn't interested in building His Church on the fruit of the tree of the knowledge of good and evil, nor on a temporary tutor like the law of Moses that provided strict rules and instructions that were designed for the immature and rebellious. So it's no surprise that the early Church bumbled through much of the process, feeling their way forward as they went. It was intended to be that way so they could have room to grow in sonship.

With all of that in mind, and given that the most obvious threat to the Church after Christ's ascension was fierce persecution from Jewish leaders who feared losing their influence and way of life (the synagogue of Satan), is it any wonder that the early Church might lean on a close relative of Jesus?

Furthermore, whether brother or cousin, its possible that James bore some physical resemblance to Jesus through shared genetics on Mary's side. That depends on whether Jesus was actually born from Mary's egg or whether she was just a surrogate host in whom the Holy Spirit provided both egg and fertilization. Scripture isn't perfectly clear on that point, and strong arguments exist on both sides. Either way, it is at least possible that James shared a family resemblance with Jesus or Mary or both. And such a resemblance could have been a comforting reminder and a point of stability for some—however superficial and carnal that comfort would be.

> He wasn't interested in building His Church on the fruit of the tree of the knowledge of good and evil, nor on a temporary tutor like the law of Moses that provided strict rules and instructions that were designed for the immature and rebellious.

But even if there was no resemblance, the simple fact that James knew Jesus much longer than most may have been enough to elevate his influence in many minds, fairly or not. Add to that mix the fact that James had a particular affinity for Jewish tradition, as well as a compassion for the struggle of Jewish believers to reconcile the boundaries of the law of Moses with the freedom of the new covenant, and his influence during that early phase of Church history is understandable.

## WHO HAS THE KEYS?

I brought all of that up because James's background helps us make sense of his judgment at the council in Jerusalem. We'll get to that in a moment, but first, here is Peter's statement on the matter of Gentiles and the law of Moses:

> After there had been much debate, Peter stood up and said to them, "Brethren, you know that in the early days God made a choice among you, **that by my mouth the Gentiles would hear the word of the gospel** and believe. And God, who knows the heart, testified to them giving them the Holy Spirit, just as He also did to us; and **He made no distinction between us and them**, cleansing their hearts by faith.

> Now therefore why do you put God to the test by plac-
> ing upon the neck of the disciples **a yoke which neither
> our fathers nor we have been able to bear?** But we
> believe that **we are saved through the grace of the
> Lord Jesus**, in the same way as they also are."
> —ACTS 15:7-11

Peter started his discourse by reminding everyone that God first used him to open the door of salvation to the Gentiles when he visited the house of Cornelius, the Roman centurion, as described in Acts chapter 10. I don't think Peter said this as a boast. It was simply the context that gave his next words more meaning. And then, as he often did, Peter cut straight to the point with a bold statement of black-and-white truth. Calling the law a burden to all, he fearlessly declared its powerlessness to bestow righteousness on anybody, Jew or Gentile.

Peter's courage is the context in which James would answer. Perhaps James was concerned Peter's definitive proclamation would cause division among the Jewish Christians. Most of them still observed the law for cultural reasons, and some—like the sect of believing Pharisees—still stubbornly clung to the law for legitimacy. That's the frame in which James stepped up to the plate:

> After they had stopped speaking, James answered, saying,
> "Brethren, listen to me. Simeon has related how God first
> concerned Himself about taking from among the Gentiles
> a people for His name."
> —ACTS 15:13-14

First, notice how James referred to Peter in front of the entire council. He called him Simeon, the old Hebrew version of Peter's original name, Simon, which means *to hear*, or *he who listens*. Perhaps James did this out of innocent familiarity and longstanding friendship with Peter. Or maybe it was a power move. Either way, whether intentional or not, the subtext of not calling him Peter (a Greek name) at that moment is fascinating.

Remember, Jesus blessed Simon and changed his name to Peter (the rock) because he boldly spoke the truth of Christ's Sonship without direction or approval from any religious authority. Then, after renaming him *the rock* and promising to build His Church upon the revelation of Christ's Sonship, Jesus made another astonishing statement:

> I will give you the keys of the kingdom of heaven; and whatever you bind on earth shall have been bound in heaven, and whatever you loose on earth shall have been loosed in heaven.
> —*MATTHEW 16:19*

The keys of the kingdom of heaven? Are those related to the key of David? Scripture doesn't say for sure, but they certainly share similarities. Binding and loosing. Closing and opening. Both deal with restricting and allowing flow from one place to another. Isn't that what Peter did when he visited Cornelius and opened the door of the gospel to the Gentiles? And now Peter was at it again: standing in front of the Jerusalem Council, speaking words about the law of Moses that could potentially blow the doors of grace wide open, not just for the Gentiles, but also for the Jewish believers, while slamming the door shut on the law of Moses.

So when James finally spoke up, saying, "Brethren, listen to *me*," and referring to Peter as Simeon (*he who listens*) in front of the entire council, including the sect of believing Pharisees, is it possible that he was undermining Peter's authority, pulling rank, and trying to dial back the full weight of Peter's words before they caused what James considered to be irreparable harm to the Church's relationship (however tenuous it was) with the Jewish Sanhedrin?

## WHICH TABERNACLE?

James then continued his statement by quoting from the Old Testament prophet Amos (see Amos 9:11-12) before applying that prophecy in a very creative way:

> With this [Peter's testimony of the Holy Spirit extending the gospel to the Gentiles] the words of the Prophets agree, just as it is written:
> 'AFTER THESE THINGS I will return, AND I WILL REBUILD THE TABERNACLE OF DAVID WHICH

HAS FALLEN, AND I WILL REBUILD ITS RUINS, AND I WILL RESTORE IT, SO THAT THE REST OF MANKIND MAY SEEK THE LORD, AND ALL THE GENTILES WHO ARE CALLED BY MY NAME,' SAYS THE LORD, WHO MAKES THESE THINGS KNOWN FROM LONG AGO.

**Therefore it is my judgment that we do not trouble those who are turning to God from among the Gentiles**, but that we write to them that they abstain from things contaminated by idols and from fornication and from what is strangled and from blood. For Moses from ancient generations has in every city those who preach him, since he is read in the synagogues every Sabbath.

—*ACTS 15:15-21 [BRACKETED TEXT ADDED FOR CLARITY]*

Okay, so James agreed with Peter, at least as far as the Gentiles were concerned. But notice the Scripture he used to support his reasoning. He pointed to a relatively obscure prophecy about rebuilding the tabernacle of David—the temporary tent David used to store the Ark of the Covenant in Jerusalem before the permanent temple was built.

The tabernacle of David was something of an enigma in the Old Testament. There were no provisions in the law of Moses for David to store the Ark of the Covenant in a separate tent in Jerusalem. Especially since the Levitical priesthood continued observing the ordinances for sacrifices and offerings and religious worship in Gibeon where the original tabernacle of Moses remained (along with the rest of the holy furniture).

One could argue that the tabernacle of David represented the ability to have faith in God outside of the law without abolishing the need to observe the law, since it existed in parallel with the tabernacle of Moses. In the context of Amos's prophecy, which specifically mentions that the rebuilding of David's tabernacle would support Gentile worship, one could also argue that Gentiles might worship God outside of the law without suggesting that Jews needed to abandon the ordinances of the tabernacle of Moses. And that seems to be what James was arguing at the council in Jerusalem.

James was willing to use the keys of the kingdom of heaven to open the tabernacle of David for the Gentiles. However, he was not willing to close the tabernacle of Moses for the Jews. Said another way, he was willing to close the door to the law of Moses as a requirement for the Gentiles, but he wasn't willing to risk offending the Jewish observers of the law by unequivocally extending that same closed door to Jewish Christians. He wasn't saying Jewish Christians *must* observe the law; he was merely dithering on the question to leave room for both perspectives.

It is telling that James concluded his judgment by stating, "For Moses from ancient generations has in every city those who preach him, since he is read in the synagogues every Sabbath." In other words, he didn't want to risk denigrating the law, which was still preached in Jewish synagogues throughout the known world as a moral and righteous standard. And he wasn't ready to proclaim to Jews everywhere (those who believed in Christ and those who didn't) that the law of Moses was no longer God's provision for their life.

## WISDOM OR FOLLY?

Was James right to deploy such a half-measure to keep the peace? And was he even successful in keeping the peace? Those are complex questions probably requiring the hindsight of eternity to untangle. Maybe he made the wisest decision possible for that transitionary period of Church history in which the physical temple in Jerusalem still existed (for a little while longer), while the Holy Spirit rapidly moved the Church toward a tabernacle of David style of worship. Maybe James's judgment offered Jewish Christians a temporary lifeline to keep up with all the changes. That's the generous way of looking at it.

Scripture doesn't say one way or the other, and maybe that is part of the lesson. After all, we aren't designed to follow some predetermined step-by-step instruction manual for perfection. God often gives us wide latitude to work things out like sons trying to learn what is pleasing to the Father. Other times He invites us to wait on Him and receive like a Bride. The freedom and maturity to figure out when to initiate versus when to wait is a prerequisite for using the key of David.

Having said that, I think James didn't go far enough in his judgment because he was still leaning too much on the crutch of the law of Moses. Perhaps, like Shebna, he saw "that the breaches in the wall of the city of David were many" and used the authority of the key of David in a way that didn't fully align with God's heart (Isaiah 22:9). Perhaps he feared the wide-open path of liberty presented to the Gentiles.

I imagine he wrestled with many questions. How would such freedom impact the Jerusalem Church? What would Jewish culture look like if Jews were no longer compelled to observe the letter of the law? Where was the balance between honoring the righteous traditions given to their fathers and embracing the fullness of Messiah? Who would arbitrate the details of what it meant to follow the spirit of the law without being bound to the letter of its specific commandments? How would he help shepherd the flock under such foreign conditions? And wasn't the letter of the law better than no law at all for those unbelieving Jews who weren't ready to embrace the new covenant?

In some ways, James faced the same challenge presented to Adam and Eve in the garden, and like them, he chose the easier path. Not that James's decision was sinful, since in this case, there was no explicit command from God one way or the other. But perhaps he missed the better path represented by the tree of life.

Unlike the forbidden fruit, no command was ever given about the tree of life. God didn't tell Adam and Eve to eat it. He didn't even tell them what it was for. It was simply there in the middle of the garden to be discovered, explored, inquired about, unpacked, and freely eaten if desired. So too is the grace available to us in the new covenant.

---

In some ways, James faced the same challenge presented to Adam and Eve in the garden, and like them, he chose the easier path. Not that James's decision was sinful, since in this case, there was no explicit command from God one way or the other. But perhaps he missed the better path represented by the tree of life.

## CHAPTER 12

# CHRIST'S SEVEN LETTERS:
# TO PHILADELPHIA, PART 3 - ANCIENT WOUNDS?

S o what? What did all of that talk about the Jerusalem Council
have to do with Philadelphia? We're almost there, but we still need
to drill down on the long-term impact of James's judgment. Stick
with me for a few more twists and turns, and then we'll tie it all together.

We've already seen that Paul wasn't entirely thrilled with the out-
come of his earlier private trip to Jerusalem when the false brethren
weren't dealt with as they should have been. Reading between the lines
of the book of Acts, I think Paul wasn't fully satisfied with James's
judgment at the council in Acts 15 either. I think that dissatisfaction
stayed with him for years and eventually led him back to Jerusalem to
address the issue.

I'll explain what I mean by that in a moment, but first, let's go back
to Galatians, where we find a fascinating encounter between Peter and
Paul. Again, this likely happened after the private meeting but before
James's judgment at the public council. I bring it up because it reveals

the root of the real issue that the council would later fail to deal with, and it demonstrates Paul's insight and passion on the subject:

> But when Cephas came to Antioch, I opposed him to his face, because he stood condemned. For **prior to the coming of certain men from James**, he used to eat with the Gentiles; but when they came, he began to withdraw and hold himself aloof, **fearing the party of the circumcision**. The rest of the Jews joined him in hypocrisy, with the result that even Barnabas was carried away by their hypocrisy. But when I saw that they were not straightforward about the truth of the gospel, I said to Cephas in the presence of all, **"If you, being a Jew, live like the Gentiles and not like the Jews, how is it that you compel the Gentiles to live like Jews?**
>
> "We are Jews by nature and not sinners from among the Gentiles; nevertheless knowing that a man is not justified by the works of the Law but through faith in Christ Jesus, even we have believed in Christ Jesus, so that we may be justified by faith in Christ and not by the works of the Law; since by the works of the Law no flesh will be justified."
>
> —GALATIANS 2:11-16

So Peter (Cephas) succumbed to negative peer pressure when "certain men from James" who were of "the party of the circumcision" arrived in Antioch. Either these men overtly convinced Peter to separate himself from the Gentiles during meals or Peter did so out of fear of their unstated opinions. Either way, James's apparent influence on this situation is hard to ignore. His support of believing Jews still clinging to the old covenant for righteousness is what empowered their desire to enforce the law on Gentiles. But this situation with Peter revealed the problem to be much deeper than a question of Gentile freedom.

If Jewish Christians were still bound in their minds to the law but Gentile Christians were not, how could there be unity between the natural and wild branches? If the converted Gentiles could live according to the grace pattern of the tabernacle of David, but converted Jews could choose to live according to the law pattern of the tabernacle of Moses in a way that set themselves apart and above the Gentiles, the result would always be division and a twisting of the truth of the gospel.

Paul's stinging rebuke should come as no surprise. This is the same guy who also said:

> There is neither Jew nor Greek, there is neither slave nor free man, there is neither male nor female; for you are all one in Christ Jesus.
> —*GALATIANS 3:28*

> You have been severed from Christ, you who are seeking to be justified by law; you have fallen from grace.
> —*GALATIANS 5:4*

To be clear, Paul was not teaching that it was wrong to follow the law of Moses. His problem was with using the law to be justified. In other words, deriving legitimacy from the law. That's what Peter did when he alienated the Gentiles just to avoid being judged by the Jews as unrighteous. Peter followed the letter of the law but broke the spirit of it. Following the law or not following the law is not what matters. What matters is the motivation behind either choice. Are we doing it as unprofitable slaves merely fulfilling what we were commanded, or are we acting in the freedom of sonship?

To be clear, Paul was not teaching that it was wrong to follow the law of Moses. His problem was with using the law to be justified. In other words, deriving legitimacy from the law.

If our righteousness is derived from faith in Christ, then even if we choose to follow the law, that choice won't lead us to break the law of Christ, which is to love God and love others. In other words, if we follow the law because we want to, we'll hold that freedom loosely and never use it to alienate others or elevate ourselves. Paul understood this principle well, and it gave him great freedom to use the law as a tool to preach the gospel:

> For though I am free from all men, I have made myself a slave to all, so that I may win more. To the Jews I became as a Jew, so that I might win Jews; to those who are under the Law, as under the Law though not being myself under

the Law, so that I might win those who are under the Law;
to those who are without law, as without law, though not
being without the law of God but under the law of Christ,
so that I might win those who are without law.
   —*1 CORINTHIANS 9:19-21*

For Peter's part, it seems he received Paul's rebuke with grace. Notice Paul called him Cephas, which is an Aramaic form of Peter. So Paul recognized the importance of Peter's role in the Body of Christ and was upholding it rather than undercutting it with his rebuke.

Paul's rebuke may be what gave Peter the conviction to stand so firmly against the idea of the law dividing between Jew and Gentile during the Jerusalem Council. Some sixteen years later, when he wrote the epistle of 2 Peter, he also spoke very highly of Paul and the profundity of Paul's wisdom:

and regard the patience of our Lord as salvation; just as
also our beloved brother Paul, according to the wisdom
given him, wrote to you, as also in all his letters, speaking in
them of these things, in which are some things hard to understand, which the untaught and unstable distort, as they
do also the rest of the Scriptures, to their own destruction.
   —*2 PETER 3:15-16*

Paul had an unquenchable passion for the redemption of Israel, but the depth of his insight into the mystery of Jesus Christ would not allow him to compromise on the role of the law of Moses in the new covenant. Years later, he would summarize his position:

Or do you not know, brethren (for I am speaking to those
who know the law), that the law has jurisdiction over a person as long as he lives? **For the married woman is
bound by law to her husband while he is living;
but if her husband dies, she is released from the
law concerning the husband.** So then, if while her
husband is living she is joined to another man, she shall be
called an adulteress; but if her husband dies, she is free
from the law, so that she is not an adulteress though she is
joined to another man.

Therefore, my brethren, **you also were made to die to the Law through the body of Christ, so that you might be joined to another, to Him who was raised from the dead**, in order that we might bear fruit for God. For while we were in the flesh, the sinful passions, which were aroused by the Law, were at work in the members of our body to bear fruit for death. **But now we have been released from the Law, having died to that by which we were bound, so that we serve in newness of the Spirit and not in oldness of the letter.**
—*ROMANS 7:1-6*

When Christ died on the cross as the "last Adam," Israel's legal obligation to the old covenant was terminated. The promises made to Abraham and his natural descendants are still active because those promises are outside the old covenant, but Israel is no longer bound to God through the law of Moses. Instead, they are free to join themselves to the "second man" under the terms of the new covenant, in which Christ is our righteousness and the letter of the law is merely a shadow in the past of the reality of God's heart.

The Gentile nations were never joined to the old covenant like Israel. Even so, the principle of Romans chapter 7 also applies to Gentiles, since the death of the last Adam severed humanity's legal connection to the fallen nature and the destructive impact of the fruit from the tree of the knowledge of good and evil. We still often choose to eat from the forbidden fruit, but we no longer need to be bound to it. Instead, we can reckon ourselves as "dead to sin, but alive to God in Christ Jesus" (Romans 6:11). So everyone has the option to eat from the tree of life by joining themselves to Christ through faith and becoming a new creation.

All of that is basic Christianity, but it wasn't basic when Paul wrote it. Paul paid a great price for these truths, and he spent much of his ministry being persecuted by the Jews for his unwavering stance on righteousness through faith in Christ alone. His teaching was a great offense to Satan since it cut to the heart of his original lie in the garden.

This doctrine was the root of Paul's teaching, and it represented so much more than a religious argument about faith versus works, or the spirit versus the letter of the law. Paul was planting seeds for the tree of life to spring up in the hearts of Jews and Gentiles alike. It was the only theology that could lead to a mature Body of Christ that walked in the creative freedom of sonship merged with bridal intimacy rather than the rigid slavery of the old covenant.

## RETURN TO JERUSALEM

As for the public Jerusalem Council, Paul accepted James's decision, though I believe he did so reluctantly. Then he spent the next ten years traveling throughout Asia Minor on missionary journeys where he was dogged at almost every step by Jewish opposition from the "synagogue of Satan." Because he loved the Jewish people, whenever he entered a new city, he preached the gospel first in the local Jewish temple—often at great peril to himself—before reaching out to the local Gentiles.

Paul had a series of great successes in Corinth and Ephesus somewhere in the middle of his third missionary journey. During that time, the unbelieving Jews were largely unable to blunt the gospel's spread for a span of 3.5 years. And that's when Paul set his heart on returning to Jerusalem for the first time since the Council. Acts chapter 19 records it this way:

> So the word of the Lord was growing mightily and prevailing.
> Now after these things were finished, **Paul purposed in the spirit to go to Jerusalem** after he had passed through Macedonia and Achaia, saying, "After I have been there, I must also see Rome."
> —ACTS 19:20-21

Notice that *Paul* purposed in the spirit. That doesn't necessarily mean that God commanded him. It was likely an act of his own will based on something he discerned in the spirit. He felt compelled by his convictions. Scripture doesn't tell us exactly what compelled him at that time, but it does provide some hints here and there:

> For Paul had decided to sail past Ephesus so that he would not have to spend time in Asia; for he was hurrying to be in Jerusalem, if possible, on the day of Pentecost.
> —ACTS 20:16

So we know at least part of the reason was to be in Jerusalem for the feast of Pentecost. This makes sense considering Paul relished his Jewish heritage and savored more than most the spiritual substance undergirding their traditions, though he didn't derive justification from any of it. Even so, there had to be more compelling him than a Jewish feast because he ignored multiple warnings along the way:

> And now, behold, bound by the Spirit, I am on my way to Jerusalem, not knowing what will happen to me there, except that the Holy Spirit solemnly testifies to me in every city, saying that bonds and afflictions await me. But I do not consider my life of any account as dear to myself, so that I may finish my course and the ministry which I received from the Lord Jesus, to testify solemnly of the gospel of the grace of God.
> *ACTS 20:22 24*

So on the one hand, Paul felt bound in spirit and compelled to go to Jerusalem, while on the other hand, the Holy Spirit kept warning him through various believers in multiple cities that he would be bound and afflicted in Jerusalem if he went. And the warnings only intensified as he continued his march toward the city of David:

> When we came in sight of Cyprus, leaving it on the left, we kept sailing to Syria and landed at Tyre; for there the ship was to unload its cargo. After looking up the disciples, we stayed there seven days; and they kept telling Paul through the Spirit not to set foot in Jerusalem.
> *—ACTS 21:3-4*

Finally, after leaving Tyre and coming to Caesarea (a port city not far from Jerusalem) Paul received the clearest warning of all while lodging with Philip the Evangelist, one of the original deacons from the earliest days of the church in Jerusalem:

> Now this man [Philip] had four virgin daughters who were prophetesses. As we were staying there for some days, a prophet named Agabus came down from Judea. And coming to us, he took Paul's belt and bound his own feet and hands, and said, "This is what the Holy Spirit says: 'In this

> way the Jews at Jerusalem will bind the man who owns this belt and deliver him into the hands of the Gentiles.'"
>
> When we had heard this, we as well as the local residents began begging him not to go up to Jerusalem. Then Paul answered, "What are you doing, weeping and breaking my heart? For I am ready not only to be bound, but even to die at Jerusalem for the name of the Lord Jesus."
>
> And since he would not be persuaded, we fell silent, remarking, "The will of the Lord be done!"
> —ACTS 21:9-14 [BRACKETED TEXT ADDED FOR CLARITY]

How do we make sense of all this? Why was Paul so bound and determined to go back to Jerusalem? Both he and the brothers and sisters warning him correctly discerned that something was up with the Jerusalem trip, but they interpreted the data in opposite ways. Paul heard the promise of opposition as evidence that he was on the right track, while everyone else heard it as a warning that he wasn't supposed to go. Who was right?

I don't think this was a question of right or wrong. I think Paul felt he had unfinished business in Jerusalem, and the Holy Spirit wanted him to know exactly what he was getting into if he went. It's possible the Lord directed him to go but Scripture leaves that point ambiguous.

Either way, I think Paul still had a bad taste in his mouth from the council some ten years earlier, and after all that he had seen and experienced in the Lord since then, he was resolved to reopen and readdress the question of the Jewish reliance on the law of Moses. What better time to address that divisive issue than during the Feast of Pentecost—the anniversary of the outpouring of the Holy Spirit and the birth of the Church?

According to the law of Moses, each Jewish family celebrated the Feast of Pentecost (also known as the Feast of Weeks) by bringing two loaves of leavened bread into the temple for an offering. Paul understood that these two loaves foreshadowed the Jews and Gentiles being brought together into the Body of Christ. What better time to appeal for unity by asking the Jews to embrace the spirit of the law while also releasing their iron grip on its letter of commandments:

> For He Himself is our peace, who has made the two one and has torn down the dividing wall of hostility by abolish-

ing in His flesh the law of commandments and decrees. He did this to create in Himself one new man out of the two, thus making peace and reconciling both of them to God in one body through the cross, by which He put to death their hostility.

   —*EPHESIANS 2:14-16, BSB*

Paul's decision to take this message to Jerusalem was courageous and honorable. The only problem is that James's well-meaning but short-sighted judgment at the council may have entrenched the position of the sect of believing Pharisees, and possibly also extinguished any chance of reformation within the greater Sanhedrin (and therefore the rest of Judaism). That's the danger and solemn responsibility of the key of David. Was it too late to fix the problem at the source? Paul was hoping it wasn't. Was he right? Let's read what happened when Paul finally arrived in Jerusalem. It's a long passage, but worth every second:

After we arrived in Jerusalem, the brethren received us gladly. And the following day Paul went in with us to James, and all the elders were present. After he had greeted them, he began to relate one by one the things which God had done among the Gentiles through his ministry.

And when they heard it they began glorifying God; and they said to him, **"You see, brother, how many thousands there are among the Jews of those who have believed, and they are all zealous for the Law; and they have been told about you, that you are teaching all the Jews who are among the Gentiles to forsake Moses, telling them not to circumcise their children nor to walk according to the customs.** What, then, is to be done? They will certainly hear that you have come. Therefore do this that we tell you. We have four men who are under a vow; take them and purify yourself along with them, and pay their expenses so that they may shave their heads; **and all will know that there is nothing to the things which they have been told about you, but that you yourself also walk orderly, keeping the Law**.

"But concerning the Gentiles who have believed, we wrote, having decided that they should abstain from meat

sacrificed to idols and from blood and from what is strangled and from fornication."

Then Paul took the men, and the next day, purifying
himself along with them, went into the temple giving notice
of the completion of the days of purification, until the sacrifice was offered for each one of them.

—ACTS 21:17-26

Houston, we have a problem! As courageous and prepared as he
was, Paul walked right into a lion's den. I don't think he expected the
spiritual assault to be quite so savage. It's sad to say that about the
church leadership in Jerusalem led by James, but I see no other way of
reading this passage. Yes, James and the elders glorified God when they
heard Paul's report of the amazing things God was doing among the
Gentiles, but they still fought to apply
the boundary of the law to Jewish Christians. That's why they turned Paul's
words around and spiritually assaulted
him with false accusations that he was
teaching Jews to forsake Moses.

Paul loved the law and the Prophets
and understood them far better than
they did. He hadn't forsaken Moses; he
had taught the deeper truths physically
foreshadowed by Moses but spiritually
realized in Christ. He wasn't telling Jews
*not* to circumcise their kids, but rather
that physical circumcision was no longer
required for righteousness. Paul taught
that if you wanted to circumcise, do it
in freedom but never out of compulsion
(see Galatians 6:15).

Sure, these accusations hadn't originated with James and the elders, but
they did nothing to correct them, and

James's well-meaning but shortsighted judgment at the council may have entrenched the position of the sect of believing Pharisees, and possibly also extinguished any chance of reformation within the greater Sanhedrin (and therefore the rest of Judaism). That's the danger and solemn responsibility of the key of David.

they used them to bully Paul into an act of religious theater to pacify
an angry mob (more on that in a moment). And then, as if doubling
down on their divisiveness, they proudly reiterated James's original
judgment that undergirded the supposed difference between Gentile

and Jewish Christians: "But concerning the Gentiles who have believed, we wrote ...."

Perhaps Paul should have seen this coming. Jesus encountered the same spiritual opposition after entering the city of David on a donkey as the heir to David's throne. Jesus eventually denounced the scribes and Pharisees who had "seated themselves in the chair of Moses" (Matthew 23:2) with an epic diatribe beginning with, "Woe to you, scribes and Pharisees, hypocrites, because you shut off the kingdom of heaven from people; for you do not enter in yourselves, nor do you allow those who are entering to go in" (Matthew 23:13).

In a sense, Jesus had entered Jerusalem to use the key of David to spiritually rebuild the tabernacle of David, but the religious leaders couldn't tolerate the freedom He was offering. They had only ever used the law of Moses to encumber and enslave themselves and others, and they couldn't see past that selfish utility.

Likewise, I think Paul hoped to work with James and the elders of the Jerusalem Church to throw the door of grace wide open to the Jews (or to help them see that the door was already wide open). He didn't expect to be blindsided by the depth to which the philosophy of those who "seated themselves in the chair of Moses" had infiltrated Church leadership.

The leaders then pressured Paul to take a Nazarite vow along with a group of other law followers. The Nazarite vow is described in Numbers chapter 6 as a temporary covenant of consecration to the Lord involving abstaining from certain foods and activities, and it required various animal sacrifices, including a sin offering.

Minus the sin offering, which was an affront to the cross, maybe it wasn't wrong in principle for Paul to take a Nazarite vow. There is some evidence in Acts that this might not have been the first time Paul took a Nazarite vow (see Acts 18:18). But to do so under coercion to placate the delusions of a self-righteous mob and prove that he kept the law? Particularly when his express purpose for

> These accusations hadn't originated with James and the elders, but they did nothing to correct them, and they used them to bully Paul into an act of religious theater to pacify an angry mob.

going to Jerusalem was to "testify solemnly of the gospel of the grace of God" (Acts 20:24)? Wasn't that essentially the same compromise for which he had rebuked Peter all those years ago? Such an action under those circumstances would undermine everything Paul stood for and kneecap his moral and spiritual authority to argue against the Judaizers. And that's exactly what happened. Paul submitted to the folly, participated in the vow, and thus proved Agabus's prophecy true: "In this way the Jews at Jerusalem will bind the man who owns this belt" (Acts 21:11).

As you read the rest of the story in Acts chapter 21, you'll see that the Church leadership's ill-advised gambit didn't work. The Jews saw through the ruse and started a riot against Paul that prompted the Roman authorities to step in. The Romans were the ones who arrested and physically bound Paul, but by that time he was already emotionally and spiritually bound by the Jews and by the Jerusalem Church leadership's abuse of spiritual authority, since they too had been influenced by the synagogue of Satan.

Paul's arrest ended his third missionary journey. There is no way to know this for sure, but it may have also significantly blunted the impact of his ministry from that point forward. God was still gracious to use the situation for His purposes by bringing Paul before many kings and government rulers to preach the gospel while he was under Roman arrest. But what could have happened if Paul hadn't compromised in Jerusalem? What level of maturity might the first-century Church have reached if Jewish and Gentile Christians could have come together as Christ intended, demonstrating the freedom and unity of the new covenant to both Israel and the Gentile world? We'll never know this side of eternity, but these questions are important to ponder. As we get closer to Christ's return, the Church will be forced to deal with the same wounds that have remained unhealed since the Jerusalem Council.

Okay, we've reached the end of our side quest. In the next chapter we'll return to the main path. Everything we just learned on the detour will illuminate the letter to Philadelphia in profound ways.

## CHAPTER 13

# CHRIST'S SEVEN LETTERS:
# TO PHILADELPHIA, PART 4 - AN OPEN DOOR

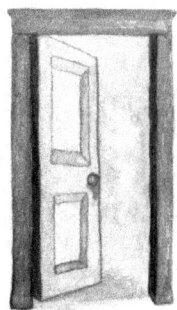

P aul's struggle against the influence of the Judaizers in the early Church provides the perfect context for understanding Christ's letter to the ruler church of Philadelphia while also reframing some of what we've already learned about the servant church of Smyrna.

Let's start with Smyrna. Remember, they suffered the blasphemy of the synagogue of Satan. They were cast into prison. They were promised temporary tribulation. Many of the main themes of their letter match up remarkably well with the flow of Paul's life. Even Christ's final exhortation to Smyrna—and the Bride's response—echoes Paul's experience at the end of his life, sitting in a Roman prison waiting for execution:

### Christ in His second letter:

> Be faithful until death, and I will give you the crown of life.
> —*REVELATION 2:10*

### The Bride's second response:

> For your love is better than wine
> —*SONG OF SOLOMON 1:2*

### Paul writing at the end of his life:

> For I am already being poured out as a **drink offering**, and the time of my departure has come. I have fought the good fight, I have finished the course, I have kept the faith; in the future there is laid up for me the **crown of righteousness**, which the Lord, the righteous Judge, will award to me on that day; and not only to me, but also to all who have loved His appearing.
> —*2 TIMOTHY 4:6-8*

Paul wrestled against the spiritual power behind the false Jews for his entire ministry. He was willing to lay down his life to build a platform for the Church to become all it was called to be, and although he lost a battle in Jerusalem, he still remained faithful until death. He died before he saw the fruit of his perseverance, but he and Luke recorded the highs and lows for the rest of us so we could understand the issues at hand, wrestle with the same questions, and benefit from the earned authority of his journey.

This aspect of Paul's life is a beautiful picture of the servant gift in action. We too must learn the lessons that Paul learned, being willing to follow the Holy Spirit into persecution and tribulation so that the servant portion of our spirit can grow in the authority necessary for participating in Christ's Unveiling. But just like Smyrna's perseverance became the foundation upon which Philadelphia would experience great breakthrough, there is an earned authority that Christ gives to those who heed the letter to the ruler church of Philadelphia:

> Behold, I have put before you an open door which no one can shut, because you have a little power, and have kept My word, and have not denied My name. Behold, I will cause those of the synagogue of Satan, who say that they are Jews and are not, but lie—I will make them come and bow down at your feet, and make them know that I have loved you.
> —*REVELATION 3:8-9*

The first promise to Philadelphia represented everything Paul had sacrificed for and so passionately desired to see. Paul once remarked that he intentionally magnified his ministry to the Gentiles in the hope that unbelieving Jews might grow jealous of the magnitude of God's favor, and thus be moved to embrace Christ (see Romans 11:13-14). That kind of jealousy is exactly what Jesus promised to Philadelphia. The ruler gift, if it learns the lesson of sacrificial service from the overcoming servant, is given an open door to bring illumination to the synagogue of Satan on a massive scale.

On one level, as we have seen, the synagogue of Satan can refer to those religious Jews who oppose Jesus as Messiah. On another level, it also refers to all pharisaical so-called Christians who oppose the free exercise of godly sonship because they derive legitimacy from a religious system rather than faith in Christ. In both cases, the open door of Philadelphia results in humility and heart-changing knowledge flowing to those who had built a false identity on the misappropriation of the spiritual treasures they received from God.

This also means that when the Body of Christ embraces the Unveiling of Jesus in this area, Christ will open a door for reaching the nation of Israel, and Israel's partial blindness will finally be removed. The gift of this open door makes sense, considering the redemptive gift of ruler, and the ruler portion of our spirit, are meant to use knowledge in creative ways to lead others into the unique freedoms for which they were designed.

## KEPT FROM THE HOUR

Another amazing promise was given to Philadelphia:

> Because you have kept the word of My perseverance, I also will keep you from the hour of testing, that hour which is about to come upon the whole world, to test those who dwell on the earth. I am coming quickly; hold fast what you have, so that no one will take your crown.
> —*REVELATION 3:10-11*

Some read this verse as a promise that the Church will be raptured before the great tribulation, but that's not what Jesus said. Putting aside the scriptural evidence for the resurrection happening sometime *after* the great tribulation (which we'll unpack later) such an assertion just doesn't make sense in the context of the seven letters.

We know the seven churches have multiple layers of meaning, including seven literal churches in ancient Asia Minor; seven seasons of Church history from the first century through to the end of the age; seven kinds of churches that will be alive on earth during the Unveiling of Christ; seven kinds of believers; and the seven portions of the human spirit. At most of those layers, it doesn't make any sense for Philadelphia to escape tribulation when the other six churches had to embrace it. The entire New Testament is an example of how the Church needs to go through tribulation to enter the kingdom of God. Let's not forget the powerful exhortation with a promise:

> Consider it all joy, my brethren, when you encounter various trials, knowing that the testing of your faith produces endurance. And let endurance have its perfect result, so that you may be perfect and complete, lacking in nothing.
> —JAMES 1:2-4

So if being kept "from the hour of testing" isn't talking about being raptured before the great tribulation, what does it mean?

First, consider that the Greek word for testing (*peirasmos*) in this verse is also translated in many other verses as "temptation." It is the same word used in the well-known and highly comforting promise about temptation:

> No **temptation** has overtaken you but such as is common to man; and God is faithful, who will not allow you to be tempted beyond what you are able, but with the **temptation** will provide the way of escape also, so that you will be able to endure it.
> —1 CORINTHIANS 10:13

God provides a way of escape so that we can endure temptation. He doesn't remove the temptation. Nor does He forcibly keep us away from tempting situations. He helps us endure so that we can escape the sin of falling to temptation by growing through the process. And yes, sometimes that means we need to find the strength to remove ourselves from the situation.

Now, remember what we learned back in book 1 from Revelation chapter 12? The great tribulation will begin as a flood of overwhelming temptation and filth poured out of the serpent's mouth. So yes, "that hour which is about to come upon the whole world, to test those who dwell on the earth" is likely a reference to the great tribulation. But what does it mean for Philadelphia to be kept from that hour?

Remember what else we learned from Revelation chapter 12? The serpent's flood won't begin until after the male child is birthed from the faithful Church. Then, just as heaven opened for Christ when He was baptized in the Jordan River, heaven will open for the "sons of God" movement of fully mature Christians who walk in sonship. *That* is the open door promised to Philadelphia. And because of that open door, Satan will be cast down to earth from his elevated position in the second heaven. Only after that casting down will the great tribulation begin.

Again, remember that a Christian's experience of the great tribulation will depend upon their spiritual maturity. In book 1 we used the three sections of the Tabernacle of Moses as a picture of three levels of maturity within the Body of Christ. How we respond to the wilderness trials of our lives largely determines our spiritual growth.

Those Christians who have spent their lives avoiding and ignoring their trials will be in the outer court. They will be forced to experience the unfiltered weight of the great tribulation because they need it the most. Some of them will succumb to the temptations associated with the great tribulation and fall away from the Faith, while others will overcome.

> God provides a way of escape so that we can endure temptation. He doesn't remove the temptation. Nor does He forcibly keep us away from tempting situations. He helps us endure so that we can escape the sin of falling to temptation by growing through the process.

Inner court Christians will experience their own set of trials during the great tribulation, but their testing will come in a wilderness of protection and nurture away from the violence of the serpent's filth.

Lastly, the holy of holies Christians will walk in mature sonship under an open heaven with full protection during the dragon's wrath.

These holy of holies Christians will inherit Christ's promise to keep Philadelphia from the hour of testing because they will have already overcome Satan in the wilderness prior to the great tribulation.

## THE OVERCOMERS IN PHILADELPHIA

What reward did Jesus promise to those in Philadelphia who embraced His Unveiling as "He who is holy, who is true, who has the key of David, who opens and no one will shut, and who shuts and no one opens" (Revelation 3:7)?

> He who overcomes, I will make him a pillar in the temple of My God, and he will not go out from it anymore; and I will write on him the name of My God, and the name of the city of My God, the new Jerusalem, which comes down out of heaven from My God, and My new name.
> —REVELATION 3:12

"A pillar in the temple of My God." A pillar speaks of strength, stability, and protection. This promise of pillars with names written on them harkens back to the construction of the temple of Solomon:

> Thus he set up the pillars at the porch of the nave; and he set up the right pillar and named it Jachin, and he set up the left pillar and named it Boaz.
> —1 KINGS 7:21

These two pillars were massive columns of bronze measuring about twenty-seven feet high and over five feet in diameter. They adorned the entrance to the Holy Place, most likely as free-standing ornaments positioned just in front of the second-story porch that looked out over the court of the priests. The priests had to pass between the pillars to reach the door to the Holy Place. However, the pillars were large enough to be visible from the outer court and likely even from passersby outside the temple courtyard.

The pillars were named Jachin and Boaz. Boaz was an immensely foundational character in Jewish history, but Jachin was not. For that reason, most scholars point to the meaning of their names rather than their personal stories to understand why these names were chosen for the two pillars.

Jachin means "He shall establish it." Boaz means "in Him is strength." Taken together, the symbolism is *He shall establish His Temple in strength.* This idea of strength, stability, and protection is a similar sentiment to what Christ said when He blessed Simon and changed his name to Peter after his revelation that Jesus was the Son of God:

> I also say to you that you are Peter, and upon this rock I will build My church; and the gates of Hades will not overpower it.
> —*MATTHEW 16:18*

Remember how Paul said that James, Peter, and John were reputed to be pillars? Again, the symbolism speaks of a person with stability derived from an unshakable revelation of Christ's Sonship that has fully defined their identity. Those who are pillars stand as reliable reminders of the nature of Christ that others can look up to and thus be drawn toward the presence of God.

The two pillars in Solomon's temple also represent God's protection over the Holy Place. Remember the context of the letter to Philadelphia: They were promised protection during the great tribulation, similar to how the Holy Place, which consisted of the inner court and holy of holies, was fully covered and protected by the presence of God. Likewise, the holy of holies saints walking as mature sons of God will be exempt from the testing of Satan's attacks while they preach and demonstrate the kingdom of God. The inner court saints, represented by the faithful Woman who fled to the wilderness, will still experience some testing, but they too will be protected from the main violence and destruction.

Just as heaven opened for Christ when He was baptized in the Jordan River, heaven will open for the "sons of God" movement of fully mature Christians who walk in sonship. *That* is the open door promised to Philadelphia.

## THREE NAMES

Unlike the pillars of Jachin and Boaz, Jesus promised to name the over-comers of Philadelphia with three names:

- the name of My God,
- the name of the city of My God, the new Jerusalem, which comes down out of heaven from My God,
- and My new name (Revelation 3:12).

We'll return to unpack multiple layers of significance from these three names later in this series. For now, I'll simply offer a teaser by mentioning that these three names stand in stark contrast to the mark of the beast, which is a three-digit number representing the name of the beast. Again, we'll cover those topics in depth when we get to Revelation chapter 13. Just know that the overcomers of Philadelphia receive a threefold spiritual mark that signifies an unassailable strength, stability, and protection because they belong to God.

## OUR REFUGE AND STRENGTH

As we draw near the end of the letter to Philadelphia, and before we learn the Bride's response, let's take a refreshing drink from the book of Psalms to anchor everything we've learned so far. As you read, think of this song as a celebration of the protection given to Philadelphia so they could continue building the kingdom with creative sonship during the great tribulation. This is our promise if we learn to see Jesus as the holy and true One Who has the key of David:

> God is our refuge and strength,
> A very present help in trouble.
> Therefore we will not fear, though the earth should change
> And though the mountains slip into the heart of the sea;
> Though its waters roar and foam,
> Though the mountains quake at its swelling pride.
>
> Selah.

There is a river whose streams make glad the city of God,
The holy dwelling places of the Most High.
God is in the midst of her, she will not be moved;
God will help her when morning dawns.

The nations made an uproar, the kingdoms tottered;
He raised His voice, the earth melted.
The LORD of hosts is with us;
The God of Jacob is our stronghold.

Selah.

Come, behold the works of the LORD,
Who has wrought desolations in the earth.
He makes wars to cease to the end of the earth;
He breaks the bow and cuts the spear in two;
He burns the chariots with fire.

"Cease striving and know that I am God;
I will be exalted among the nations,
I will be exalted in the earth."
The LORD of hosts is with us;
The God of Jacob is our stronghold.
—*PSALM 46*

## THE BRIDE'S RESPONSE

So what was the Bride's response to her Bridegroom's astounding promise? Could she recognize and synthesize the profound themes embedded in His words? Would she see how it connected with His earlier letter to Smyrna, combining to paint a picture of servant leadership that called her to something so much greater and more impactful than obedience? And would she see more than some simple pledge of ease and escape for those who merely did what they were told? Would she hear the invitation to follow His example of selflessness, and thus learn to lead with an unbridled creativity that opened doors of grace for others against the gates of hell?

Her answer was immense. Standing for the first time from her desk, as if the faith-filled action could catapult her words more quickly to His heart, she proclaimed with unbound expectation:

Draw me after you, and let us run together!
—*SONG OF SOLOMON 1:4*

It was the perfect reply for the ruler gift and a sublime recognition of God's intended sequence.

"Draw me after you ...." She didn't ask for His command, nor did she simply seek to know what she must do next. She wanted freedom to hear His heart and follow after Him. She sought open doors that never shut, so every step she took could be a free response of love to the expressions of His heart.

"And let us run together!" She didn't ask Him to do all the work while she watched from safer walkways. Nor did she want Him to slow His pace to make her feel more sure about the chase. No, it was as if she were saying, "I'll learn the cadence of Your heart so we can run together, side by side, synchronized in vibrant strides of freedom!"

And it was only in
That wild place of trust
Where she could confidently leave
Her worn-down older paths
Without fear of being lost
Or broken on the way.

A higher path awaits—
One where snare and pitfall couldn't reach.
A path no human knowledge could uncover
And no rigid law could ever tame.

A better trail that He had blazed
And now He beckoned her to join,
So together they might show the way
Of freedom and fulfillment
To the rest of His creation.

## CHAPTER 14

# CHRIST'S SEVEN LETTERS:
# TO LAODICEA

We're there! We've made it to the last letter: Laodicea, the lukewarm church. There's probably more commentary available on the church in Laodicea than the other six churches combined. If you've studied Laodicea then you may recognize certain sections of the path we're about to travel. Still, I advise you to be alert and expect a wholly unique experience in the steps ahead.

To set the stage, remember where we've been so far. If we view the letters to the seven churches as invitations to Christ's Unveiling, then that means Christ is waiting for some generation of Christians to finally step up and respond appropriately to each letter in successive order to demonstrate their willingness to embrace the process. The Unveiling won't commence until the Bride has responded to all seven letters.

A right response to each letter simply means that we have ears to hear what He is saying and have turned to face Him so that we are positioned for His Unveiling. It also means that we are expecting Him to reveal Himself to our spirit in these seven areas. However, it doesn't mean that we have fully matured in each area.

The first six letters focused on the right and wrong actions that keep the Body of Christ distracted and unprepared for the Bridegroom's Unveiling. As we'll see in this chapter, the seventh letter deals with essence rather than action.

> To the angel of the church in Laodicea write:
>
> The Amen, the faithful and true Witness, the Beginning of the creation of God, says this:
>
> 'I know your deeds, that you are neither cold nor hot; I wish that you were cold or hot. So because you are lukewarm, and neither hot nor cold, I will spit you out of My mouth. Because you say, "I am rich, and have become wealthy, and have need of nothing," and you do not know that you are wretched and miserable and poor and blind and naked, I advise you to buy from Me gold refined by fire so that you may become rich, and white garments so that you may clothe yourself, and that the shame of your nakedness will not be revealed; and eye salve to anoint your eyes so that you may see. Those whom I love, I reprove and discipline; therefore be zealous and repent.
>
> Behold, I stand at the door and knock; if anyone hears My voice and opens the door, I will come in to him and will dine with him, and he with Me. He who overcomes, I will grant to him to sit down with Me on My throne, as I also overcame and sat down with My Father on His throne. He who has an ear, let him hear what the Spirit says to the churches.'
>
> —REVELATION 3:14-22

The letter to the angel of the church in Laodicea is an exhortation to the mercy portion of the human spirit. It beckons to the part of our human spirit that was made to align with the Spirit of the Fear of the Lord. As our spirit reflects that color of God's light into our soul and body, we become more like Jesus in that area and shine that aspect of His character back out to the world.

In the fractal of seven, the essence of the Spirit of the Fear of the Lord and the mercy redemptive gift are exemplified in God's sabbath rest. During the first six days of creation, God expressed various aspects of His nature through the external product of His Words in action. That means we learned about God's attributes mainly through observing how creation responded to Him. On the seventh day, God revealed His deepest essence—His nature at rest—through His presence and nothing else. He expressed Himself through a state of being rather than doing. On the seventh day, the I AM was simply the I AM. Likewise, we'll find that everything Jesus says to Laodicea revolves around His undiluted nature at rest.

> On the seventh day, the I AM was simply the I AM. Likewise, we'll find that everything Jesus says to Laodicea revolves around His undiluted nature at rest.

## THE INTRODUCTION

In every other letter, Christ's introduction referenced at least one external attribute or action. But to Laodicea, He leaned entirely on His internal essence. Again, His nature at rest:

> The Amen, the faithful and true Witness, the Beginning of
> the creation of God, says this …
> —*REVELATION 3:14*

"Amen" is a word of Hebrew origin that means firm or trustworthy. It is used throughout the New Testament, often by Christ in the Gospels, where it is also translated as surely, verily, or truly. For example, consider what Jesus said to Nicodemus:

> **Truly, truly**, I say to you, we speak of what we know and
> testify of what we have seen, and you do not accept our
> testimony.
> —*JOHN 3:11*

Truly, truly. Or, amen, amen. It's like saying, "You can take it to the bank." In other words, what He says is so sure to come to pass that it's as if it has already happened. There is no difference between His Word and reality because His Word is the seed from which reality springs.

Similar to "the Amen," He is also "the faithful and true Witness." In this context, faithful means to be worthy of faith. He is worthy of faith, not just because everything He says is true, but also because whatever is true is true because He said it. And the reason for that is found in His next attribute: "the beginning of the creation of God."

Although this attribute references creation, it is still a state-of-being title rather than an action. It doesn't say that He began (past tense action) creation. It says He *is* the beginning. So, yes, He initiated creation, but the point is that creation was derived from the seed of His essence, and all things are meant to reach their full potential only by coming into rest with who He IS. This concept will make more sense as we continue with the letter.

## LAODICEA EXAMINED

Unlike the first six churches, Jesus had no compliments for Laodicea. He jumped straight into the correction phase and never looked back:

> I know your deeds, that you are neither cold nor hot; I wish
> that you were cold or hot. So because you are lukewarm,
> and neither hot nor cold, I will spit you out of My mouth.
> —*REVELATION 3:15-16*

Notice that He starts with "I know your deeds," but then proceeds to describe their state of being rather than their actions. He didn't say that their *deeds* were neither cold nor hot. He said, "*You* are neither cold nor hot … *you* are lukewarm." The critique isn't about their deeds. To Sardis He said, "I have not found your deeds completed," but that's not the case with Laocidea (Revelation 3:2). He wasn't saying their deeds were bad, nor was he saying they needed to do more deeds. He knew their deeds, but He addressed their internal nature.

In this analogy, to be cold or hot is not about good or bad, wrong or right. It's about a state of being different than the surrounding environment. Hot water is good to warm you up in a cold environment. Cold water is good to cool you down in a hot environment. Lukewarm water does neither because it has reached homeostasis with its surrounding environment.

Being hot or cold is about our internal nature being completely synchronized with God's nature in whatever way is appropriate for the moment. The divine nature of I AM is never altered by His environment. He is the catalyst to which all things respond. If we rest in Him and draw from His divine nature, then we too will be a catalyst that brings life to our environment:

> Abide in Me, and I in you. As the branch cannot bear fruit of itself unless it abides in the vine, so neither can you unless you abide in Me. I am the vine, you are the branches; he who abides in Me and I in him, he bears much fruit, for apart from Me you can do nothing.
> —*JOHN 15:4-5*

When God rested on the seventh day, He didn't enter a state of homeostasis with creation. At the end of the sixth day, creation was everything it was designed to be at that time, but an insurmountable chasm still existed between it and God's holiness. Creation was good because God spent six days making it good, but it was not yet holy, because it was not yet one with Him. So God rested alone on that day, separate and entirely "other than" everything else.

The same juxtaposition exists between the first six letters and the seventh letter. God called everything He created on each of the six days "good." Likewise, a right response to the first six letters would be to see the nature of Christ that He was pinpointing when He compared our works with His works and assent in our hearts: "Yes, He is good in that way!" But even after responding correctly to the first six letters, an insurmountable chasm still exists between our nature and God's holiness to the degree that we have not come to rest—to draw life from—that aspect of His nature. And that is what Christ is addressing in the letter to Laodicea.

> In this analogy, to be cold or hot is not about good or bad, wrong or right. It's about a state of being different than the surrounding environment.

When Jesus called out Laodicea's lukewarmness, He wasn't just correcting some subset of lazy and self-satisfied Christians who needed to take their faith more seriously. He was challenging all of us! Compared to the unfiltered, unrestrained fullness of God's holiness, we are all lukewarm. No matter how on fire we are, no matter how devoted and righteous our lifestyle, we are all lukewarm compared to the Holy One.

Don't get me wrong—we can and must seek to act like Jesus. We should model our works after His. There are temporal and eternal rewards for living the sacrificial lifestyle of a bondservant in His name:

> Jesus said, "Truly I say to you, there is no one who has left house or brothers or sisters or mother or father or children or farms, for My sake and for the gospel's sake, but that he will receive a hundred times as much now in the present age, houses and brothers and sisters and mothers and children and farms, along with persecutions; and in the age to come, eternal life."
> —*MARK 10:29-30*

> For we must all appear before the judgment seat of Christ, so that each one may be recompensed for his deeds in the body, according to what he has done, whether good or bad.
> —*2 CORINTHIANS 5:10*

So yes, good works are important but they can never bridge the gap between us and the holiness of God's divine nature. God's sabbath rest demonstrated that His holiness is not dependent on His works. The first six days of his wonderful creation flowed out of His holiness but were not the source of His holiness. Likewise, no amount of righteous deeds will make us holy or unite us with Christ. We are only holy as we rest in Him. Our good works are meant to be the overflow of an internal life that abides in Him by faith. That's how we synchronize with His catalytic nature.

Whenever we get it backward—whenever we view our actions as the source of our holiness, or our works as a source of righteousness, or our sacrifices as the source of our legitimacy—then we

Whenever we get it backward—whenever we view our actions as the source of our holiness, or our works as a source of righteousness, or our sacrifices as the source of our legitimacy—then we are no longer resting in Christ's work.

are no longer resting in Christ's work. And that is exactly why Christ rebuked Laodicea. They were trusting in a form of self-righteousness that kept them disconnected from the source and, therefore, lukewarm.

## SEQUENCE OF CREATION

This brings up an interesting question. If our good works are supposed to flow out of our rest, then why is the letter to Laodicea last instead of first? Or why did God work for six days before displaying His holiness at rest? The pattern almost seems backward.

The message in God's creation sequence becomes clearer when you look at the larger pattern. God was at rest before the beginning, but nothing else existed to observe Him in that state. So the internal nature-at-rest of the Creator remained hidden even as He demonstrated many aspects of His character through six days of work.

His final masterpiece was a man and a woman created in His image, whom He then commissioned to replicate His beauty and order to the rest of the world. But to do that, they would have to observe what He had planted in His garden and combine that knowledge with an understanding of His character as revealed through the six days of creation. In other words, just seeing the final result of the garden wasn't enough; they needed to understand what these things revealed about God based on the order and details of each creation day.

But even that wasn't enough because, without the Sabbath, Adam and Eve had no picture of God's nature outside of creation. They had no reference to help them understand God's deepest motivation: His internal nature at rest that motivated Him to create in the first place. And that's why God rested on the seventh day *after* humanity was around to observe it.

God's rest demonstrated both the source and the destination of His works. It provided an anchor point for Adam and Eve as they sought to understand His handiwork. They didn't get to see how He had created everything. They only saw the end result and had to reason backward to understand the how and why. But what they did see of God was His rest. That was the final, enduring imprint He left them, and it was the only reference point in the creation story from which they could draw as they sought to unpack the meaning behind His works.

Without seeing God at rest in His holiness, they might have assumed that God had somehow created the universe just to aggrandize
Himself, or to make Himself a wealthy Lord of other creatures. But observing the utter separateness of I AM at rest would have grounded
Adam and Eve in the reality that God was wholly self-sufficient and beyond creation. He wasn't there to take. He was the source, and even after completing the original creation, He intended to give out of the
overflow of His inexhaustible resources. And through His giving, He
intended to elevate all things into congruence with His holiness.

As they studied the puzzle of weather systems or the water cycle or
the pollination of flowers or the germination of a seed or the birth of a
sparrow or the formation of precious stones or the path of the constella-
tions, they could unpack various attributes of God's character, but always their understanding was meant to be filtered through that enduring image of God at rest. A holy God, so alone, so completely other-
than His creation, yet so clearly inviting a companion to receive and
share in His rest. That means at each step in Adam and Eve's journey to
understand and replicate God's works, they were meant to draw upon
the power of His rest—to remember that God is the all-sufficient source
for every good work and every good work that flows from Him leads to
His rest.

I'm belaboring on this point because it has immense implications
for the Unveiling of Jesus Christ, just as it had immense implications in
Genesis. When the serpent tempted Adam and Eve to eat the fruit from
the tree of the knowledge of good and evil, he was convincing them to
disconnect from God as the source of their works. From that point on,
their works would flow out of their knowledge of good and evil, as
would their sense of righteousness and legitimacy. In other words, their
motivation became self-righteousness rather than trusting in God's nature.

## REMEDY FOR SELF-RIGHTEOUSNESS

Let's bring this back to Laodicea. Jesus warned Laodicea that He would
spit them out of His mouth for the lukewarmness of their self-righteousness. It was a judgment similar in many ways to Adam and Eve being banished from the Garden of Eden.

Some translations say, "I am about to spit you out of my mouth." Either way, it is clear from the context that the judgment was not yet final, and there was still room for Laodicea to repent. That was the whole reason for the warning of such harsh rejection. The warning was an expression of the Spirit of the Fear of the Lord.

The Spirit of the Fear of the Lord reveals the insurmountable chasm between our nature and God's nature. It pinpoints the areas in our hearts where we rely on self-righteousness rather than resting in Christ's nature. But the goal of the fear of the Lord is to draw us into His rest, not to keep us separate; to connect us to God's holiness, not to entrench us in our failure.

The hope embedded in the Spirit of the Fear of the Lord becomes more visible as Christ continues His correction of Laodicea:

> Because you say, "I am rich, and have become wealthy, and have need of nothing," and you do not know that you are wretched and miserable and poor and blind and naked, I advise you to buy from Me gold refined by fire so that you may become rich, and white garments so that you may clothe yourself, and that the shame of your nakedness will not be revealed; and eye salve to anoint your eyes so that you may see. Those whom I love, I reprove and discipline; therefore be zealous and repent.
> —*REVELATION 3:17-19*

Again, Jesus was correcting Laodicea's internal state of being, not their actions. He was correcting the self-righteous heart behind their deeds, not their actual deeds. They saw themselves as rich, satisfied, and fulfilled when they were actually "wretched and miserable and poor and blind and naked" because they were standing outside of God's rest and separated from His righteousness. They were disconnected from the source.

Perhaps Laodicea had read the other six letters. Perhaps they had heard Christ's challenge to align their deeds with His, but rather than leaning on the revelation of Jesus embedded in

> The goal of the fear of the Lord is to draw us into His rest, not to keep us separate; to connect us to God's holiness, not to entrench us in our failure.

each letter, they leaned on the fruit from the tree of knowledge of good and evil. Whatever the case, it seems they adjusted their external actions without connecting to His rest. As a result, they were not internally conformed to His image.

What was Christ's advice to remediate their condition? It wasn't a command to do more deeds, to try harder, or work more diligently. It was a challenge to return to the source. He invited them to "buy" a few things from Him:

- "Gold refined by fire so that you may become rich,"
- "white garments so ... the shame of your nakedness will not be revealed," and
- "eye salve to anoint your eyes so that you may see."

## REFINED IN THE FIRE

"Gold refined by fire" speaks of the testing of our faith:

> In this you greatly rejoice, even though now for a little while, if necessary, you have been distressed by various trials, so that the proof of your faith, being more precious than gold which is perishable, even though tested by fire, may be found to result in praise and glory and honor at the revelation of Jesus Christ ...
> —1 PETER 1:6-7

Again the testing described here isn't about perfecting our works but purifying our faith. Jesus said to buy the gold refined in the fire *from Him*. His works are perfect because everything He did flowed from His state of being holy, and because He was wholly at rest in the Father. Likewise, when tribulation comes to challenge our faith in Christ, our answer must be to lean more and more upon faith in His righteousness and less on our own understanding. In other words, trials are meant to disabuse us of our reliance on the fruit from the tree of the knowledge of good and evil, and to drive us to rest more deeply in Christ. If we embrace our trials with great joy in this life, we will be found rich with "praise and glory and honor" when Christ is revealed because we will be revealed as one with Him.

## WHITE GARMENTS

"White garments" speak of righteous acts:

> "Let us rejoice and be glad and give the glory to Him, for
> the marriage of the Lamb has come and His bride has
> made herself ready." It was given to her to clothe herself in
> fine linen, bright and clean; for the fine linen is the right-
> eous acts of the saints.
> —*REVELATION 19:7-8*

To be fair, the fine linen spoken of in Revelation chapter 19 has additional connotations that we'll discuss later. But it is probably safe to
say that the white garments recommended to Laodicea, as well as the
ones promised to the overcomers of Sardis, are also related to the righteous acts of the saints. However, my point is that Jesus didn't command
Laodicea to *earn* their white garments *with* righteous acts. He advised
them to buy white garments from Him. How do we buy something
from Christ? Especially if we are wretched, miserable, poor, blind, and
naked? What do we have that we can give in exchange? Obviously, the
answer is that Jesus offers every bit of Himself to us free of charge. The
only thing required is that we recognize our need so that we can then
turn to Him:

> Come, all you who are thirsty, come to the waters; and you
> who have no money, come, buy and eat! Come, buy wine
> and milk without money and without cost.
> —*ISAIAH 55:1, NIV*

In other words, our righteous acts must flow out of an abiding faith
in His finished work. The clearer we see Jesus, and the more we lean on
His righteousness, the less we'll need to manufacture our own works or
lean on any other legitimacy crutch to magnify our worth. And it is
from that place of abiding rest in Him that our most authentic and con-
sequential acts of service will flow—because our motivations will be
pure.

## EYE SALVE

Laodicea was so blinded by self-righteousness that they couldn't see how utterly naked and destitute they were before God. Their good works were no better than filthy rags. They had done all of the right things on the outside but never dealt with the inside. They had observed His works, and maybe even emulated some of them, but they never connected to His rest and therefore couldn't understand what His works revealed about His heart.

Remember Christ's statement about the eye being the lamp for the body? In book 1 we saw how that verse describes the way that the eyes of our spirit are meant to receive illumination about the nature of Jesus from the seven Spirits of God. Now let's look at that verse again in its greater context because it ties back to the very same self-righteousness that Jesus was addressing in Laodicea:

> Whenever you fast, do not put on a gloomy face as the hypocrites do, for they neglect their appearance so that they will be noticed by men when they are fasting. Truly I say to you, they have their reward in full. But you, when you fast, anoint your head and wash your face so that your fasting will not be noticed by men, but by your Father who is in secret; and your Father who sees what is done in secret will reward you.
>
> Do not store up for yourselves treasures on earth, where moth and rust destroy, and where thieves break in and steal. But store up for yourselves treasures in heaven, where neither moth nor rust destroys, and where thieves do not break in or steal; for where your treasure is, there your heart will be also.
>
> **The eye is the lamp of the body; so then if your eye is clear, your whole body will be full of light. But if your eye is bad, your whole body will be full of darkness. If then the light that is in you is darkness, how great is the darkness!**
>
> No one can serve two masters; for either he will hate the one and love the other, or he will be devoted to one and despise the other. You cannot serve God and wealth.
> —*MATTHEW 6:16-24*

Like hypocrites who only feel important and valuable when others notice their good works, Laodicea did some right things for all the wrong reasons. In today's vernacular, we might call that virtue-signaling. They were storing up false and fleeting treasures that made them feel wealthy on earth but left them eternally destitute before God. That's why Jesus equated self-righteousness with serving wealth rather than God. No man can serve two masters.

When the eyes of our hearts are focused on external perceptions of right and wrong according to the knowledge of the forbidden fruit, we become spiritually blind and poor and naked because we cannot perceive our need for the true riches hidden in Christ:

> I pray that the eyes of your heart may be enlightened, so that you will know what is the hope of His calling, what are the riches of the glory of His inheritance in the saints, and what is the surpassing greatness of His power toward us who believe.
> —*EPHESIANS 1:18-19*

Every treasure we need is hidden in Christ, and the riches of His inheritance are in us when we abide in Him because He also abides in us. When we lean on anything other than what we already have in Jesus to increase our worth, we are essentially repeating Adam and Eve's sin and reaching again for the forbidden fruit.

## ZEALOUS REPENTANCE

Even after using the Spirit of the Fear of the Lord to warn Laodicea of eternal judgment, Jesus still lovingly redirected their eyes back to Him as the source:

> Those whom I love, I reprove and discipline; therefore be zealous and repent.
> —*REVELATION 3:19*

What does it mean to be "zealous and repent"? Self-righteousness is often a wrong response to the trials of life. When faced with a challenge, sometimes we don't trust God's heart and provision, so we manufacture zealous deeds that, despite appearances, are focused on making us feel good about ourselves. They look good to others rather than flowing out of a heart of love. Isn't that the natural state of all things since the fall? Self-righteous zeal is just one side of the fruit from the tree of knowledge of good and evil, and it only brings us into homeostasis with the world. In other words, it makes us internally lukewarm, regardless of our external appearance.

Jesus specifically told Laodicea that His discipline flowed out of His love. He then added, "*Therefore* be zealous and repent." That means the antidote to self-righteousness is to understand that God's heart behind trials is to unite us with Him. If we can see that, then we can zealously turn to Him as the source of the provision that we need to overcome the trial and be transformed.

The ultimate challenge and purpose of all of life's difficulties is to learn how to recognize Him as the provision. That was the message behind God's seventh-day rest: to see the holy otherness of I AM as an invitation to become one with Him rather than as a harsh judgment of separation. And that is what Jesus was offering to Laodicea:

> Behold, I stand at the door and knock; if anyone hears My voice and opens the door, I will come in to him and will dine with him, and he with Me.
> —*REVELATION 3:20*

Before God ever kicked Adam and Eve out of the garden in Genesis chapter 3, they had already closed the door of their hearts to Him out of shame and self-righteousness born from the fruit of the forbidden tree. That's why they covered themselves with fig leaves (self-righteousness) and hid themselves from His presence (shame). When God replaced their self-made leafy coverings with garments He had made from animal skins, He was previewing His intended remedy for both.

Christ's finished work on the cross tore down the dividing wall of God's judgment toward us, and now He reaches past our shame to knock on the doors of self-righteousness that we have erected to protect ourselves from a God that we have wholly misunderstood. He knocks and invites us to

> The ultimate challenge and purpose of all of life's difficulties is to learn how to recognize Him as the provision.

dine with Him. To rest and receive sustenance from Him. To partake of His unmitigated holiness free of charge. And the reward for turning from our self-righteousness and opening our door is stunning:

> He who overcomes, I will grant to him to sit down with Me on My throne, as I also overcame and sat down with My Father on His throne. He who has an ear, let him hear what the Spirit says to the churches.
> —*REVELATION 3:21-22*

To sit down on His throne?! What an unfathomable offer of oneness with God! In the same way that Jesus sits at the right hand of the Father, not in subordination, but in complete unity and equality with the Ancient of Days, we are invited to sit with Christ on His throne. Paul explained Christ's exalted position in this way:

> For this reason also, God highly exalted Him, and bestowed on Him the name which is above every name, so that at the name of Jesus EVERY KNEE WILL BOW, of those who are in heaven and on earth and under the earth, and that every tongue will confess that Jesus Christ is Lord, to the glory of God the Father.
> —*PHILIPPIANS 2:9-11*

Many scholars believe "the name which is above every name" is a reference to YHWH (pronounced Yahweh). It was the holy name of I AM that God revealed to Moses at the burning bush. There are many theories and controversies surrounding the proper use and pronunciation of Yahweh, but none of that matters for this discussion. The point is that Jesus shares the name above every name with the Father, so all praise and glory given to Jesus is also praise and glory given to the Father. There is no contention because they are perfectly harmonized in unity of essence.

We are offered the same oneness with Christ. We can tap into the spirit of that oneness today by resting in Him, but the ultimate promise of the new covenant will be realized through the resurrection at the end of the age when our mortal flesh puts on immortality in the image of Christ. Then we will become spiritually, inseparably one with Jesus in the way that a husband cleaves to His wife and the two become one flesh. So too are we destined to inherit the fullness of the divine nature, not as a result of our good works, but by allowing our trials to drive us to rest in Him.

## THE MERCY RESPONSE

With all of that in mind, let's return to the Song of Solomon to learn the Bride's response. Remember, we have imagined the Shulamite Bride-to-be sitting in front of her vanity, alone in her bedroom, while she read each of the seven letters from her fiancé. With every sentence, her emotions rose and fell like waves upon a sandy shore of hopes and dreams. The untamed beauty of His promises ... the fierceness of His vows ... they crashed over her with equal parts excitement and trepidation to continually reshape her expectations. And then she opened His letter to the mercy portion of her spirit, and she found herself undone again in ways she never expected.

> His other letters spoke of lofty deeds and noble goals.
> They beckoned her to higher places,
> While every single one of her desires
> For unsightly selfish smallness
> Drifted further from her soul.
>
> But this letter hit differently.
> It cut her to the quick,
> Challenging her deepest motivations
> With savage disregard for many of the charities
> And sacrifices for which she was most proud.

"Lukewarm?!" She recoiled at the word.

As she struggled through His ardent admonition, she thought back to their early days of courtship. In Ephesus He called her spirit to return to her first love. Hadn't she said yes?!

"May He kiss me with the kisses of His mouth," was her reply! How, then, could she still be lukewarm? Wasn't love her primary motivation for every deed?

And then in Smyrna when He offered her a cup of suffering, hadn't she responded appropriately: "Your love is better than wine!"

And in Pergamum, when she embraced her responsibility to live a holy and acceptable life amidst the darkness, she agreed: "Your oils have a pleasing fragrance!"

And in Thyatira, had she not embraced the wilderness trials that produced refined character: "Your name is like purified oil!"

And in Sardis, had she not pledged to steward every resource like a wise virgin: "Therefore the maidens love you!"

And finally in Philadelphia, had she not invited the difficult and unknown path of challenge and creative response: "Draw me after You and let us run together!"

"What then?!" she agonized. "Is nothing I do enough to make me ready for the King?!" But even as the question flexed and strutted in her mind, a humble answer came to speak the truth: "This isn't about me, or anything I have or haven't done!"

All those things were good and right and had brought her to this place, but now He wanted her to see the deeper truth ... the reality that had stared her in the face from the beginning though she couldn't see. And now, to embrace the encounter He desired, she would have to turn aside, like Moses had at Horeb, to see the burning bush. The I AM was inviting her into His presence, not to walk or run or do anything at all, but just to be with Him.

And like Moses, she would have to remove her sandals, along with every other accessory that helped her get stuff done but shielded her from who He really was.

"The I AM," she finally realized, "is calling me to Himself, so obviously what *I do* is not the point. Maybe what He has done isn't even the main point right now ... but who *He is*."

As these new ideas swirled and danced inside her spirit, they cast a new illumination upon a verse she knew so well:

> He made Him who knew no sin to be sin on our behalf, so
> that we might become the righteousness of God in Him.
> —2 CORINTHIANS 5:21

All her righteous acts, and every sin and stumble, amounted to absolutely nothing in His presence. "When I abide in the reality that I am the righteousness of God, then I truly enter the presence of I AM and become one with His holiness!"

It was all at once a wonderful and terrifying thought. It offered liberation from every opinion and judgment she had ever feared, while somehow searing her more deeply with the weight of who He was. She sensed that somewhere from beyond the veil through which He beckoned her, He would show her things about His heart she had never imagined. And she sensed it would change her forever. He would take the deepest things about her that felt most vulnerable—those tender things she hid for fear of rejection and abandonment—and He would cover them in divine light so glorious that no fear could ever penetrate. Somehow His very essence—His nature at rest—would accomplish this impossibility. And she longed for such intimacy, though it terrified her to the core!

And then it hit her all at once: A tidal wave of faith and hope and love that swept her off her feet and drew her toward the wild ocean of His essence He was promising to share. She didn't even struggle as peace and awe consumed her. She just surrendered to its promise, singing out one simple statement of prophetic longing for an Unveiling that she knew was soon to start:

> The king has brought me into his chambers.
> —SONG OF SOLOMON 1:4

She knew she wasn't literally in His chamber yet. At least not in the fullest sense of the idea. But the abundant weight of His seven invitations was finally unfolding in her mind, wrapping all around her like layers of impending, irresistible reality. His promises were sure! He seemed so close, she could almost reach out and touch Him. It was time for her to take the next step into His plan ...

## Chapter 15

## Spiritual Furniture

It may not feel like it, but we've already come a long way. The letters to the seven churches were invitations to engage with the book of Revelation as bondservants rather than unprofitable slaves. To prepare us to overcome in the wilderness rather than fall away from the faith. To reorient our perspective so that we long for the time of His Unveiling with bridal expectations rather than fear of separation. To realign the eyes of our spirit so that we can receive in each way He intends to reveal Himself.

Now that we have some experience with Christ's intended Unveiling process through the fractal of seven, subsequent encounters will flow more naturally and require less preparation. That's another reason why every second spent with the seven letters was worth the time.

Beginning in the next chapter, we'll follow John as he enters the heavenly throne room of God, as described in Revelation chapters 4 and 5. In the throne room, we'll see many fantastical displays, including God on His throne, the four living creatures, the twenty-four elders, the seven Spirits of God, the sea of glass, a scroll with seven seals, and the Lamb Himself. But to get the most out of that discussion, we first need to take another detour to gather important context about the throne room.

## THE HEAVENLY PATTERN

Think back to the Old Testament tabernacle. In one sense, the tabernacle of Moses can be viewed as a physical representation and foreshadowing of the Body of Christ (both Jew and Gentile believers), particularly during this temporary "wilderness journey" that is our life here on earth *before* Christ's return. The transient nature of the tabernacle was a picture of the temporary nature of the current creation as well as the impact our physical bodies have on our relationship with God.

As we discussed in book 1, the tabernacle analogy applies to us on an individual and corporate level. Each of us is a tabernacle with three parts: spirit, soul, and body. These three parts correspond to the holy of holies, inner court, and outer court. At the same time, the entire Body of Christ is a corporate tabernacle.

Beyond what it represents for the Body of Christ, the tabernacle of Moses (and everything in it) is a shadow of a larger heavenly reality:

> They serve at a sanctuary that is a copy and shadow of what is in heaven. This is why Moses was warned when he was about to build the tabernacle: "See to it that you make everything according to the pattern shown you on the mountain."
> —*HEBREWS 8:5, NIV*

When Moses encountered God on Mount Sinai, he received much more than the Ten Commandments. During that visitation, God's throne room descended upon the mountain like a heavenly tabernacle. Moses was then instructed to build the physical tabernacle patterned after what he saw of that throne room.

In that way, everything John experiences in God's throne room, beginning in Revelation chapter 4, ties back to the tabernacle of Moses. To truly appreciate the significance of what John saw, we need at least a basic understanding of the tabernacle. In this chapter, we will build out that understanding.

I should note that the temple of Solomon eventually replaced the tabernacle as God's dwelling place on earth—at least for a season of Israel's history. The temple was primarily modeled after the Mosaic tabernacle, with additional embellishments and significantly more grandeur. Since Solomon's temple was built as a permanent structure, in some ways it was a symbolic picture of the new creation. In other words, when compared to the transient tabernacle, the temple foreshadowed the grandeur of our new creation bodies and the permanence of how God intends to dwell with humankind for all of eternity in the New Jerusalem.

Having acknowledged that distinction, for the purposes of this particular discussion, we are going to treat the tabernacle and the temple as interchangeable, since they both derived their form and function from God's heavenly throne room.

In a sense, we are working backward. Typically, we would start with the original precedent to understand the subsequent copies. But in this case, we'll go in reverse. We'll seek a deeper understanding of the throne room by studying the shadow it cast in the Old Testament through the tabernacle of Moses.

A deep study of the tabernacle of Moses, let alone the temple of Solomon, could (and has) filled volumes. Every detail, right down to the colors, fabrics, materials, shapes, relative placements, and precise dimensions, is rich with layered symbolism. We can't possibly unpack all of that in this book. Instead, we will spend this chapter focusing on just a few key details about the seven items of holy furniture in the tabernacle. Each item of furniture plays a role in the throne room, and as you might expect, they synchronize with the fractal of seven. After this overview, we'll return to John's vision in the next chapter to apply the information to our journey through Revelation.

## OVERVIEW OF THE FURNITURE

Based on the heavenly pattern he saw on Sinai, Moses was commanded to build seven items of furniture for use in the tabernacle service. Detailed instructions for the construction and placement of each item can be found in Exodus chapters 25, 27, and 30. In obedience to God's command, Moses then instructed the Israelites to follow the pattern he was given for these furniture items down to the smallest detail. The names of the items are as follows:

1. Altar of burnt sacrifice
2. Brazen laver
3. Table of showbread
4. Golden lampstand (menorah)
5. Golden altar of incense
6. Ark of the covenant
7. Mercy seat

For context, here is a simple overhead diagram of how these items were arranged relative to the tabernacle, moving from outside to inside (the direction in which we approach God):

TABERNACLE FURNITURE LAYOUT (NOT TO SCALE)

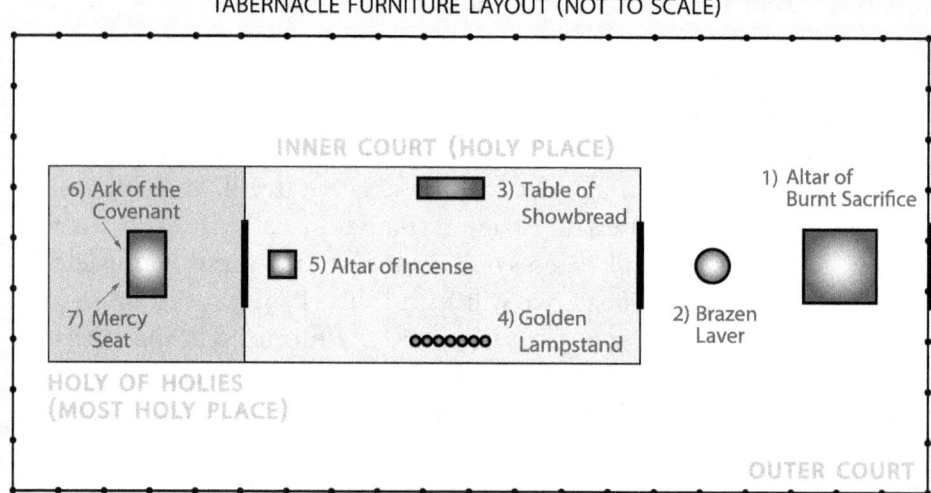

Again, the goal here is to provide a basic overview of the sacred furniture to help us recognize each item when it appears in Revelation. We won't expound on every detail, but rather review their general purpose and touch on a few details specific to our journey. The spiritual parallels are virtually endless, especially when you begin unpacking their different applications against the various versions of the tabernacle in Scripture, such as God's throne room, the Body of Christ, the ministry of Christ, the individual believer, the new Jerusalem, etc. Such a study would be fascinating and rewarding, and it would certainly enhance our experience of Revelation. But for the sake of time, we'll stick to the bare essentials.

One more note about this tabernacle discussion. We'll talk a lot about priests in this chapter. The Old Testament priesthood was Levitical, but if we want to apply the same principles to the new covenant, we need to think in terms of the Melchizedek priesthood.

The Levitical priesthood was a temporary system that set aside a single tribe for full-time ministry. It was established because of Israel's hard heart and slave mindset. But the Melchizedek priesthood is open to every believer. And just as Melchizedek was both king and priest, it unites the so-called sacred with the so-called secular. It calls each one of us to find the purpose for which He made us and to walk it out like mature sons in the mold of Christ. In other words, the Melchizedek priesthood isn't just for pastors, priests, worship leaders, missionaries, or any other vocation that the institutional church typically considers full-time ministry.

## ALTAR OF BURNT SACRIFICE
(See Exodus 27:1-8)

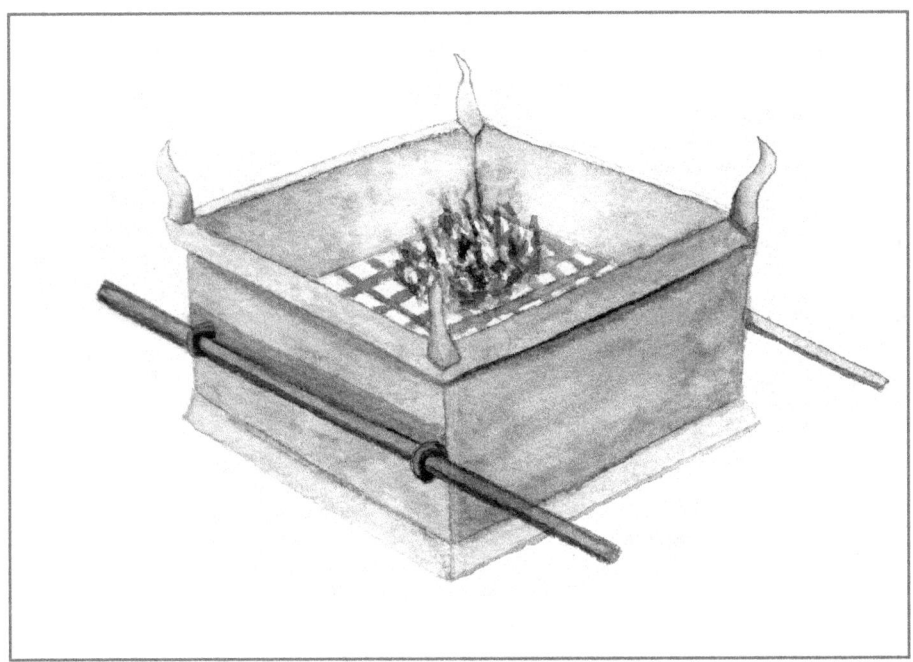

The first item encountered when entering the outer court was the altar of burnt sacrifice—sometimes called the brazen altar. It was a large hollow box built from acacia wood and overlayed inside and out with copper (or possibly a copper alloy like bronze or brass, depending on who you ask), standing 4.5 feet high and 7.5 feet square. In the simplest terms, it was a giant grill.

As the name suggests, the altar of burnt sacrifice was used to burn animal and grain offerings unto the Lord. It was the largest of the tabernacle furniture, and it would have dominated the perspective of anyone first stepping into the outer court. The smoke from its sacrifices was considered a sweet aroma to God and could be seen rising into the sky even from passersby outside the tabernacle.

Of note, the altar also had four horns, or angular protrusions, extending upward from the four corners of its structure. These horns represented the power and authority of the altar, just like animal horns are an external sign of an animal's strength, vigor, and dominance among its herd. In other words, the services performed on the altar were effective, reached in all directions to the ends of heaven and earth, and could not be challenged by any other spiritual force. The altar had effective spiritual authority over the works of the enemy.

Some scholars believe the bottom corners of the altar were installed on top of rocks so that the structure was high enough off the ground for priests to shovel out the old coals and ash to keep the fire tended. File this little detail away because it will come alive for us in book 3.

Acacia is a dense and highly durable wood with strong resin that makes it resistant to decay and insects. It was a practical choice with symbolic meaning. As we'll see in a moment, acacia was used in all three sections of the tabernacle, though only the altar of burnt sacrifice was acacia overlaid with copper.

Copper was a relatively abundant base metal with good heat-conducting properties. It, too, was a practical choice with symbolic meaning. Copper was only used in the outer court.

In the context of the holy furniture, decay-resistant acacia wood speaks of the humanity of Christ, or, more specifically, the incorruptible nature of His sinless humanity:

For You will not abandon my soul to Sheol; Nor will You
allow Your Holy One to undergo decay.
—*PSALM 16:10*

Copper, on the other hand, speaks of the fading glory of the old
covenant. In a broader sense, it also speaks of the temporary and subtle
way that God's divine nature is expressed in the first creation—like shadows of greater glory to come. Moreover, because copper was only used in
the outer court, it also speaks of the aspects of Christ's ministry that are
directed at and available to the whole world. That stands in contrast to
those aspects of His ministry that are directed at the Body of Christ (i.e.,
those who are already born again). More on that in a moment.

Many Christians assume that because Jesus Christ fulfilled the law
of Moses and paid the debt for our sin on the cross, the altar of burnt
sacrifice has no application in the new covenant. True, there is no longer
a need for a physical temple, much less animal sacrifices, but the altar of
burnt sacrifice represents so much more than appeasing the justice of
God.

Consider that five different kinds of sacrifices were offered on the
altar (as described in Leviticus chapters 1-7), and only two had anything
to do with sin. The three most common sacrifices were voluntary offerings of dedication, worship, and thanksgiving. Of those three voluntary
offerings, some involved animals, and others involved grains and fine
flours combined with oil and frankincense. Without getting into all of
the symbolism of the sacrificial laws, my point is that most of these offerings were voluntary acts of faith meant to draw the worshiper's heart
nearer to God.

The principle behind the altar of burnt sacrifice still has direct application to us today—especially for those seeking to move through the
outer court and closer to God through a bondservant lifestyle. It was
this very principle that Paul referred to in Romans chapter 12:

Therefore I urge you, brethren, by the mercies of God, to
present your bodies a living and holy sacrifice, acceptable
to God, which is your spiritual service of worship.
—*ROMANS 12:1*

While we're on the subject of Romans 12, this is a good time to apply the fractal of seven. As the first of the seven items of furniture, the

brazen altar aligns with the redemptive gift of prophet and the Spirit of the Lord. Many of the attributes of God seen on the first day of creation are also reflected in the altar of burnt sacrifice. On the first day, God sowed Himself (the Word) into the void like a seed that initiated everything. In a sense, that initial sowing also represented the first sacrifice out of which all life flows (unless a grain of wheat falls into the earth and dies, it abides alone). I'm not saying that God experienced pain or death in that moment, but speaking into the void to initiate creation *was* a sacrifice for God, because it created a reality where God's will would no longer be the *only* will, and He knew that decision would eventually necessitate His incarnation and death.

As we'll see in the book of Revelation, there is a spiritual version of the altar of burnt sacrifice in the temple in heaven. It represents the place where God receives the sweet aroma of the voluntary sacrifices we make in our lives to draw nearer to Him—whether they be spiritual, emotional, or physical sacrifices of time, energy, or other resources. And even beyond those voluntary offerings, whenever we experience involuntary pain, loss, or injustice in our lives, if we choose to sacrifice our right to be bitter or our license to judge God in those situations, He receives that heart attitude of faith as the sweetest of aromas.

Note that the brazen altar is the only item built from acacia overlaid with copper. That unique combination represents an aspect of Christ's ministry that is temporary. By that, I mean the spiritual significance of the altar of burnt sacrifice applies to the current creation, but it will have no ongoing role in the eternal state of the new creation after Christ's millennial reign is complete and all things have become new:

> Then I saw a new heaven and a new earth; for the first heaven and the first earth passed away, and there is no longer any sea.
>
> And I saw the holy city, new Jerusalem, coming down out of heaven from God, made ready as a bride adorned for her husband.
>
> And I heard a loud voice from the throne, saying, "Behold, the tabernacle of God is among men, and He will dwell among them, and they shall be His people, and God Himself will be among them, and **He will wipe away every tear from their eyes; and there will no longer be any death; there will no longer be any mourn-**

**ing, or crying, or pain; the first things have passed away."**
*—REVELATION 21:1-4*

We'll unpack these verses later in this series when it is time to discuss the new Jerusalem. My point right now is that once all of creation is summed up in Christ and God has become all in all, there will no longer be any need for pain or sacrifice. Then, the aspect of Christ's ministry represented by the brazen altar will have passed away with the first heaven and the first earth.

## BRAZEN LAVER
(See Exodus 30:17-21)

The brazen laver was the second item in the tabernacle, and it stood in the outer court between the altar of burnt sacrifice and the Holy Place. It was a washing bowl made entirely of hammered copper (again, possibly bronze or brass), filled with water. The priests used it to clean their hands and feet before and after their service to the people at the altar of burnt sacrifice and before and after entering the Holy Place for their service to God.

No dimensions were given for the brazen laver in the law of Moses, though it would have been small enough to be easily lifted by a single person since it had no built-in rings for transportation poles like most of the other furniture. The permanent model made for Solomon's temple was called "the molten sea" (see 1 Kings 7:23), and it was impressively large: sixteen feet in diameter and eight feet high.

The copper for the brazen laver had a peculiar origin. It came from polished copper mirrors donated by the Israelite women who served the original builders of the tabernacle outside the door to the Tent of Meeting while the tabernacle was under construction (see Exodus 38:8).

The fact that the laver was crafted from burnished copper mirrors was significant. When the priests stared down into the water-filled laver under an open sky, the reflection provided a moment for honest self-reflection. It was an opportunity to refocus their minds and emotions on God so their service could be performed with clean hands *and* a pure heart.

In this way, the brazen laver filled with water represents the Word of God. More specifically, it points to the process through which our minds are renewed as we meditate on the Word:

> For if anyone is a hearer of the word and not a doer, he is like a man who looks at his natural face in a mirror; for once he has looked at himself and gone away, he has immediately forgotten what kind of person he was. But one who looks intently at the perfect law, the law of liberty, and abides by it, not having become a forgetful hearer but an effectual doer, this man will be blessed in what he does.
> —*JAMES 1:23-25*

> Husbands, love your wives, just as Christ also loved the church and gave Himself up for her, so that He might sanctify her, **having cleansed her by the washing of water with the word**, that He might present to Himself the church in all her glory, having no spot or wrinkle or any such thing; but that she would be holy and blameless.
> —*EPHESIANS 5:25-27*

Note that this cleansing process at the brazen laver of God's Word is a prerequisite before entering the Holy Place for deeper encounters with

Christ's nature. Remember the parallel we drew between Romans 12:1 and the altar of burnt sacrifice? Well, the next verse of that chapter is an allusion to the brazen laver:

> Therefore I urge you, brethren, by the mercies of God, to present your bodies a living and holy sacrifice, acceptable to God, which is your spiritual service of worship. **And do not be conformed to this world, but be transformed by the renewing of your mind, so that you may prove what the will of God is, that which is good and acceptable and perfect.**
> —*ROMANS 12:1-2*

So, the brazen laver produces transformation through the renewing of our minds. In some ways, this entire book series is my attempt to guide us to the brazen laver. That's where our minds are cleansed and renewed and expanded and prepared for deeper encounters with Christ's nature when the full Unveiling begins in the Holy Place.

All of our talk about the Unveiling is still only talk. It's like seeing through a cloudy mirror. It is not the face-to-face encounter we desire, but it is an essential prerequisite to getting there:

> For now we see in a mirror dimly, but then face to face; now I know in part, but then I will know fully just as I also have been fully known.
> —*1 CORINTHIANS 13:12*

As the second of the seven tabernacle furniture items, the brazen laver aligns with the redemptive gift of servant and the Spirit of Wisdom. Like the atmosphere created on the second day of creation, it provides cleansing, protection, and refreshment for soul and body. It filters out the impurities of life so that the light and life of God can flow to us.

On another level, it also represents the expanse—or the firmament—that God spoke into existence on the second day to separate the waters above (heavenly realm) from the waters below (earthly realm). More on that when we get to the throne room scene.

Lastly, remember what we said about the spiritual significance of copper with the brazen altar? Likewise, the copper of the brazen laver speaks of the temporary nature of its application to the first creation. I don't mean to suggest that the Word of God is temporary. We know that heaven and earth will pass away, but His Words will never pass away (see Matthew 24:35). The copper basin of the brazen altar represents the vessel through which we currently experience the Word of God. It is the dim mirror of our perception. It includes the temporary, imperfect filter of our soul's ability to hold and meditate upon His perfect Word. That is what will pass away when we see Him face to face.

In Revelation 4:6, John encounters the spiritual version of the brazen laver in the form of a "sea of glass like crystal," which carries all of the qualities we've just discussed. We'll unpack the role of the sea of glass in due time, but for now, recall the verse we read about the new heavens and new earth in light of the brazen laver's temporary nature:

> Then I saw a new heaven and a new earth; for the first heaven and the first earth passed away, **and there is no longer any sea.**
> —*REVELATION 21:1*

**TABLE OF SHOWBREAD**
(See Exodus 25:23-30)

The table of showbread was the third item of holy furniture. It stood in the inner court, just inside and to the right of the veil separating the inner and outer courts. It was a rectangular table made from acacia wood overlaid with pure gold. It had a raised lip, or ornamental rim, extending around the perimeter of the tabletop like a golden crown.

On the table were twelve round loaves of unleavened bread, divided into two stacks of six: one loaf for each tribe of Israel. The bread was called the showbread (or *bread of presence* in some translations), which literally means *face bread* in Hebrew.

Also on the table were various utensils made of pure gold, including dishes for the two stacks of bread, bowls for frankincense placed on top of the bread stacks, jars for wine, and cups for receiving the wine offering.

The showbread miraculously stayed fresh while it sat in the presence of God for seven days. At the end of the week on the Sabbath it was replaced with new loaves while the priests ate the old loaves and drank the wine offering in God's presence. At that time, the priests would also take the frankincense that sat in golden bowls atop the showbread and burn it on the altar of incense. This was done as a substitution for burning the bread, since the showbread was technically considered a food offering to God.

Only the Levitical priests were allowed in the Holy Place, so when they ate the twelve loaves, drank the wine, and burned the frankincense, they stood in for the other twelve tribes, like elders representing the entire nation.

In contrast to the copper used in the outer court, the pure gold overlay of the table of showbread represented the untarnished, unmixed, eternal glory of God. Every item of furniture covered in or constructed from pure gold speaks of some aspect of Christ's ministry that applies to the formation of the new Jerusalem and will eternally persist as an ongoing service in the new heavens and earth.

The Last Supper of Christ contained many of the principles foreshadowed in the table of showbread. The table represented the ministry of Jesus: the acacia wood of sinless humanity covered in glorious divinity. During the Last Supper, He offered the bread and wine of His new covenant to each of the twelve apostles, who were representatives of the entire Church. All who eat the flesh and drink the blood of His new covenant become part of His Body.

The table's raised ornamental border—its golden crown—speaks of Christ's Kingship. It also speaks of the kingship that is available to His people as kings and priests in His kingdom. Remember, He promised the overcomers from His Body the reward of sitting down with Him on His throne. At the table of showbread He offers that aspect of Himself as we metaphorically eat His flesh and drink His blood.

That's nice religious language, but what does it mean? Do we fulfill the principles of the table of showbread simply by participating in the holy sacrament of communion? No, communion is important, but it is symbolic of something much deeper.

To eat His flesh and drink His blood means to internalize His nature. To meditate on His Word and ruminate on His character. To unpack the life-giving nutrients hidden in the substance of who He is. To allow those nutrients to permeate our members until they become an inseparable part of our being, incarnated in our lives. Like eating and drinking, it is not a one-time event but a continual process that lasts a lifetime.

The table of showbread also speaks of healthy community. Just as the Levitical priests ate the showbread for the entire nation, it is good and wise to receive teaching from leaders who have dedicated their lives to unpacking life-giving principles from the Word of God. But there is a higher calling available in the Melchizedek priesthood. In the new covenant, everyone is invited to receive directly from Christ. We all have the responsibility and privilege to eat the bread of His presence directly from His table, and to learn to unpack the specific nutrients we are uniquely designed to receive.

We each have our own tribe—our own loaf of bread, so to speak—specifically designed to nourish us with those attributes of Christ most related to our calling. That also means that we can learn from each other and thus partake of all aspects of Jesus. But we must have our own direct connection to God or the process breaks. Paul alluded to that very reality in Romans chapter 12, right after describing the spiritual application of the altar of burnt sacrifice (in verse 1) and the brazen altar (in verse 2):

> For through the grace given to me I say to everyone among you not to think more highly of himself than he ought to think; but to think so as to have sound judgment, as God has allotted to each a measure of faith.
> —*ROMANS 12:3*

In John's vision of the heavenly throne room, the table of showbread appears in the unexpected form of twenty-four elders sitting on twenty-four thrones. That connection may not be immediately obvious yet, but it will make sense when we unpack it in the context of Revelation chapter 4.

As for the fractal of seven, the connections to the redemptive gift of teacher, the Spirit of Understanding, and the third day of creation are probably obvious at this point, given everything we just discussed about communion and the unpacking of nutrients from the Word of God. Let's move on to the fourth item.

## GOLDEN LAMPSTAND
(See Exodus 25:31-40)

The golden lampstand, or menorah, was a seven-branched lampstand hammered out of a single piece of pure gold. It was crafted to resemble an almond tree with a central trunk—or servant branch—out of which six other branches grew (three on one side, and three on the other). Each branch was decorated with bulbs and flowers and topped with a cup to hold a lamp.

The fuel for the seven lamps was pressed olive oil refined to the purest possible quality to produce the brightest light with minimal smoke. According to rabbinic tradition, the wicks for the lamps were made from strips cut from the worn-out linen garments of the priests. The oil was renewed daily by the high priest who tended the lamps twice a day—in the morning and evening—to ensure that at least one lamp burned at all times. Although not explicitly stated in Scripture, it is thought that only the light of the central stem was kept lit during the day, and then all seven lamps were lit in the evening.

The seven-branch lampstand was the only light source in the Holy Place. It illuminated both the table of showbread and the altar of incense. However, rabbinic tradition considered the lampstand to be an external extension of the supernatural light of God's glory that dwelled behind the veil above the mercy seat. In other words, the menorah light represented the glory of God visibly sown into creation.

Exodus mentions many other details about the construction of the lampstand, adding enough layers of symbolism to fill an entire book. As a whole, some rabbis describe the menorah as a picture of Israel. Others, a picture of the perfect law of God. Christians typically see it as either the written Word of God, the Holy Spirit, or the Body of Christ.

Some truth can be mined from all of these perspectives. However, the lampstand was pure gold, not acacia covered in gold, so we're talking about the pure divine essence of God with no human component. For that reason, and considering everything we've learned about the fractal of seven, we're going to focus on one interpretation: the golden lampstand is a symbol of the Holy Spirit expressing the fullness of God's light through the seven Spirits of God.

If you want to say that the burning fires on the lamps were the actual seven Spirits of God while the golden lampstand itself was Jesus (the pre-incarnate Word of God), that's fine too. In reality, each of the seven items of holy furniture represents something about Christ. But for now, we're going to focus on the seven Spirits of God. Particularly because that aligns with the seven lamps of fire (which are the seven Spirits of God) that appear before the throne in John's vision.

In the fractal of seven, the golden lampstand represents the redemptive gift of exhorter and the Spirit of Counsel. Remember, the celestial lights were created on the fourth day to illuminate the earth, to energize the seed lifecycle through photosynthesis, to declare the heavenly glory of God, and to govern times and seasons. Likewise, we need the illumination of the Holy Spirit—particularly, the sevenfold light containing the principles of God's essence—if we want to receive the full depth of nourishment available at the table of showbread. Not only does it show us what to eat and when, but it empowers the conversion factor of life flowing from God's Spirit to our spirit (the photosynthesis analogy).

Jesus Christ, our High Priest, determines the sequence and timing of when the lamps are trimmed, establishing the ebbs and flows of when we should be receiving from Him (at the table of showbread) or giving to Him (at the altar of incense). More on that in a moment.

## GOLDEN ALTAR OF INCENSE
(See Exodus 30:1-10)

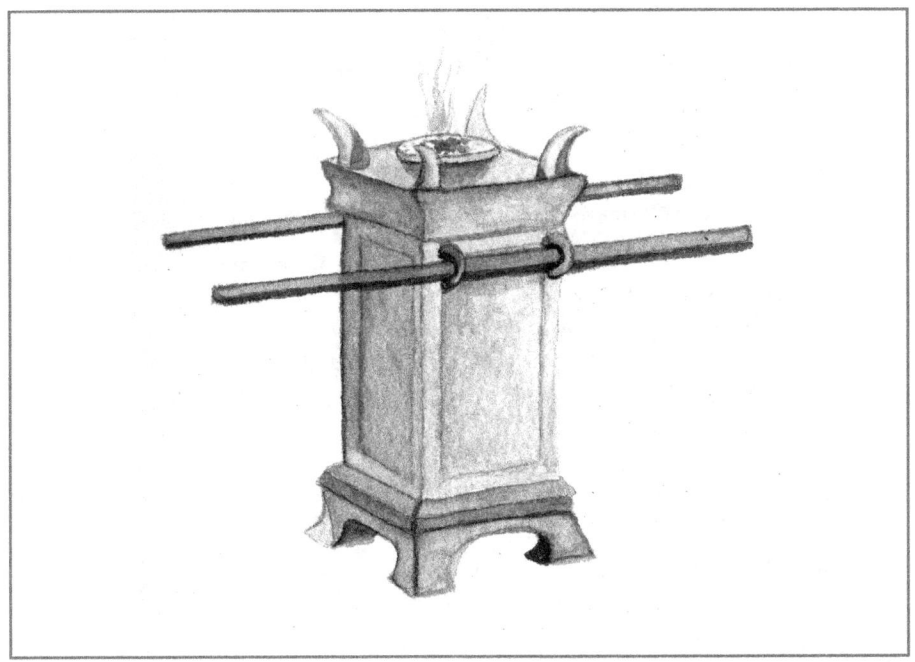

The golden altar of incense was the fifth piece of holy furniture in the tabernacle. Built from acacia wood overlaid with pure gold, it was a small altar standing right in front of the veil that led into the holy of holies. Though separated from the ark of the covenant by the veil, it was placed in alignment with the ark to symbolize that the aroma of its incense would rise continually before the Lord.

Like the table of showbread, the altar of incense had a raised ornamental lip of gold crowning its top edge, symbolizing the Kingship of Christ. Like the altar of burnt sacrifice, it had four horns symbolizing its authority, strength, and reach. However, the altar of incense was not a grill. It was more like an ornate box with a bowl built on top to hold live coals for burning incense. Some believe the bowl was just a receptacle for holding a removable golden censor, meaning the coals and incense were actually burned inside the censor. Either way, the only thing allowed to be burned on this altar was a special blend of sweet-smelling incense.

The burning coals came from underneath the altar of burnt sacrifice (see Leviticus 16:12). God explicitly forbade the burning of any "strange fire" upon the altar—that is, any fire that did not come from the coals of the altar of burnt sacrifice, which He had originally lit with fire from heaven. Tradition suggests that the coals were routinely replaced every morning and evening when the high priest tended the menorah lamps. At that time, the priesthood would also refresh the incense. In this way, the Holy Place was continually filled with the sweet aroma of burning incense.

Burning incense speaks of the prayer and praise that we give to God:

> O LORD, I call upon You; hasten to me!
> Give ear to my voice when I call to You!
> May my prayer be counted as incense before You;
> The lifting up of my hands as the evening offering.
> —*PSALM 141:1-2*

Scripture doesn't say at which side of the altar the priest stood when burning the incense. I assume he faced the holy of holies since the incense was offered to God (who dwelled behind the veil), though I can't find any definitive information either way. Perhaps it doesn't matter, but the question is fascinating, and it offers a good example of different ways to think through these symbols.

For instance, if the priest stood on the west side, between the altar and the holy of holies, his work would be better illuminated by the lampstand, but he would be facing the people rather than God's presence. Perhaps that is a picture of the thanksgiving we offer when life seems good during times of plenty, when we are walking in the clarity of revelation we have already received from God, or when we are interceding for someone else based on the leading of the Holy Spirit.

If the priest stood on the east side of the altar facing the holy of holies, he would have been staring at the veil separating him from the ark of the covenant, and the light of the lampstand may have cast shadows on the altar. Perhaps that is a picture of the prayers we offer by faith during the trials of life when God seems far away and the path ahead is difficult to discern. Times of famine. Either way, both types of prayer are a sweet aroma to God.

Like the table of showbread, the altar of incense ultimately represents the ministry of Christ. He is the High Priest who ever lives to make intercession for us (see Hebrews 7:25). His ministry also provided the conduit through which our intercession and praise can rise to the throne room as a sweet fragrance to God.

On the other hand, whereas the table of showbread was primarily about Christ initiating and us responding, the altar of incense is primarily about us initiating and Christ responding. And the ministry of both were synchronized to the schedule of the high priest tending the lampstand in the evening and morning. We'll learn how that applies to the heavenly temple later.

Like the altar of burnt sacrifice, there is a spiritual version of the altar of incense in the heavenly temple, and like it's sister altar, it doesn't explicitly appear until later in the book of Revelation. We'll find hints of its services beginning in Revelation chapter 4, but we won't see it's largest role until book 3.

In the fractal of seven, the golden altar of incense aligns with the redemptive gift of giver, and with the Spirit of Might. Remember, birds and fish were the first creatures designed with the instincts to be fruitful and multiply through intentional physical intimacy and the sacrificial nurturing of their young. They were the first stewards in the natural world. Obviously, we can receive from God like baby chicks from a mother hen, but in this instance, the metaphor applies best in the other direction.

When we practice drawing near to God to give Him our prayers and praises, He draws near to us to receive them. In the process we learn how to be better stewards of His gifts and resources. And like a mother sacrificially nurturing her child until it reaches maturity, our consistent offering of thanksgiving and intercession produces godly character in us while also moving the mighty hand of God on our behalf.

## ARK OF THE COVENANT
(See Exodus 25:10-16)

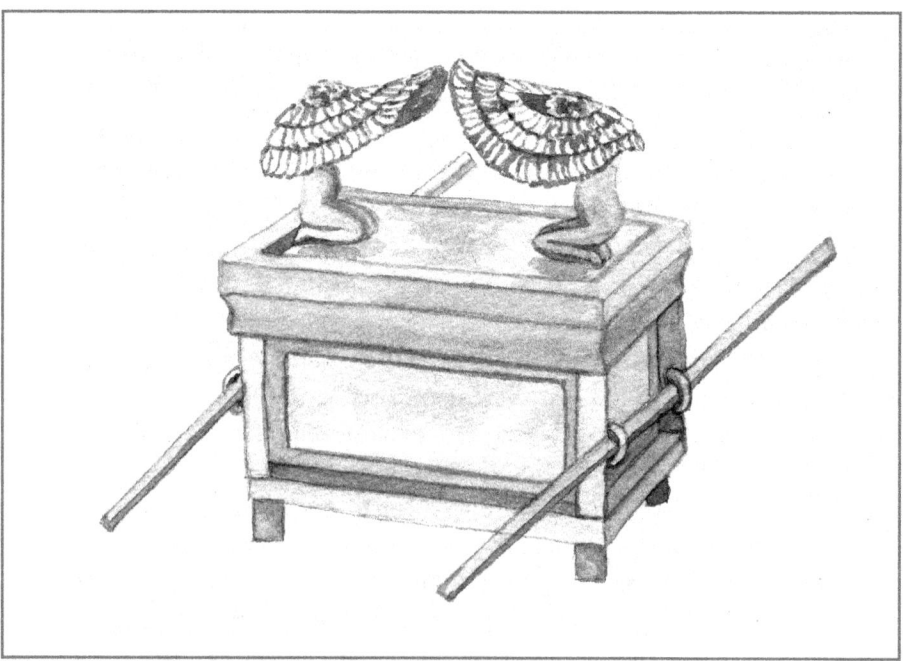

The ark of the covenant was the sixth piece of holy furniture. Located behind the veil in the holy of holies, the ark was built from acacia wood overlaid inside and out with pure gold. It stood about twenty-seven inches high, twenty-seven inches in breadth, and forty-five inches wide. It was a hollow box with a separate cover called the mercy seat. Like the table of showbread and the altar of incense, it had an ornamental golden crown-like molding around the top of the box upon which the mercy seat sat.

The mercy seat was a solid piece of pure gold formed into the shape of two cherubim overlooking a flat golden cover. Most images (including mine) show the ark and the mercy seat together since the mercy seat was always covering the ark. Technically, though, the mercy seat is the seventh item of furniture, so we'll discuss it separately. For now, let's just focus on the box of the ark itself.

Four golden rings were built into the sides of the ark, two on each side, with two poles of gold-covered acacia wood inserted into the rings. Although the altars of burnt sacrifice and incense, and the table of showbread also had rings and poles, those poles were only inserted when their items were being transported. With the ark, God commanded that the poles should never be removed. Some scholars believe the practical reason for this was to ensure the ark could be quickly moved in case of attack. Whether or not that was true, the four rings and two polls contain spiritual symbolism as well. More on that in a moment.

It was called the ark of the covenant because it contained the Ten Commandments—the testimony of God's covenant with Israel written on two stone tablets by the finger of God. There is some debate about whether the ark also contained a pot of manna and Aaron's rod that budded. Certain verses in Exodus and Numbers suggest those items may have been placed *next* to the ark, while the wording of Hebrews 9:4 suggests they were *inside* the ark. Perhaps both were true at different times in Israel's history. Either way, the primary purpose of the ark was to house the two tablets that were the testimony of God's covenant. Hence the name.

The ark of the covenant represents Jesus. While the other furniture made of acacia wood covered in gold (the table of showbread and the altar of incense) also represented some aspect of Christ's ministry to His Body, the ark is the clearest picture of Christ's essence: the Word made flesh. He is the holder of God's covenant. He is the ultimate summation and expression of God's law—the perfect law of love written on the tablets of our heart. And like the two original stone tablets, He is both the righteousness and justice of God made manifest to humanity. As such, like the ark of the covenant, He is the foundation of the throne of God:

> Clouds and thick darkness surround Him; Righteousness and justice are the foundation of His throne.
> —PSALM 97:2

As we'll see when we get to the seventh item of furniture, the cover of the ark represents the throne of God, which is a throne of mercy and grace. In that way, the ark can be seen as the foundation that holds up God's throne. Because Jesus became a human and faithfully fulfilled the Word of God, fully demonstrating its righteousness and justice, He is now the solid ground upon which God's eternal judgments can be merciful and gracious without violating His nature. Don't worry If that concept feels a bit fuzzy right now; we'll come back to it later when we see Christ in the throne room in Revelation chapter 5.

The four rings on the ark represent the four gospels. They enable the message of Christ to be mobilized. And the two poles are like the feet that transport the good news of Jesus.

As the sixth item of furniture, the ark aligns with the redemptive gift of ruler, and with the Spirit of Knowledge. Consider that Jesus is the example of what it looks like for humanity to fulfill their sixth-day mandate and walk in true sonship. In other words, as the ark, He led the way by demonstrating how to live in freedom—with the spirit of the law of love written on our hearts—rather than as slaves forever trying to live up to an external list of commandments to compensate for misreading our Father's heart.

Isn't that the ultimate expression of the ruler gift? Helping creation discover God's heart so everyone and everything can find the freedom and wholeness for which it was designed?

As you might expect, the true ark of the covenant—Jesus Christ—appears in John's throne room vision. Throughout the book of Revelation, Jesus manifests in many different ways. In this book, we'll see Him as a lamb standing before the throne in Revelation chapter 5, fulfilling much of the spiritual symbolism of the ark. But later, in Revelation chapter 11, during the sounding of the seventh trumpet, John describes seeing the temple of God in heaven opening up and the ark of the covenant appearing in the temple. We'll see why that happens and what it means in book 3.

## THE MERCY SEAT
(See Exodus 25:17-22)

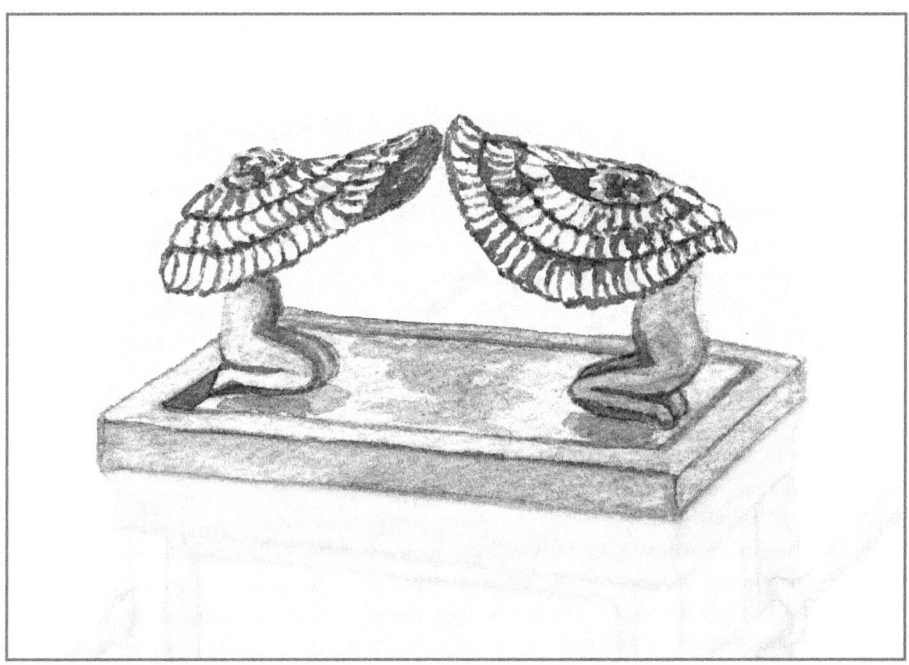

As I mentioned earlier, the mercy seat was the final piece of holy furniture. It was a solid piece of pure gold hammered into a flat cover with two cherubim on top. The cherubim faced each other from each side of the cover. We are not told exactly what these cherubim looked like, beyond that their faces looked down at the mercy seat and their wings were outstretched over it like a covering.

It was there, between the cherubim and above the mercy seat, that the glory of God resided. And it was there, on the flat open space of the mercy seat, that the high priest would sprinkle the blood of the sin offerings when He entered the holy of holies on the Day of Atonement:

> There I will meet with you; and from above the mercy seat, from between the two cherubim which are upon the ark of the testimony, I will speak to you about all that I will give you in commandment for the sons of Israel.
> —*EXODUS 25:22*

> And the LORD said to Moses: "Tell your brother Aaron not to enter freely into the Most Holy Place behind the veil in front of the mercy seat on the ark, or else he will die, because I appear in the cloud above the mercy seat."
> —LEVITICUS 16:2, BSB

The mercy seat represents the throne of God. The cloud is His awesome and terrifying manifest presence. In the old covenant only the high priest could enter beyond the veil, and even he could only enter one day a year for a special ceremony on the Day of Atonement. But in the new covenant, Christ's work on the cross has torn down the veil of separation and the enmity of the law. We are now invited to enter boldly into the holy of holies where God speaks from His throne as a righteous King extending grace and as a just Judge extending mercy:

> Therefore, since we have a great high priest who has passed through the heavens, Jesus the Son of God, let us hold fast our confession. For we do not have a high priest who cannot sympathize with our weaknesses, but One who has been tempted in all things as we are, yet without sin. Therefore let us draw near with confidence to the throne of grace, so that we may receive mercy and find grace to help in time of need.
> —HEBREWS 4:14-16

As you may have guessed, the heavenly version of the mercy seat features prominently in John's vision of the throne room, complete with living cherubim performing a similar function to what we see in the tabernacle model. It's probably equally obvious at this point that the mercy seat aligns with the redemptive gift of mercy, and with the Spirit of the Fear of the Lord.

We'll expand further on those details in the next chapter in the context of John's throne room vision. For now, let's close out this detour by reviewing the overall pattern formed by the tabernacle furniture. This review should help anchor these symbols in something a little more concrete and launch us forward better equipped to understand Revelation chapter 4.

## THE PATH INWARD

At the risk of oversimplifying or even trivializing everything we just learned, I invite you to think about the furniture as the general sequence of spiritual growth available to all Christians. As you might expect, the path also follows the original pattern God established for us with the creation story, but I'll let you practice drawing those parallels on your own this time.

We start outside the tabernacle of Christ's Body until we embrace His work on the cross at the altar of burnt sacrifice. We can either camp there, merely thankful for His sacrifice, or we can choose the path of a bondservant by presenting our own bodies as a living sacrifice upon the same altar. If we choose to move inward, He teaches us to wash in the water of His Word at the brazen laver, which prepares us to step into the Holy Place where we learn to become His Bride.

Once we step into the inner court of the Holy Place as bondservants, we begin learning how to receive spiritual sustenance and strength by unpacking the nutrients of His ways at the table of showbread, aided by the Holy Spirit's sevenfold illumination of the Word through the golden lampstand. During that process, we also learn to offer the deepest, most sincere meditations of our heart on the altar of incense as a sweet aroma to Him.

And once we synchronize with the rhythms of His heart, He leads us into the holy of holies as a Bride leaning on her Beloved. There, we encounter Christ fully unveiled, and we learn how to walk in true sonship with Him.

Finally, in that place of complete unity with Christ, we encounter the mercy seat, where eternal life begins.

Again, this is just a general pattern that shouldn't be applied too strictly to the sequences of life or to the path ahead. Although the fractal of seven does outline the steps we'll take through Revelation, we are not going to specifically map the seven items of furniture repeatedly to the seven letters, seven seals, seven trumpets, and seven bowls. It might be more helpful to see them as representing the entire process, from start to finish, of the Unveiling of Christ. But even that is not my reason for dwelling on this subject.

Instead, I want us to focus on how the symbolism of this furniture enriches our understanding of the throne room scene starting in the next chapter. Also, each item of furniture provides important context for recognizing certain landmarks that we'll soon encounter on the journey. So keep them in the forefront of your mind as we move forward.

## CHAPTER 16

# THE THRONE ROOM - PART 1:
# THE ONE ON THE THRONE

Now we're ready to move back onto the main path where we'll step into the second phase of John's vision. Let's pick the trail back up starting in chapter 4 of Revelation. If the first three chapters of Revelation gradually positioned us for the best experience of Christ's Unveiling, then chapters 4 and 5 will propel us into the most exciting stages with our eyes firmly focused on the treasure.

In this final section of book 2, we'll follow John as he enters God's throne room in heaven. We'll advance one verse at a time, taking time to learn about the main players and properly establish the scene for the primary drama that will begin unfolding in book 3. Along the way, we'll layer in some of what we learned about the tabernacle furniture to enhance our understanding. Finally, we'll end this book with a compass check from the Song of Solomon to see how it all relates to the Bride narrative.

Now would be a good time to remember my exhortation at the beginning of this book: Simplicity and practicality aren't always the best metrics of utility. Sometimes, exercising faith and patience to engage with the majestic complexity of the mysterious will lead us to the most transformational paths through Christ's Unveiling. The section ahead contains a mountain of majestic complexity, and no shortage of exciting detours to keep you on your toes. Consider it a great opportunity to exercise more of your faith and patience, and to further purify and refine your imagination with healthy doses of creative exegesis.

## SO WHAT?

To that end, and to help increase your anticipation and fortitude for this leg of the journey, I'm going to preemptively address the question that usually comes *after* all of the exposition: So what? How will this information help us in our daily lives?

To be honest, I cannot directly tie some of what we are about to discuss to a practical life principle. Beyond pointing out the general appearance of the fractal of seven, I also won't try to turn this Revelation chapter 4 throne room scene into some seven-step process for transformation that will help you love your neighbor better or overcome the influences of darkness in your life or the lives of your family, your coworkers, or your community. Don't get me wrong—the truths in these chapters of Revelation have the power to accomplish all of those things in our lives, but you won't get that just from reading some words.

So what, then? Why should we spend so much time unpacking John's vision of the throne room of God? I mean, beyond the basic reason I already gave for studying Revelation chapters 1 through 5. Yes, we know it provides essential context to help us keep our eyes fixed on Christ throughout the rest of Revelation, and we'll see that it establishes the anchor point around which everything else in Revelation revolves. Those are great reasons, but they are future-focused. How will a study of the throne room help us now, even before we get to the rest of Revelation?

The way I see it, meditating on John's vision of the heavenly throne room is one of the most impactful biblical disciplines we can practice. In a world so dominated by the tyranny of the temporal, nothing is more practical than being wholly and fully grounded in the reality of the One on the throne at the center of time and space. Imagine how your life would change if you were literally transported to heaven to see God sitting on His throne. What if you temporarily experienced the full power of His presence with your five senses? How would that encounter recontextualize everything else in your life?

Obviously, we can't control whether or not God chooses to transport us to His throne room as He did for John. But even though we may not be able to conjure such literal encounters, we can and should meditate on His Word as if our imagination brings us close. The invisible reality experienced by John and recorded for our benefit is meant to grow in our thoughts until it becomes the foundation upon which our worldview is built. That means more than just knowing God is on His throne in a general sense. We are invited to ruminate on the details of His throne room until the truths they reveal about reality invade every fiber of our being. Like the table of showbread, it's not just a search for information but a way to practice the presence of God. What better way is there to fulfill the exhortation in Hebrews:

> In a world so dominated by the tyranny of the temporal, nothing is more practical than being wholly and fully grounded in the reality of the One on the throne at the center of time and space

> Therefore let us draw near with confidence to the throne of grace, so that we may receive mercy and find grace to help in time of need.
> —HEBREWS 4:16

## THE DOOR IN HEAVEN

In that light, and without further ado, Revelation chapter 4 begins where the letters to the seven churches left off:

> After these things I looked, and behold, a door standing open in heaven, and the first voice which I had heard, like the sound of a trumpet speaking with me, said, "Come up here, and I will show you what must take place after these things."
> —REVELATION 4:1

"After these things I looked …." After what things? The original vision of Christ walking among the lampstands and the seven letters that unpacked the meaning of that vision. That experience was the prerequisite that prepared John (and us) to see the next phase of the divine encounter of Revelation.

"A door standing open in heaven …." This is the same open door that Jesus gave to the ruler-church of Philadelphia: the one that opened because they walked in sonship and learned how to employ the keys of heaven. It's the same door that opened in heaven when Christ was baptized in the Jordan River before entering His ministry. This same door opened in Revelation chapter 12 when the male child was born and was caught up to the throne of God.

It's no accident that right before this part of John's vision, Jesus had been knocking on Laodicea's closed door. It is as if our response to His first six letters produces an open door into the authority, resources, and perspective of heaven. But then the final letter addresses the self-righteous part of our hearts that keeps us separated from God behind self-imposed doors of fear and shame. Once we open the doors we've shut and allow Him to teach us how to rest in Him, we'll see the door He has already opened in heaven beckoning us to a higher reality.

> The invisible reality experienced by John and recorded for our benefit is meant to grow in our thoughts until it becomes the foundation upon which our worldview is built.

Notice that this open door also aligns with the Bride's response to the seventh letter: "the king has brought me into His chamber" (Song of Solomon 1:4). The heavenly door leads to the King's chamber. In the tabernacle metaphor, it leads into the Holy Place (the inner court), where the holy of holies is fully visible because its veil is already torn down by Christ's atonement.

"Come up here, and I will show you what must take place after these things." The Unveiling involves more than just our initial consent to the terms of engagement outlined in the seven letters. It starts with our consent, but after that, a series of events *must take place*. And as we'll see shortly, those events must be initiated by Christ Himself in response to our "yes."

> Immediately I was in the Spirit; and behold, a throne was
> standing in heaven, and One sitting on the throne.
> —*REVELATION 4:2*

"Immediately I was in the Spirit ...." When Jesus said, "Come up here ..." it wasn't just another invitation requiring a response. It was a command that immediately altered reality. In many ways, this is a preview of the same process and power that He will use to initiate the final stage of the resurrection and transformation of our earthly bodies before the marriage supper of the Lamb:

> For the Lord Himself will descend from heaven with a
> shout, with the voice of the archangel and with the trumpet
> of God, and the dead in Christ will rise first. Then we who
> are alive and remain will be caught up together with them
> in the clouds to meet the Lord in the air, and so we shall
> always be with the Lord.
> —*1 THESSALONIANS 4:16-17*

> Behold, I tell you a mystery; we will not all sleep, but we
> will all be changed, in a moment, in the twinkling of an
> eye, at the last trumpet; for the trumpet will sound, and the
> dead will be raised imperishable, and we will be changed.
> —*1 CORINTHIANS 15:51-52*

We'll unpack these verses later in the series when we get to the seven trumpets. My point is that after the seven letters, John experienced a transformative event that foreshadows the future time when our mortal flesh will put on immortality.

To be clear, this door in heaven wasn't the resurrection. It doesn't seem that John's body was transformed or translated in any way. It is more likely that his human spirit was transported to heaven for a preview of Christ's Unveiling in much the same way that the sons of God will experience an open heaven at the beginning of the second half of the seventieth week. Both cases are examples of the impact of Christ's Unveiling: first on spirit, then on soul, and eventually on body.

This shouldn't be surprising. Remember, like all biblical messianic prophecies, the Unveiling follows the lifecycle of a seed and unfolds in ever-increasing stages of maturity. Put another way, we will experience the power of Christ's Unveiling in waves of increasing intensity. When a sufficient portion of the Church finally responds appropriately to Christ's seven letters, the first wave of the Unveiling will begin, and it will be accompanied by a corresponding leap forward in spiritual maturity for those who heed it.

## SPIRITUAL THOUGHTS

One more note on John being "in the spirit." As we'll see in a moment, John encounters many amazing and mysterious things while in the spirit in heaven. In the first few verses alone, he sees thrones, the likeness of gemstones, lightning and thunder, living creatures with animal features, human elders with crowns, a sea of glass, and flames of fire. And it only gets weirder from there. Was John seeing heaven as it really is? Or was he receiving a divinely curated vision of symbolic pictures with metaphoric meaning?

I believe the answer is yes to both. John saw heaven as it really is: Chapter 4 of Revelation is probably best understood as a typical day in the throne room of God before the Unveiling begins. Yet the spirit realm is about feeling, sensing, and experiencing reality on multiple simultaneous levels that our physical brains struggle to comprehend and explain. As such, the language and expression of the spirit world is often deeply symbolic while also revealing the deepest truth of reality. So we'll treat these events as though John were literally in heaven, seeing actual events while experiencing them through the highly symbolic language of the spirit. Discerning how to interpret those symbols and where to draw the line between literal and metaphorical fulfillment is the challenge and adventure of sonship led by the Holy Spirit:

> Now we have received, not the spirit of the world, but the Spirit who is from God, so that we may know the things freely given to us by God, which things we also speak, not in words taught by human wisdom, but in those taught by the Spirit, combining spiritual thoughts with spiritual words.
>
> But a natural man does not accept the things of the Spirit of God, for they are foolishness to him; and he cannot understand them, because they are spiritually ap-

praised. But he who is spiritual appraises all things, yet he himself is appraised by no one.
—*1 CORINTHIANS 2:12-15*

So, let's move forward with a sense of wonder, anticipation, and excitement while leaving room for our understanding to grow and change as we mature in Christ.

## THE THRONE ROOM

Now back to our verse in Revelation:

Immediately I was in the Spirit; and behold, a throne was standing in heaven, and One sitting on the throne.
—*REVELATION 4:2*

"Behold, a throne was standing in heaven ...." This will become clearer as we keep reading, but this throne is the mercy seat at the center of the heavenly temple. More on that in the next chapter. But first, the fact that Christ wants us to behold His Unveiling from the third-heaven perspective available in the throne room of God is significant. Only from that elevated position can we see everything that transpires as it really is, unfiltered by second-heaven distractions or first-heaven defilements. Only with our eyes fixed on the throne will we behold the events of Revelation from the proper viewpoint.

"One sitting on the throne." Again, it all starts with the One; the I AM; the ALL who initiated creation so that He would no longer be alone. In the nomenclature of the Trinity, this is God the Father. The One, resting alone in His holiness, waiting for His plan to come to fruition. He is more than just the center of the heavenly temple; He is the center of the universe. The anchor point of all dimensions of eternity, time, and space. The heart of reality. And yet He exists outside of those things, tethered to creation through His throne and His Word.

Everything else that we read in the book of Revelation from this point forward ultimately revolves around the One working through Christ to bring all things into congruence with His throne. That's why it is important to read these visions and wrestle with their mysteries. What John beheld is far beyond our minds to comprehend, but the very act of imagining and staring at the throne room scene with a desire to know

Him is an act of faith that gradually recenters our perspective around Him.

## STONES AND COLORS

> And He who was sitting was like a jasper stone and a sardius in appearance; and there was a rainbow around the throne, like an emerald in appearance.
> —*REVELATION 4:3*

"Like a jasper stone and a sardius in appearance ...." John's description of God on the throne is both fascinating and perplexing. It must have blown his mind and exceeded his vocabulary because all he could do was draw from natural things to make imperfect comparisons. I don't know how precisely we are meant to interpret the imagery of these gemstones since John was clearly grasping for words to convey an overwhelming spectacle, but let's try to unpack a few relevant details for the next few steps of our journey.

Every commentary I've read on this verse points to the colors of the gemstones as significant. The problem is that scholars aren't entirely certain about the identity—let alone the color—of some of these stones. Read a dozen commentaries and get half a dozen opinions on the color of jasper, for instance. The problem only increases when you look for other appearances of gemstones in Scripture.

> What John beheld is far beyond our minds to comprehend, but the very act of imagining and staring at the throne room scene with a desire to know Him is an act of faith that gradually recenters our perspective around Him.

The twelve gemstones on the high priest's breastplate (see Exodus 28) are a good example. Among widely respected Torah scholars, there are no less than thirty variations on the identity of those stones depending on how the Hebrew words are translated. Different Bible versions demonstrate the same frustrating lack of consensus.

Consider the aforementioned jasper stone. Some say the jasper of Revelation 4 was dark opaque green. Others, milky white. Still others, crystal clear. If it was white or clear, we could hypothesize that it represents either God's holiness or righteousness. But dark opaque green? It's hard to say based solely on the color.

On the other hand, a sardius (sometimes translated as carnelian) is widely agreed to be fiery red like a ruby. So perhaps the sardius speaks of God's mercy ... or maybe His justice?

An emerald is green, possibly speaking of God's grace ... or peace ... or eternal life. You see, even when we know the gem's color, we can't be dogmatic about the meaning of the color.

Having mentioned those caveats to ensure we hold our interpretations loosely, what happens if we apply fractal principles to the gemstones? Putting aside that some of the gemstones in Scripture are subject to great uncertainty, what happens if we just pick a translation and go with it? In that scenario, what lists could we use to help derive some divine characteristics from gemstones?

After our tabernacle furniture discussion in the last chapter, you might be inclined to start with the list of twelve gemstones in the high priest's breastplate found in Exodus 28. Chronologically, that is the first significant list of gemstones in Scripture. However, I'd like to take you in a different direction. Ezekiel prophesied about a list of gemstones that appeared at the dawn of creation in a context that might be more directly tied to the throne room of God than even the high priest's breastplate. Let's start there:

> You were the seal of perfection, full of wisdom and perfect in beauty.
>
> You were in Eden, the garden of God; every precious stone was your covering: The **sardius**, **topaz**, and **diamond**, **beryl**, **onyx**, and **jasper**, **sapphire**, **turquoise**, and **emerald** with gold. The workmanship of your timbrels and pipes was prepared for you on the day you were created.
>
> You were the anointed cherub who covers; I established you; you were on the holy mountain of God; you walked back and forth in the midst of fiery stones. You were perfect in your ways from the day you were created, till iniquity was found in you.
> —*EZEKIEL 28:12-15, NKJV*

This is part of a larger prophetic judgment in which Ezekiel draws several esoteric parallels between the human king of Tyre and a spiritual being described as "the anointed cherub who covers." As we'll see later, Ezekiel knew a thing or two about cherubim (plural of cherub). This particular *anointed* cherub is thought by many Christians to be a reference to Satan before he rebelled against God. I tend to agree, though the specific identity of the anointed cherub is immaterial for this conversation. Right now, we're only seeking a better understanding of the gemstones.

Consider how much this passage resonates with heavenly throne room overtones: Eden, the garden of God, was a primordial shadow of the future reality of the new Jerusalem with the throne room at its center. Cherubim are typically associated with the throne and glory of God. That was true of the tabernacle, and we'll see it again in both Revelation and Ezekiel. Even Ezekiel's mention of "the mountain of God" is consistent with other throne room allusions, including Mount Sinai, where Moses first saw the throne of God descend, and Mount Zion, where the temple of Solomon eventually resided. Some scholars even suggest that Eden itself was originally planted on a high mountain.

In that throne room context, nine stones covered the anointed cherub: sardius, topaz, diamond, beryl, onyx, jasper, sapphire, turquoise, and emerald. We will leave gold off the list, since that is just a metal in which gemstones are set. These nine stones are a picture of nine character traits of God that sparkle and shimmer in the light of His glory, just as gemstones on a cherub would as they receive the overflow of light emanating from God's throne. They can also be seen as nine divine attributes that take shape and grow in creation through close proximity to God's presence.

We'll come back to the cherubim later because they play a major role in the throne room scene. But first, how do we identify the nine character traits represented in these nine gemstones? How about the nine fruits of the Spirit? Aren't they similar in function, growing in the light of the Holy Spirit and reflecting the character of God?

> But the fruit of the Spirit is love, joy, peace, patience, kindness, goodness, faithfulness, gentleness, self-control; against such things there is no law.
> —GALATIANS 5:22-23

Using this fractal approach, we arrive at the following potential interpretation:

- Sardius (or carnelian or ruby) = love
- Topaz = joy
- Diamond (or crystal) = peace
- Beryl = patience
- Onyx = kindness
- Jasper = goodness
- Sapphire (or lapis lazuli) = faithfulness
- Turquoise = gentleness
- Emerald = self-control

Now, what happens if we apply this fruits of the Spirit motif to the Revelation chapter 4 vision of God's throne room? Remember the verse we're working with:

> And He who was sitting was like a jasper stone and a sardius in appearance; and there was a rainbow around the throne, like an emerald in appearance.
> —*REVELATION 4:3*

The jasper stone would be goodness, the sardius would be love, and the emerald would be self-control. Again, we can't be dogmatic—this is only one potential interpretation—but isn't it beautiful how well they align? It makes sense to think of the appearance of the One on the throne as the source of all goodness (jasper) and love (sardius). We know that God *is* love, but goodness is also one of the main intrinsic characteristics of His holiness. Remember Christ's statement to the rich young ruler?

> And Jesus said to him, "Why do you call Me good? No one is good except God alone."
> —*MARK 10:18*

Why would Jesus correct someone for calling Him good when He was, without a doubt, good? Perhaps the reason is that pure, undiluted goodness is directly related to the glory of God on His throne—a glory that Christ had temporarily set aside to be incarnated as a human bondservant. Only the One sitting on the throne, alone in His holiness, emanates undiluted goodness like a jasper stone.

This idea of God's goodness being the primary expression of His divine glory was echoed in Moses's encounter on Mount Sinai:

> Then Moses said, "I pray You, show me Your glory!" And He said, "I Myself will make all My goodness pass before you, and will proclaim the name of the LORD before you; and I will be gracious to whom I will be gracious, and will show compassion on whom I will show compassion."
> —EXODUS 33:18-19

When Moses asked to see God's glory, God showed him all of His goodness. So it makes sense that John would see the glow of a jasper stone representing goodness emanating from the One on the throne.

"And there was a rainbow around the throne, like an emerald in appearance." It also makes sense to think of the rainbow as a visual expression of God's self-control (emerald) ... especially considering His covenant with Noah to never again destroy the earth with water.

Speaking of that rainbow, we described it in book 1 as the light of God's glory refracted and reflected into the colors of the rainbow around the throne. Yet, here we read that the rainbow was "like an emerald in appearance." How can a rainbow, which by definition is *many* colors, appear like an emerald, which is only green? If the shining was just a green hue, why call it a rainbow? If it was many colors, why say it appeared like an emerald?

To add to the puzzle, consider the prophet Ezekiel's vision of the throne room, some seven hundred years before John's vision:

> Now above the expanse that was over their heads there was something resembling a throne, like lapis lazuli in appearance; and on that which resembled a throne, high up, was a figure with the appearance of a man. Then I noticed from the appearance of His loins and upward something like glowing metal that looked like fire all around within it, and from the appearance of His loins and downward I saw something like fire; and there was a radiance around Him. **As the appearance of the rainbow in the clouds on**

**a rainy day, so was the appearance of the sur-
rounding radiance.**
—*EZEKIEL 1:27-28*

So Ezekiel also saw the Holy One sitting on His throne with a rain-
bow-like radiance surrounding Him, though Ezekiel didn't mention an
emerald-like appearance. Rather, he suggested the radiance looked like
the rainbow of many colors found in the clouds after a storm.

We can only speculate about the discrepancy between Ezekiel's and
John's descriptions. Perhaps John also saw a rainbow of many colors but
noticed green as the most prominent color. Or maybe John saw a green
rainbow in that moment because God wants us to know that the grace
of His self-control (emerald) will temper every judgment that proceeds
from His throne during the Unveiling.

At the end of the day, whether or not we are right about our gem-
stone interpretations, we know that John saw a glorious overflow of colors radiating from God on the throne, like shimmering flecks of irides-
cent gemstones. I imagine it was like looking at the sun through a kalei-
doscope and trying to pick out the most prominent hues as they danced
and darted uncontrollably through his field of vision. The colors and
gemstones matter, but perhaps their greatest significance will be experienced during the Unveiling rather than described second-hand ahead of
time.

## CHAPTER 17

# THE THRONE ROOM - PART 2: AROUND AND BEFORE

N ow that our perspective is unshakably anchored to the One on the throne, let's find out what else John saw in the throne room:

> Around the throne were twenty-four thrones; and upon the thrones I saw twenty-four elders sitting, clothed in white garments, and golden crowns on their heads.
> —*REVELATION 4:4*

"Around the throne were twenty-four thrones ...." Notice that the vision now contains a total of twenty-five thrones: God's throne in the middle, plus twenty-four other thrones around the One. The exact positioning of these other thrones isn't clear. Some read it as a complete circle around the One. Others see a semicircle, either in front or behind the One. Still others are convinced of twelve thrones on the left and twelve thrones on the right. I prefer to think of them as surrounding the throne in a complete circle, almost like the markings on a sundial or an analog clock. I'll explain why later, but legitimate arguments exist for each configuration, so let's keep an open mind.

## THE TWENTY-FOUR ELDERS

Sitting on the twenty-four thrones were twenty-four elders. They wore white garments and had golden crowns on their heads. Beyond that, the fact that they are called elders suggests they are spiritually mature and of sufficient experience and faithfulness to be trusted as examples, and to judge and teach others with honor, dignity, and respect. Such was the main role of the elders in both Old and New Testament Scriptures.

Who or what are these twenty-four elders? Scripture doesn't offer any definitive answers, but maybe we can make a few deductions from the text. Let's start with a list of the logical options, in no particular order:

- The elders are representative symbols instead of individual beings.
- The elders are angels (i.e., spiritual messengers).
- The elders are some other kind of spiritual rulers (i.e., the heavenly council mentioned earlier).
- The elders are disembodied human spirits.
- The elders are glorified saints (i.e., humans with new creation bodies).

Obviously these are only the top-level categories under which more specific options could be enumerated. Before we drill down further, we should define each category and see if any can be easily eliminated as options.

## THE ELDERS ARE ONLY SYMBOLIC?

We'll get this one out of the way first. Do the twenty-four elders need to be actual sentient beings, or can they just be non-personal symbolic representations of some spiritual truth? This question is different than asking whether we *can* identify them as individuals, or whether they *can* represent something else. It is possible for them to be emblematic of something while also being real beings. The option we are discussing is whether they are real beings that actually exist in heaven or only symbolic constructions in the way that people in dreams are typically only constructs of our mind. I know this sounds like an esoteric question, but it matters.

Considering that John held interactive conversations with at least one of the twenty-four elders (see Revelation 5:5 and 7:14), and since we believe this experience wasn't just a figment of John's imagination, I think it is safe to say that the elders are sentient beings that actually exist in reality. They are not just visual constructs in a spiritual vision, who are merely representative of some idea or concept.

## THE ELDERS ARE ANGELS?

Next, we can be reasonably certain that these elders are not angels because they are later mentioned in a common scene separately from the angels:

> Then I looked, and I heard the voice of many angels around the throne and the living creatures and the elders; and the number of them was myriads of myriads, and thousands of thousands ...
> —*REVELATION 5:11*

If there are elders *and* angels in the same scene, then the elders aren't angels. Of course we've already seen that *angel* is an imprecise term, often used indiscriminately in Old and New Testaments to describe both human and non-human messengers. To further complicate matters, sometimes angel is a catch-all label to describe all manner of supernatural beings, while other times (as in Revelation 5:11) a clear distinction is drawn between beings of different rank and role. Let's put all of that aside for the sake of this discussion. In the context of this throne room scene we'll consider the angels standing around the throne as lower ranking spiritual beings with a messenger role rather than a governing one (since there were an innumerable quantity of them and they are further away from the throne). In that way, the elders are not considered angels (based on Revelation 5:11), so we can take that option off the list.

## THE ELDERS AS NON-HUMAN SPIRITUAL RULERS?

Could the twenty-four elders represent some other order of non-human spiritual beings, like angels but with a higher rank than the myriads standing at a distance around the throne? Beings that are faithful and subservient to their Creator and have an important role to play in the administration of His heavenly temple? In other words, could these be some subset of the morning stars and/or the sons of God spoken of in Job, similar to what the Psalmist described as a "council of the holy ones" among the heavenly beings surrounding God?

> For who in the skies can compare with the LORD? Who among the heavenly beings is like the LORD? In the council of the holy ones, God is greatly feared, and awesome above all who surround Him.
> —PSALM 89:6-7, BSB

While I like this option and I think it has a lot of merit, I also have a few reasons to take us in a different direction. Firstly, Revelation 4:4 describes the elders with features that directly harken to the promises Christ gave to the overcomers of the seven churches. Remember, they sat on thrones (the promise to Laodicea), they wore white garments (the promise to Sardis), and they had golden crowns (similar, if not exactly the same, as the promise to Smyrna). That certainly doesn't mean the elders have to be overcoming Christians. It could simply indicate that the glorified state of overcoming Christians will be similar to these heavenly beings. Even so, there is only one other place in Scripture where non-human spiritual beings are described as wearing crowns, and in that case it's talking about demonic entities who have "*something like* crowns of gold" (Revelation 9:7, BSB). Something like crowns of gold isn't actual crowns of gold. Instead, the description suggests counterfeit crowns representing a false authority and a pretense of victory. Kind of like Satan's claim to be the star of the morning. My point is that legitimate crowns in Scripture are reserved for humans, and in a spiritual context are almost always tied either to Christ (who earned His crown as a human) or the crowns He gives His people for suffering with Him.

That seems like a significant (though hardly conclusive) connection between the twenty-four elders and humanity. The connection grows when you consider that the Greek word for the elders' crowns is *stephanous*, which was typically used to describe a wreath or garland awarded to victors in ancient athletic games. It was more a crown of honor earned for victory than the kind inherited by a monarch. Again, not conclusive, but wouldn't a victor's crown be an award given to humans, not to supernatural beings never born to suffer the wilderness of earth?

Secondly, and perhaps more importantly, it would take an entire book to build out the biblical case for a heavenly "council of the holy ones" made up of non-human supernatural beings. As I mentioned earlier, others have already done that better than I ever could, and our focus in this series needs to stay firmly attuned to Christ's Unveiling. So while this option could very well be true, we can't take the time to build out all of the framework necessary for understanding why such a non-human council would even matter and what impact it would have on our experience of the Unveiling. Instead, there is another option for the elders that I think is better suited for the path we are taking in this series. It doesn't preclude the existence of a non-human heavenly council of holy ones, but it does suggest that the twenty-four elders may be something else entirely. But before we discuss that option, let's talk about another one we can probably cross off our list ...

> Legitimate crowns in Scripture are reserved for humans, and in a spiritual context are almost always tied either to Christ (who earned His crown as a human) or the crowns He gives His people for suffering with Him.

## THE ELDERS ARE DISEMBODIED HUMAN SPIRITS?

If the elders' attributes are more inline with humanity, could they be disembodied human spirits of saints? In other words, Old Testament or New Testament saints who died after living on earth, and are now in heaven *before* the resurrection of the dead? This option is also possible, but I find it less plausible than even the non-human divine council option. Firstly, the white garments, crowns, and thrones are rewards attributed to Christ's Unveiling, so we shouldn't expect to see disembodied human spirits enjoying those rewards *before* the resurrection associated with Christ's return. Moreover, we'll encounter other references to disembodied spirits in the throne room scene as we move forward, and although they too will be given white robes, the Greek word for *robes* in those cases is different than the white garments worn by the elders and those promised to the overcomers of Sardis. Also, in none of those cases are the disembodied spirits given crowns or thrones. More on that in book 3.

There is a variation of this option that I want to mention, though I hesitate to go too far down this road right now. Consider that disembodied human spirits in heaven don't *necessarily* have to be the spirits of saints who have fallen asleep in Christ, or of Old Testament saints awaiting the resurrection. There is also a school of thought that God created all human spirits (or apportioned them out from His Spirit, as the thinking goes) way back at the beginning of time on the first day of creation. Under that scenario, pre-born human spirits would somehow be at God's side awaiting the season He elects to send them to earth at the time of conception. That's when they would join with their newly created human body in the womb. Moreover, if that scenario is true, then these pre-born human spirits could also account for any mention in the Old Testament of sons of God, heavenly hosts, council of the holy ones, etc. ...

Having recognized that option, and putting aside the many theological questions it would raise, all of the same issues still exist for them to be the twenty-four elders. Remember, the crowns and white garments and thrones are still best seen as rewards apportioned out to resurrected and glorified saints who have already experienced Christ's Unveiling. So I'm not a fan of viewing the twenty-four elders as either disembodied or pre-bodied human spirits (if the latter is even a thing).

## THE ELDERS ARE GLORIFIED SAINTS?

And then there was one: glorified saints. "Wait a minute," you might be thinking. "How can the elders be glorified saints if the Unveiling of Jesus Christ hasn't happened yet at this point in the throne room scene? How did they get glorified?!" At least I hope you are thinking something along those lines because it would mean you've been paying close attention to the details.

We haven't spent much time talking about the chronology of end-time events since reviewing "The Hourglass" of Daniel's seventy-week prophecy in book 1, so I can understand if the problems with viewing the elders as glorified saints with resurrection bodies isn't already obvious. Not to mention, I told you that building a chronological timeline of end-times events is one of the least important exercises (and most fraught with peril, I might add) for a life-giving journey into the Unveiling. So if you're not even thinking about chronology yet, you are doing well.

Even so, there are a few guideposts that we should keep in mind. For instance, we know from Christ's own words, Paul's teachings, and many verses in Revelation, that believers won't receive their glorified, new creation bodies until after Christ's Unveiling (see Mark 13:24-27, 1 Corinthians 15:52, and Revelation 20:4 for examples). It is okay if you are not convinced of that point yet, but hopefully you've at least come to see the resurrection of the saints as the primary fruit of His Unveiling, not the seed that leads to it.

In order for the twenty-four elders to be glorified saints, wouldn't we have to say that their appearance in the heavenly throne room happens *after* the Unveiling of Christ and *after* the resurrection of believers? In other words, wouldn't we have to accept a rapture event that removes Christians from the earth before the majority of Revelation unfolds? Obviously, some eschatological theories teach exactly that, but if you've made it this far with me, you already know why we should reject that idea: It misses the whole purpose and power of Christ's Unveiling. It circumvents the most intense earthly trials that will act as contractions to help form us into His unveiled image.

So baring some "wibbly-wobbly, timey-whimey" (to quote Doctor Who) nonlinear paradoxical time travel explanation requiring us to abandon all hope of constructive biblical exegesis, haven't we eliminated our last option? Doesn't that mean the elders cannot be glorified saints? Not exactly. Consider this mysterious event from the story of the crucifixion:

> And Jesus cried out again with a loud voice, and yielded up His spirit. And behold, the veil of the temple was torn in two from top to bottom; and the earth shook and the rocks were split. **The tombs were opened, and many bod-**

> **ies of the saints who had fallen asleep were raised;**
> and coming out of the tombs after His resurrection they
> entered the holy city and appeared to many.
> —MATTHEW 27:50-53

When Christ died, many Old Testament saints were physically raised from the dead and given new creation bodies. Unless you want to contend that this event describes only a temporary raising from the dead like Lazarus and that these saints eventually died again, this passage must be describing something of a first-fruits resurrection—an early sample of the power of the full resurrection that is reserved for the final harvest at the end of the age.

Does that mean all Old Testament saints were raised at that time? That is theologically unlikely for numerous reasons, including the fact that it specifies "many bodies of the saints" were raised, not all the saints. Rather, it seems only a subset of those buried in and around Jerusalem experienced this first-fruits resurrection. Perhaps it included some mix of the patriarchs, matriarchs, prophets, kings, and peasants of the Old Testament. It may have even included some contemporaries of Christ who believed in His messiahship but died before His work on the cross (for instance, Simeon and Anna from Luke 2:25-38, or John the Baptist). We can't know their identities, but we know they were a privileged few to experience something so immensely special and unique in human history.

Have you ever wondered what happened to these resurrected saints? Surely they didn't stay behind on earth. Christ eventually ascended to the right hand of the Father after appearing to many in His new creation body. These resurrected saints must have followed Him into the throne room.

Could the twenty-four elders be taken from these resurrected (and therefore glorified) saints? I know this is far from conclusive, but for me, this option checks the most boxes and presents the least number of problems. Going forward, I'm going to keep this option in the forefront of my mind as the most likely identity of the elders. The heavenly council of non-human spiritual beings is a close second. It may even be possible for both to be true—a council composed of twelve non-human divine beings and twelve glorified saints. But before we go down another rabbit trail, let's just say that the jury is still out.

## A NUMBER OF SIGNIFICANCE?

Now let's consider some other attributes of the elders. First, why are there *twenty-four* elders? The answer somewhat depends on their identity, but the basic logic of what we are about to talk about can be applied whether the elders are humans or non-humans or both. Here is an overview of the more common theories:

- There are twenty-four to represent the whole Body of Christ, with twelve for the natural branches (believing Jews) and twelve for the wild branches (believing Gentiles).
- There are twenty-four to represent the whole will and purpose of God for creation, with twelve for the Old Testament and twelve for the New Testament portions of His plan. Or perhaps twelve for the first creation and twelve for the second creation.
- There are twenty-four to represent the twenty-four divisions of priests who served day and night in the temple (see 1 Chronicles 24) and/or the twenty-four divisions of musicians who offered twenty-four hour singing and music to the Lord (see 1 Chronicles 25). More on this in a moment.
- They are literally the twelve patriarchs of Israel (the sons of Jacob) combined with the twelve apostles of Christ. (I'm sure you can see the problem with this option already).

One or more of these options can be true at the same time. Or none of them. Again, it is unwise to be too rigid.

Of these four options, I see a lot of truth in the first three (more on them in a moment), but obviously the fourth one doesn't work if the elders are not disembodied human spirits (since the apostles haven't experienced the resurrection yet.) And even if we say they *could* be disembodied human spirits, wouldn't John have mentioned something if he saw his best friends (and himself) sitting on glorious thrones in heaven?

Moreover, it is hard to imagine the twelve sons of Jacob sitting around the throne of God as elders. Rewards and positions in heaven are based on faithful sacrifice and servanthood. In other words, our inheritance in the afterlife is a meritocracy based on God's judgment of our character and deeds on earth, not an aristocracy based on the influence of our natural family line. The Old Testament account of the lives of the sons of Jacob hardly screams "elders worthy of veneration."

So minus the literal patriarchs and apostles option, I encourage you to think about the role of the elders through the other three lenses as we move forward. Having said that, while fruit can be gleaned from our discussion about who the elders may or may not be, it is probably less fruitful to speculate too much about their individual identities. I find it more helpful to think about what they represent as a group based on their actions. In other words, since God wants us to know that they exist but didn't tell us who they are, let's move forward with an eye toward learning whatever He wants us to know about the office of eldership in heaven, and perhaps the righteous government of God as expressed through humanity.

## DIVISIONS OF TIME

One important attribute of the twenty-four elders that may not be immediately obvious is their relationship with time. Hence the reason I said I like to imagine them sitting in a circle around the throne like the markings on a sundial or an analog clock. To explain what I mean, we'll need to weave together a few different concepts.

First, consider that time is a structure that God created. And though our perception of it is relative and our understanding limited, we only interact with the spatial dimensions of physical and spiritual creation through the structure of time.

So whether time is a dimension or a concept or a measurement, it can be defiled by sin and death just like physical and spiritual space. Especially when those defiling influences are perpetuated across a duration of time. And it can also be redeemed by the blood and sanctified by the faithful application of Christ's righteousness:

> See then that you walk circumspectly, not as fools but as wise, redeeming the time, because the days are evil.
> —EPHESIANS 5:15-16, NKJV

Second, consider that elders are seasoned saints who have experienced God's faithfulness over a long period of time, and they have responded with their own faithfulness through many difficult circumstances. When someone experiences God's faithfulness over a period of time and responds by exercising their own faithfulness, they earn a level of authority over the passage of time itself. They have learned to use time wisely by synchronizing with God to accomplish His agenda in His time-frame. In other words, they have learned to "redeem the time," and can teach others to do the same.

So whether time is a dimension or a concept or a measurement, it can be defiled by sin and death just like physical and spiritual space. Especially when those defiling influences are perpetuated across a duration of time.

Third, consider how King David divided the priests and the minstrels in 1 Chronicles chapters 24 and 25. We won't read those chapters here because they are long and full of names and genealogies. The important point to note is that David split the priests from the houses of the sons of Aaron into twenty-four divisions to form a twenty-four-week recurring rotation for the temple service. He then split the families of the three chief musicians into twenty-four divisions to form a twenty-four-hour recurring rotation of perpetual musical praise in the temple. These two services functioned together to keep time and space within the temple consecrated and holy so that God's presence could manifest there and the priests could move in and out of the temple without introducing defilement.

I suggest that the twenty-four elders in the heavenly throne room (along with the four living creatures, whom we'll talk about in a moment) perform a similar function. Given that one of the defining characteristics of an elder is someone who has earned authority by being faithful across a period of time, part of the role of the twenty-four elders is to exercise their authority through actions that sanctify time—or at least creation's perception and experience of time.

This allows humans to come into God's presence in the throne room. Perhaps it also enables us to see and understand why time unfolds the way it does and helps us synchronize with God's intended role for us in time. This will make more sense after we read the verses describing what the elders actually do in heaven. More on that shortly.

## TWO POSTURES OF TIME

There is at least one other level on which the elders sanctify time. Remember, there are twenty-four elders, likely broken into two sets of twelve, just as the twenty-four-hour day is divided into two twelve-hour evening/morning, or night/day periods:

> Jesus answered, "Are there not twelve hours in the day? If anyone walks in the day, he does not stumble, because he sees the light of this world. But if anyone walks in the night, he stumbles, because the light is not in him."
> —*JOHN 11:9-10*

I took that verse out of context, but it shows that ancient Jews divided the day and night into twelve-hour increments. The twelve-hour segments align well with the twenty-four elders: one elder per hour, with the Old Testament elders for the evening and the New Testament elders for the morning.

Why is that important? Remember the fractal of two? Evening and morning, night and day, female and male, receiving and giving? If we look at the whole of redemptive history through the fractal of two, the Old Testament was like the evening portion of time, and the New Testament is like the morning portion of time.

In the Old Testament, God primarily gave while creation received. Obviously, we can't apply that grid too strictly to every event in every way, but in general, the flow of the Old Testament was all about creation receiving the seed of Christ until His incarnation.

After Christ confirmed the New Testament through His death and resurrection, His experience with time flipped from morning/male/giving to evening/female/receiving. Christ now sits in heaven waiting for His Body on earth to multiply the seed He sowed

When someone experiences God's faithfulness over a period of time and responds by exercising their own faithfulness, they earn a level of authority over the passage of time itself.

and thereby make His enemies His footstool. So, in a sense, we are now meant to engage with time from a day/work/sowing/giving posture, while Jesus is now experiencing the flow of time from an evening/rest/waiting/receiving posture.

I admit this is a rather esoteric concept with unclear practical application, but it does at least provide a fascinating lens through which to view the broad strokes of history. It also adds context to some of the elder's actions, who, if they are indeed first-fruits of the resurrection, are heavenly examples for the Body of Christ on earth. If we think of the twenty-four elders as representing both the natural and wild branches of the Body of Christ, then they have earned authority over both aspects of time. The twelve elders of the old covenant were faithful overcomers during the evening/receiving hours of history, and the twelve elders of the new covenant were faithful overcomers during the day/giving hours.

As we'll see in a moment, the elders' actions in the throne room will help to cleanse and redeem the flow of time—or at least humanity's perception of time—in preparation for Christ's Unveiling.

## TWO STACKS OF BREAD

Now think back to the table of showbread. It was an acacia table overlaid with pure gold, crowned with a golden ornamental molding, and it held twelve loaves of bread (divided into two stacks of six) for the twelve tribes of Israel. Can you see how this parallels the twenty-four elders?

Of course, rather than twelve loaves, the heavenly new covenant version doubles up on that number: twenty-four loaves, perhaps for twenty-four glorified humans wearing golden crowns, representing both the natural and wild branches of Christ's Body.

Just like the bread of the presence sat in the Holy Place absorbing the presence of God all week long, these elders continually sit in the presence of God. The eating of the showbread on the morning of the Sabbath is also an important symbol, but we'll discuss that later in this series.

Moreover, the twenty-four elders also have a connection to the altar of incense, a point we'll come back to in the next chapter. Their relationship with time, their role in the throne room, and their connection to both the table of showbread and the altar of incense will become clearer after we layer in some of the other things John saw in the throne room.

## REVERENCE AND AWE

> Out from the throne come flashes of lightning and sounds
> and peals of thunder ...
> —*REVELATION 4:5*

This verse is about the throne of the One, not the thrones of the elders. The "flashes of lightning and sounds and peals of thunder" are often associated throughout Scripture with the manifest presence of God. But notice that they emanate from the throne, not from God Himself. Indeed, we've already seen that goodness and love are what John saw emanating from God. So these terrible and frightening signs of lightning, sounds, and peals of thunder are related to His throne, not His essence. And that makes sense, considering the throne of God is the inspiration for the seventh item of holy furniture in the tabernacle: the mercy seat, which aligns with the redemptive gift of mercy and the Spirit of the Fear of the Lord.

> Reverential awe is the required heart attitude for clearly beholding God's nature as He is rather than as we want Him to be. We need to be in a posture of awe to truly comprehend the reality of His goodness and love.

Remember how the Israelites responded when they experienced these same phenomenon at Sinai as God descended upon the mountain in a cloud of fire?

> So it came about on the third day, when it was morning,
> that there were thunder and lightning flashes and a thick
> cloud upon the mountain and a very loud trumpet sound,
> so that all the people who were in the camp trembled.
> —*EXODUS 19:16*

Fear and trembling were logical responses for Israel. However, as discussed in book 1, the Fear of the Lord is not intended to drive us away. Yes, it will have that effect on the parts of our being that are enslaved to shame and determined to remain separate from Him—those parts of our hearts that have an expectation of judgment from God. But the goal of the Fear of the Lord is to draw us into a posture of awe and reverence. Reverential awe is the required heart attitude for clearly beholding God's nature as He is rather than as we want Him to be. We need to be in a posture of awe to truly comprehend the reality of His goodness and love. Awe is the only posture that leads us to rest in Him and become like Him. Any view of God's goodness and love that is not filtered through reverential awe of His throne will cause us to miss the target of who He is.

## BEFORE THE THRONE

> And there were seven lamps of fire burning before the throne, which are the seven Spirits of God; and before the throne there was something like a sea of glass, like crystal
> ...
> —*REVELATION 4:5-6*

"Before the throne" means somewhere out in front of and facing the throne. In the same way that the inner court and outer court were *before* the holy of holies and leading toward it.

Two things were described as being before the throne: "seven lamps of fire ... which are the seven Spirits of God," and "something like a sea of glass." They were described separately because they did not occupy the same space, and the first (the lamps of fire) was closer to the throne than the second (the sea of glass). As we keep reading, we'll find that the seven Spirits of God were likely positioned within the ring of the twenty-four elders, while the sea of glass was outside the elders.

## SEVEN SPIRITS OF GOD

Some artists depict the lamps of fire in the throne room as a Menorah (seven-branch lampstand)—or even as seven separate Menorahs—standing before the throne. That is understandable given that the seven Spirits of God were almost certainly the inspiration and original pattern for the Menorah. But the Greek word used here for lamps is *lampades,* which is more about something that gives radiant light. *Lampades* doesn't necessarily require the presence of a lampstand or candlestick. In any case, the focus here is the *lamps* of fire, not lampstands. The seven lamps of fire are probably best viewed as seven self-sustaining, radiating lights of pure fire.

Like the twenty-four elders, the seven lamps of fire also have a time component. They express the principles of God's character in a specific sequence over a span of time that establishes His kingdom in creation. We saw this with the seven days of creation and the letters to the seven churches, and we'll see it again in other contexts throughout the Unveiling.

As with the exhorter redemptive gift that it exemplified, whenever the high priest would prepare to trim and light

> Like the twenty-four elders, the seven lamps of fire also have a time component. They express the principles of God's character in a specific sequence over a span of time that establishes His kingdom in creation.

the Menorah lamps in the evening and morning, the services at the table of showbread and the altar of incense would follow. Likewise, there may be a sense in which the seven lamps of fire govern the sequence and flow of time in the throne room, at least as far as it is experienced by creation.

This is only speculation, but perhaps the seven Spirits of God take the attributes of the One on the throne (who exists outside of space and time) and shine them into space and time. Based on the tabernacle pattern, it is likely that the seven lamps are between the twenty-four elders and the central throne.

I don't know if the lights of the seven lamps are necessary for the twenty-four elders to see the One—that seems unlikely given the glory emanating from God—but their position suggests that they play some role in the seeing process. There must be a way in which they influence the elders' sight, just as the Menorah provided the light by which the priests ministered in the Holy Place. More on that when we get to the four living creatures.

## A SEA OF GLASS?

Also before the throne was "something like a sea of glass ...." Don't you love John's imprecise description here? Was this an actual sea, or was it just *something like* a sea? Was it a crystal-clear body of water so calm that it looked like glass? Or was it made of something solid and crystal-clear, like glass? Was it as vast as a sea stretching to the horizon, or was it something smaller and more self-contained? It seems John wasn't quite sure himself, so we'll leave those questions open for now. Either way, this sea of glass aligns with the brazen laver in the outer court of the tabernacle. It is a place for introspection and washing in the water of the Word of God before approaching the throne.

It may not be immediately clear just yet in the context of Revelation chapter 4, but the sea of glass (like the brazen laver before it) also represents the expanse, or firmament, that was hammered out on the second day of creation to separate the waters above from the waters below. In a sense, it separates the physical realm from the spiritual realm. I'll explain why I say that in the next chapter when we discuss the four living creatures.

Lastly, the sea of glass may also specifically represent the second heaven, which is between the first and third heaven, but we'll talk about that later in this series when we get to Revelation chapter 15.

## CHAPTER 18

# THE THRONE ROOM - PART 3:
# FOUR LIVING CREATURES

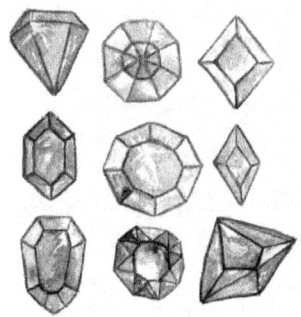

W e've arrived at one of the more cryptic elements of the throne room scene: the four living creatures. We'll camp here for a while to work through the complexity since some of the details are downright puzzling to visualize:

> and in the center and around the throne, four living creatures full of eyes in front and behind. The first creature was like a lion, and the second creature like a calf, and the third creature had a face like that of a man, and the fourth creature was like a flying eagle. And the four living creatures, each one of them having six wings, are full of eyes around and within; and day and night they do not cease to say,
> "HOLY, HOLY, HOLY is THE LORD GOD, THE ALMIGHTY, WHO WAS AND WHO IS AND WHO IS TO COME."
> —*REVELATION 4:6-8*

If you've studied the book of Revelation before, you may have seen various artists' renditions of the four living creatures. And if you're anything like me, those renditions caused more questions than they answered. I won't pretend that I've found all the answers. In fact, by the time you're done with this chapter, you'll probably have deeper questions. I only hope to help you ask some of the right questions—the ones that better prepare us for Christ's Unveiling.

As we unpack these Scriptures, we'll draw from several similar encounters recorded by the prophets Ezekiel and Isaiah. I say similar, but their encounters also contain discrepancies that have puzzled Christians for millennia.

Ezekiel encountered spiritual beings called cherubim near God's throne, but his descriptions varied slightly from what John saw. Isaiah also saw heavenly beings near the throne, but he called them seraphim. And although Isaiah's seraphim shared some similar features with John's living creatures, they varied even further from Ezekiel's cherubim.

Again, I can't reconcile all these mysteries, but I have a few insights that might keep us moving in the right direction. As we'll see in a moment, Revelation's four living creatures are something of an amalgamation of Ezekiel's and Isaiah's spiritual beings, both in form and function. At the end of the day, I think it is fair to call John's creatures cherubim, in as much as they fulfill the role of the golden cherubim built into the mercy seat of the tabernacle of Moses (as did Ezekiel's cherubim). It may not be equally fair to call them seraphim, but we'll get into that shortly.

Let's parse through the details of John's experience and then compare it to what Ezekiel and Isaiah saw. For the sake of time, we won't read all three encounters. Instead, we'll step through the verses in Revelation and sprinkle in details from the other prophets wherever there are significant differences. Our goal here is to better understand how the four living creatures relate to Christ's Unveiling, not to develop a comprehensive theology on different orders of spiritual beings.

## CREATURE CHARACTERISTICS

John described the four living creatures as being "in the center and around the throne." In the center of what? Remember the larger context: one throne encircled by twenty-four other thrones. There were also seven lamps in front of the throne inside the ring of elders, and a sea of glass in front of the throne but outside the ring of elders. So, for the creatures to be in the center and around the throne means they were likely positioned in a circle around the one throne, inside the ring of elders, and inside the lamps of fire. Clear as mud, right? Perhaps a visual will help:

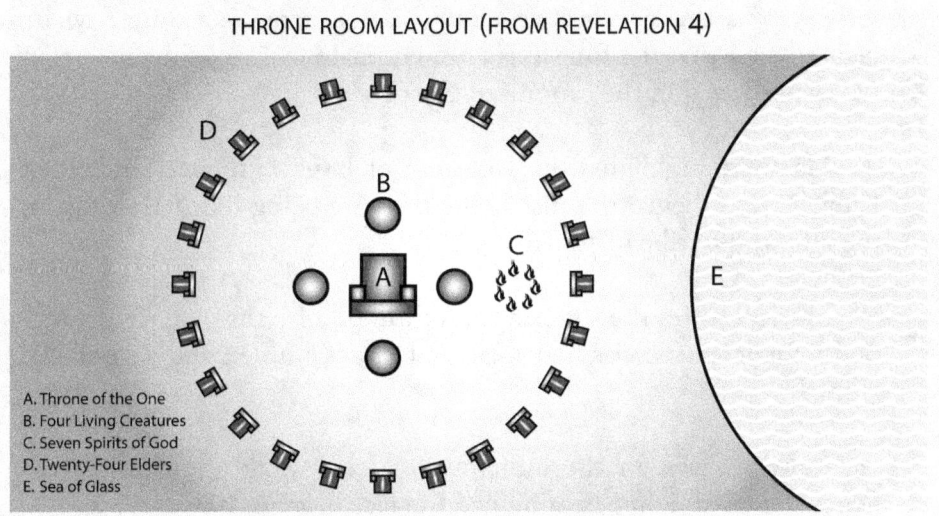

THRONE ROOM LAYOUT (FROM REVELATION 4)

A. Throne of the One
B. Four Living Creatures
C. Seven Spirits of God
D. Twenty-Four Elders
E. Sea of Glass

The living creatures were assigned a specific order (first, second, third, and fourth), so we know the order matters in the context of John's vision. We'll see why in book 3.

The first living creature was like a lion. The second was like a calf. The third had the face of a man, and the fourth was like a flying eagle. Each creature had six wings.

Some of these details are perplexing. For instance, the third creature had a *face* like a man, but the other three were *like* a lion, calf, and flying eagle. Does that mean they also had the body and legs of their specific creature? If so, why did the man just have the *face* of a man? And what about the flying eagle? All of the creatures had wings. So, if the eagle had the body of an eagle but the same wings as the other living creatures, then why was it specifically called a *flying* eagle? Wouldn't they all have been flying? Like I said, puzzling to visualize.

I prefer to think of each living creature as having the head, body, and legs of the animal it resembles, and to assume that the eagle was the only one actually using its wings for flight. Your mileage may vary.

This viewpoint takes the appearance of John's living creatures even further away from what Ezekiel and Isaiah saw, but I'll explain why in a moment. For now, regardless of what their bodies looked like, we can at least agree that their faces must have resembled the stated creatures, and that's probably the most important thing to focus on.

So, what is the significance of the four different creatures? Many scholars suggest that the four likenesses correlate with the four flavors of Christ as portrayed in the canonized Gospels:

- **Matthew** highlights the Kingship of Jesus as the descendent of King David—hence the first living creature being like a **lion** (as in, the lion of the tribe of Judah).

- **Mark** features the suffering servanthood of Jesus—hence the second living creature was like a **calf** (a beast of burden and a sacrificial animal).

- **Luke** focuses on the humanity of Jesus as the Son of Man—hence the third living creature had the face of **man**.

- **John** dwells on Jesus' divinity as the Son of God and the incarnate Word—hence, the fourth living creature was like a **flying eagle**.

I generally agree with this "four Gospels" perspective. It makes sense and fits with some other things we'll see from the four living creatures in book 3. However, it also begs a question when you compare this to what Ezekiel saw in Ezekiel chapter 1.

Rather than four living creatures, each with a different face, Ezekiel saw four living "beings" (later called cherubim), each with their own set of four faces. All four of Ezekiel's cherubim had the face of a lion on the right, an ox (a similar symbol to a calf) on the left, a man in the front, and an eagle, presumably, in the back.

Of note, Ezekiel also stated that each of the cherubim had four wings, the body and hands of a man, straight legs, and the cloven feet of a calf. Like John's creatures, they were full of eyes covering their bodies and wings. There are other details related to where they were and what they did, but we'll come back to that later.

So, as far as appearances go, there are many potential differences, depending on how we read John's description in Revelation. Perhaps we could overlay Ezekiel's description of the bodies, hands, legs, and feet onto the creatures in Revelation since John doesn't explicitly describe those, but that feels like a stretch. Either way, the faces and number of wings (four versus six) are clearly dissimilar. The question is why? What can we learn from these differences?

One possibility is that Ezekiel's cherubim are just different beings than the living creatures in Revelation. This seems unlikely, given how strikingly similar they are with strange features that are otherwise unique in Scripture.

Alternatively, what if they are the same beings, only seen from different perspectives at different periods in redemptive history? Ezekiel was viewing an Old Testament version of the cherubim before the incarnation of Christ and the manifestation of the gospel. If the cherubim are designed as reflections of the four main aspects of Christ expressed in the Gospels, then maybe it makes sense for the Old Testament prototype to be slightly veiled and not yet fully unpacked. Just as the Word of God was still in seed form at that time, perhaps the cherubim in Ezekiel's visions represented a primordial or prenatal expression of the Gospels—a jumble of faces rather than fully formed separate expressions of Christ's ministry.

## MOTION AND SOUND

There's a third possibility that is tied to the second. What if the discrepancies in their appearance also stemmed from the different locations in which they appeared? John saw them after he was spiritually transported to the temple of God in the third heaven realm. There, they stood in perfect peace around the throne of God, worshiping day and night in a holy environment.

On the other hand, Ezekiel encountered them on earth in highly defiled spaces. First, near the River Chebar outside of Babylon. Later, he saw them in the defiled temple of Solomon in Jerusalem when God brought him there in a vision to observe His glory departing the earthly temple because of the idol worship perpetrated by the priesthood. In both of Ezekiel's encounters, the cherubim were not in their natural habitat of the third heaven surrounding the throne of God in peace and rest. Instead, they were in the second heaven in the space typically occupied by the powers of darkness.

These vastly different environments may also explain the variation in their wings and the disparity in their actions. Remember, Ezekiel saw four wings while John saw six. The number of wings may relate to the level of heaven in which they operate. When they manifest in the second heaven—as when Ezekiel saw them—they have four wings (two pairs) to demonstrate their authority in the first and second heavens. When they manifest in the third heaven—as they were in Revelation—they have six wings (three pairs) to demonstrate their authority in all three heavenly realms.

> In both of Ezekiel's encounters, the cherubim were not in their natural habitat of the third heaven surrounding the throne of God in peace and rest. Instead, they were in the second heaven in the space typically occupied by the powers of darkness.

What about their actions? In Ezekiel chapter 1, the cherubim were seen entering the atmosphere near Babylon in advance of the appearance of God on His throne. In fulfillment of that role, they stood in a tight circle, back to back, each with two wings outstretched and touching the wings of the other cherubim on either side. They moved as a single unit, darting back and forth, up and down, like lightning bolts across the dimensions of first- and second-heaven space. Sounds also accompanied the movement of their wings:

> I also heard the sound of their wings like the sound of abundant waters as they went, like the voice of the Almighty, a sound of tumult like the sound of an army camp ...
> —EZEKIEL 1:24

Abundant waters, the voice of the Almighty, and the tumult of an army encampment. In other words, the powerful sounds of cleansing, authority, and warfare. Like a digital eraser moving across a computer screen or a laser burning impurities from a surface, everything about their sound and movement was intended to wash, protect, and cover the physical and spiritual atmosphere (first and second heavens) into which God was about to manifest.

When their preparation was complete, God did appear on His throne, though He appeared above a crystal-like expanse spread out over the outstretched wings of the cherubim.

> Now over the heads of the living beings there was something like **an expanse, like the awesome gleam of crystal**, spread out over their heads.
> —*EZEKIEL 1:22*

> Now **above the expanse that was over their heads** there was something resembling a throne, like lapis lazuli in appearance; and on that which resembled a throne, high up, was a figure with the appearance of a man.
> —*EZEKIEL 1:26*

As a quick side note, what does this crystal-like expanse remind you of? Remember the sea of glass that John saw in the throne room? The one that correlates to the brazen laver? The one we likened to the expanse that God created on the second day of creation to separate the waters below from the waters above? In the natural, that second-day expanse was the physical atmosphere surrounding and protecting the earth, but in a spiritual sense, it was also the second heaven, which separates the physical heaven from the third heaven where God dwells. Here, in Ezekiel, we see the throne of God appearing "above the expanse" of the sea of glass.

It is almost like the cherubim cleansed the first- and second-heaven atmosphere so that Ezekiel could see from earth, up through the sea of glass, into the third-heaven throne room. For some reason, it was important for Ezekiel to see the throne of God in the context of the surrounding earth rather than to be transported into heaven like John was.

> Everything about their sound and movement was intended to wash, protect, and cover the physical and spiritual atmosphere (first and second heavens) into which God was about to manifest.

Compare that to Revelation, where the four living creatures remained relatively still around the throne in third-heaven space rather than in a tight formation underneath it. There were no wing sounds or movements necessary to cleanse defilement or war against darkness. Instead, the creatures made a continual proclamation of praise into the atmosphere, amplifying the awe and reverence already emanating from the throne.

## ISAIAH'S SERAPHIM

So between the different periods of redemptive history in which they were seen and the disparate environments into which they appeared, perhaps we have a satisfactory explanation to bridge the gap between Ezekiel's cherubim and John's four living creatures. Without heading off down another long and winding rabbit trail, let's quickly overlay Isaiah's experience to see if it harmonizes with everything we just learned:

> In the year of King Uzziah's death I saw the Lord sitting on a throne, lofty and exalted, with the train of His robe filling the temple. Seraphim stood above Him, each having six wings: with two he covered his face, and with two he covered his feet, and with two he flew. And one called out to another and said,
> "Holy, Holy, Holy, is the LORD of hosts, the whole earth is full of His glory."
> —ISAIAH 6:1-3

Okay, so there are some major differences and a few similarities. The most obvious difference is that they are called seraphim instead of cherubim or living creatures. We'll unpack the name seraphim in book 3 when we get to Revelation chapter 6 and the breaking of the seven seals. Not that the seraphim appear in that chapter, but a deeper look at their name and role in the throne room will make more sense in the context of what happens in Revelation 6 and beyond. For now, let's set their distinctive name aside.

What about the other differences? Isaiah doesn't mention how many seraphim were present. It may have been four, but we just don't know. Related to that, we also don't know anything about their faces, since their faces were covered by their wings. It's not impossible that they had faces like the cherubim of Ezekiel or living creatures of Revelation, but we just don't know. Lastly, unlike the cherubim and living creatures, there is no mention of the seraphim being covered in eyes.

As for their wings, they had six wings like the living creatures in Revelation rather than four like the cherubim in Ezekiel. Given that the seraphim were seen in the heavenly temple of God, it makes sense that they had six wings for navigating the third heaven.

## LOCATION LOCATION LOCATION

Notice that Isaiah's seraphim were flying *above* the Lord's throne in heaven, whereas Ezekiel's cherubim were *below* the throne on earth, and John's were *around* the throne in heaven. Again, these differences in relative location and role may help account for some of the differences in appearance.

In Isaiah, when the seraphim declared, "Holy, Holy, Holy, is the Lord of Hosts, the whole earth is full of His glory ...," they were preparing the physical earth for the righteous judgments of God, and they were preparing Isaiah to declare those judgments. Again, we'll see how that relates to the Unveiling in book 3.

In that context, it makes sense that the seraphim flew *above* the throne with their faces and feet covered. They were not looking at the throne. They were not directing their words at God. They were speaking *about* God and projecting it down to the earth.

In Ezekiel, everything about the appearance of the cherubim *under* the throne supported their job to cleanse and protect a finite area of physical and spiritual atmosphere, and to participate in the transport of the appearance of the throne of God through that area.

In Revelation, the four living creatures were *around* the throne with uncovered faces. They were positioned to behold the glory of the One on the throne and to fully manifest the four-fold diversity of the gospel of Jesus Christ. From that position, they continually proclaimed His holiness throughout all of time into the rest of the throne room. More on that in a moment.

## CONCLUSIONS?

I've just thrown a ton of details at you, along with a healthy mixture of exegesis and speculation. Have we seen enough to decide if the four living creatures, cherubim, and seraphim are different versions of the same beings?

I think John's and Ezekiel's creatures are the same, while Isaiah's seraphim are something altogether different. To be fair, though, there are other details in Ezekiel's and Isaiah's encounters that we haven't addressed yet, so the question may be premature. Especially for the seraphim.

We'll look at some of those other details in book 3 when we see how the four living creatures participate in Christ's Unveiling. For now, we can at least use the variations we've seen in their appearance and actions to enrich our understanding of John's throne room scene as we move forward.

## COVERED IN EYES

What else did John say about the four living creatures? Here is where we left off:

> And the four living creatures, each one of them having six wings, are full of eyes around and within; and day and night they do not cease to say,
> "HOLY, HOLY, HOLY is THE LORD GOD, THE ALMIGHTY, WHO WAS AND WHO IS AND WHO IS TO COME."
> —*REVELATION 4:8*

Each living creature was "full of eyes in front and behind." And their wings were "full of eyes around and within." In other words, their entire bodies were covered in eyes. The same was true of Ezekiel's cherubim. So, what are these eyes?

Remember how the seven Spirits of God were described as both seven eyes and seven flames? The eyes received light and the flames gave light. Contrast that with the living creatures, who have eyes but no flames. Aside from the fact that the living creatures likely have many more than just seven eyes, it is fair to assume that their eyes have a similar function to those of the seven Spirits of God. Maybe they aren't exactly the same in practice and execution since the fractal of seven isn't in play, but the eyes of the living creatures must at least have *something* to do with receiving light. After all, that's what eyes are for.

Along those lines, consider again the nine kinds of gemstones that covered the anointed cherub:

> Every precious stone was your covering: The **sardius**, **topaz**, and **diamond**, **beryl**, **onyx**, and **jasper**, **sapphire**, **turquoise**, and **emerald** ...
> —*EZEKIEL 28:13, NKJV*

Prior to this prophecy, Ezekiel had already encountered the four cherubim on two separate occasions and observed that they were covered in eyes (see Ezekiel 10:12). As with John, the description of being covered with eyes was his best attempt at describing a mind-blowing vision with human words. On the other hand, the prophecy in Ezekiel 28 about the anointed cherub covered in every precious stone was directly dictated by God.

So, I see two possibilities: Either the anointed cherub was completely different from the four cherubim in that one was covered in gemstones while the others were covered in eyes ... Or the two attributes are descriptions of the same phenomenon seen from different perspectives, with Ezekiel describing them as eyes and God stating they were gemstones.

I don't know which of these options is true, but in either case, there are at least general similarities between the eyes and gemstones. Both are meant to take in every possible angle of the prismatic glory shimmering out from the throne of the One. If there is anything to learn from their differences, then perhaps the gemstones on the anointed cherub would have directly reflected God's glory back out through their various shapes and hues. In that case, perhaps the eyes on the four cherubim would have only observed, absorbed, and internalized the lights so that their glory could be declared outward in a different way.

Related to that, consider that the four living creatures in Revelation repeated a nine-fold phrase, divided into three sets of three (similar to how the nine gemstones were separated into three sets of three):

> Holy[1], holy[2], holy[3]
> is the Lord[4] God[5] the Almighty[6]
> who was[7] and who is[8] and who is to come[9]
> —*FROM REVELATION 4:8 [PARENTHESES MINE]*

> … Sardius, topaz, and diamond,
> Beryl, onyx and jasper,
> Sapphire, turquoise, and emerald …
> —FROM EZEKIEL 28:13, NKJV

Could this nine-part phrase be how the living creatures respond to nine particular aspects of God's character that their eyes/gems are specifically tuned to behold? Again, this is only speculation. I don't know if this alignment is significant. I just find the similarities fascinating.

Notice that the proclamation of the living creatures isn't directed to God. They don't say, "Holy, holy, holy are *You* ...." No, like the seraphim, they speak outward toward creation. But, in this particular case, they are around the throne, able to look directly at the One while proclaiming His glory outward to the rest of the throne room rather than down to the earth.

Whereas the cherubim in Ezekiel cleansed space with their movement and sound, the living creatures in Revelation take the character traits of God that they perceive with their many eyes and relay them as a continual proclamation of God's preeminence over all of time: past, present, and future ("who was and who is and who is to come"). They are almost like a metronome in the throne room, establishing a rhythm of praise about God's holiness.

## INTERVALS OF TIME

Now think about the frequency of their proclamation: "day and night they do not cease to say." Does that indicate a constant, unending chant on a forever loop? Or does it simply mean they say it at least once every day and once every night for all eternity? Or something in between those two extremes? It's hard to say, but we'll find that John describes the four living creatures saying and doing other things in Revelation chapters 5 and 6. That would be difficult to do if they were constantly chanting the first phrase over and over again without a pause between sets.

Whatever the interval of their day-and-night proclamation, it always engenders an effusive response from the twenty-four elders:

And when the living creatures give glory and honor and thanks to Him who sits on the throne, to Him who lives forever and ever, the twenty-four elders will fall down before Him who sits on the throne, and will worship Him who lives forever and ever and will cast their crowns before the throne, saying, "**Worthy are You**[1], our **Lord**[2] and our **God**[3], to receive **glory**[4] and **honor**[5] and **power**[6]; for You **created all things**[7], and **because of Your will they existed**[8], and **were created**[9]."
—*REVELATION 4:9-11* {*PARENTHESES MINE*}

Notice the synchronization between the elders and the living creatures. As often as the living creatures proclaim God's preeminence over time, the twenty-four elders respond with an act of unabashed, unrestrained reverence, followed by their own nine-part statement of worship directed back at God.

I recognize that their statement could be parsed differently, and that it doesn't necessarily have to be viewed in nine parts. And even if we agree on nine parts, I don't have any insight into the significance of that model, nor am I ready to speculate how it might align in some mysterious way with the nine fruits of the Spirit. I just think the pattern is too striking to ignore, so I present it to you as a potential point of study and meditation with the Holy Spirit.

Is there anything else we can we see about the elder's response as a whole? Remember what we said about the elders' relationship to time in the last chapter? By their very nature, elders are those who have redeemed the time they were given. As such, they have a level of earned authority over time. Here, we see the elders responding to the proclamation of God's preeminence over time by throwing themselves to the ground and casting down their crowns at His feet. In other words, they take their earned authority and offer it to the King in humble acts of worship. We'll see how this ties into everything else in a moment.

Again, it's hard to picture any of this happening on a forever loop with no pause or breath in between intervals, but there is certainly some type of frequently recurring schedule marked by the words day and night. Maybe we can't know—or don't need to know—the exact rhythm, but there are some general patterns here that can tie this entire throne room scene together and help us understand some of the mechanics of the next phase of the Unveiling of Jesus Christ that John experiences in Revelation chapter 6.

To that end, let's take all of these seemingly disparate details about the throne room and connect them back to the pattern of the tabernacle furniture that we learned a few chapters ago. At the risk of belaboring the obvious, we'll step through each piece of furniture again, this time moving from the inside out to follow the flow of the life of God outward to His creation. For now, we'll focus on the Holy Place (the holy of holies and inner court), since this section of John's vision doesn't deal much with the outer court (beyond the mention of the sea of glass).

## HOLY OF HOLIES PATTERNS

Remember the diagram showing the overview of the throne room? Here it is again:

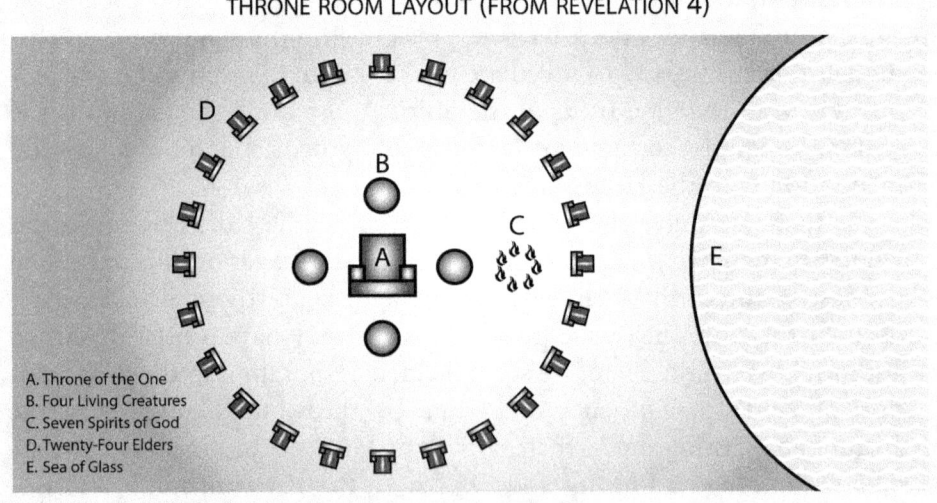

THRONE ROOM LAYOUT (FROM REVELATION 4)

A. Throne of the One
B. Four Living Creatures
C. Seven Spirits of God
D. Twenty-Four Elders
E. Sea of Glass

At the center of everything is the throne of the One, which aligns with the mercy seat. Upon the throne sits the One, just as the glory of God dwelled above the mercy seat.

Notice that John didn't describe the *face* of the One on the throne. The reason for this ties into the role of the four living creatures, which have the same role as the cherubim covering the mercy seat. Consider that John was able to clearly behold the face of the glorified Christ at the beginning of Revelation. There, he described the face of Christ as shining like the sun, and His eyes were like flames of fire (see Revelation 1). Christ's face is visible because He is the image of the invisible God sown into time and space. But with the One on the throne—who abides outside of creation and therefore outside of time and space—there is only a general description of His body with zero mention of His face.

This experience is the same throughout Scripture whenever a person encounters God on His throne. Whether it was Isaiah, Ezekiel, Daniel, or even Moses, nobody ever describes God's face. Moses tells us why:

> Then Moses said, "I pray You, show me Your glory!" And He said, "I Myself will make all My goodness pass before you, and will proclaim the name of the LORD before you; and I will be gracious to whom I will be gracious, and will show compassion on whom I will show compassion." **But He said, "You cannot see My face, for no man can see Me and live!"**
> —*EXODUS 33:18-20*

"You cannot see My face!" Why? What's in a face? We can learn a lot about someone by listening to their words and observing their body language, but nothing compares to what we can learn by seeing their face. The face is a firehose of information about a person's inner life. Unless they practice to deceive, their character, emotions, and deepest thoughts are manifested on their face.

God has no guile or deception, so His face is the unadulterated expression of His innermost essence. Perhaps that is where the nine fruits of the Spirit come in. Love, joy, peace, patience, kindness, goodness, faithfulness, gentleness, and self-control are the deepest and purest expressions of God's heart—His inner life. So, while His words and actions do demonstrate the fruits of the Spirit in ways we can observe, and the overflow of certain attributes like His love and goodness can be seen as the glory emanating from His body, the strength with which they radiate from His countenance is like the unbridled force of an infinity of supernovas. No mortal human can survive God's unfiltered demeanor.

Hence, the covering cherubim. The four living creatures full of eyes (and maybe nine kinds of gems?) stand between God and the rest of creation, filtering that which can't be seen into something that can only be comprehended through the message of the gospel of Jesus Christ. And this they proclaim, not just in their appearance as a lion, a calf, a man, and a flying eagle, but also through the words they declare into the throne room.

Before we move outside of the holy of holies into the inner court to see the other furniture, you're probably wondering about the ark of the covenant. So far, we haven't seen anything related to the ark in John's throne room experience. But remember, I mentioned earlier that the ark of the covenant represents Christ Himself. Rest assured, Jesus will make an appearance in the throne room in the next chapter. Later in this series, we'll also find the ark of the covenant specifically mentioned in a different context toward the end of the book of Revelation. So stay tuned.

## INNER COURT PATTERNS

The inner court of the Mosaic tabernacle housed three pieces of holy furniture. Moving from inside out, they were the golden altar of incense, the seven-branched lampstand (menorah), and the table of showbread. The altar of incense was about giving intercession and praise to God, the table of showbread was about receiving the life of the new covenant from Him, and the menorah provided light for both services.

There is an altar of incense in the heavenly throne room, but, as with the ark, it isn't specifically mentioned until later in the book of Revelation. For that reason, we'll save a more detailed discussion of the heavenly altar of incense for book 3 of this series. However, some of the services performed at the altar of incense are alluded to through the actions of the twenty-four elders, which we'll discuss shortly.

What about the menorah? We already know that in the context of the heavenly throne room, the menorah represents the seven lamps of fire, which are the seven Spirits of God. Recall that the menorah was considered to be the external, physical illumination of the spiritual glory of God that filled the holy of holies behind the veil. In that way, it connected and synchronized the inner court services to the holy of holies. If you extend that idea to the throne room, then the flames of the seven

Spirits of God provide the necessary illumination for the twenty-four elders to do what they do.

As we mentioned earlier, the role of the twenty-four elders corresponds to both the service of the table of showbread and the altar of incense. In a sense, they can been seen as the priesthood that tended both pieces of furniture, as well as being the personification of the showbread and the incense. Like the two stacks of bread, they sit in the overflow of God's presence in the inner court, facing the throne of the One, constantly receiving from and reveling in His glory. And just as there was a constant fragrance filling the inner court from the incense burning on the altar of incense, we'll find that the elders also participate in offering praise to God.

So, follow the flow with me: the life and light of God's glory shine perpetually from the One on the throne. They are filtered through the four living creatures into regular proclamations of God's holiness spoken outward toward creation to sanctify time and space in the heavenly holy of holies. The life and light of the One are also indirectly refracted into the rest of the throne room through the seven-fold flames of the seven Spirits of God. In turn, the twenty-four elders perceive God's glory—and understand the proclamations of the living creatures—through the light of that seven-step progressive revelation of God's character. In response, at the proper time, the twenty-four elders offer their prayer and praise in regular demonstrations of worship that sanctify time and space in the inner court of the throne room. And all of that is merely in preparation for the main drama ...

---

While His words and actions do demonstrate the fruits of the Spirit in ways we can observe, and the overflow of certain attributes like His love and goodness can be seen as the glory emanating from His body, the strength with which they radiate from His countenance is like the unbridled force of an infinity of supernovas. No mortal human can survive God's unfiltered demeanor.

## CHAPTER 19

# THE THRONE ROOM - PART 4:
# OF SCROLLS AND SEALS

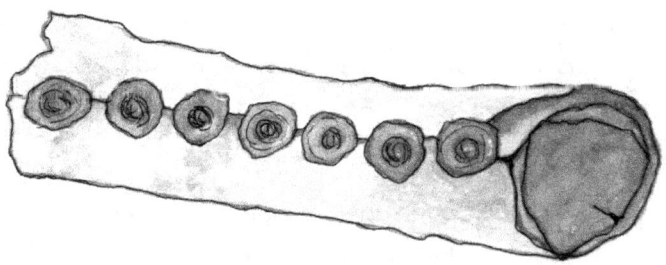

T he stage is set. Most of the key players in the throne room are in position. What happens next will introduce the inciting in- cident and the primary protagonist for the drama surrounding the consummation of the ages.

As we move forward with the scene, it is important to note that there were no chapter breaks when John originally wrote the book of Revelation. The throne room scene described in Revelation chapter 4 connects seamlessly to what we are about to read from chapter 5. To- gether, they represent one continuous progression that leads to Christ initiating His Unveiling:

> I saw in the right hand of Him who sat on the throne a
> scroll written inside and on the back, sealed up with seven
> seals. And I saw a strong angel proclaiming with a loud
> voice, "Who is worthy to open the scroll and to break its

seals?" And no one in heaven or on the earth or under the
earth was able to open the scroll or to look into it.
—*REVELATION 5:1-3, NAS*

## THE SEALED SCROLL

So now we have God the Father holding a sealed scroll written inside
and on the back. A large part of the drama surrounding the Unveiling
stems from the unsealing of this scroll. Like so many other aspects of
Revelation, there are diverse theories about the scroll's meaning, appearance, and the timing of when its seals will be opened. There is even debate about whether or not any seals have already been opened in the
past.

If you are anything like me, you're feeling something between giddy
excitement and frustrating impatience as you wait to talk about what
happens when the seven seals are broken, and to discuss how the seven
trumpets and the seven bowls relate to those seven seals. Those topics
represent some of the most thrilling sections of our journey, especially
after we spent so much time in this book trudging through the deep
forest just to get here. For ardent treasure hunters like us, the sealed
scroll beckons like the promise of a mysterious clearing peeking through
the trees up ahead ... one whose allure is accentuated by the unmistakable thunder of a waterfall growing louder with every step forward. It's
everything we can do to keep from dropping our packs and running
toward the enticing light and sound that await us. But that clearing will
be the main focus of book 3, and we still have a few important steps to
take before we get there. Remember, there is joy to be found in the
lessons of each footfall. So stick with me just a little longer to make sure
we can truly appreciate the excitement when we get there.

To that end, let's take some time to unpack the symbolism of the
sealed scroll. We'll begin our discussion by dealing with some low-hang-
ing fruit related to its description.

The Greek word used for scroll in these verses is *biblion*. A few Bible
versions (including the older New American Standard version from
1995 that I use throughout most of this series) render it as *book* instead
of *scroll*, but most scholars agree that what John saw in the hand of the
Father was likely a scroll made of papyrus. Or at least it resembled such.
So let's just be clear that it wasn't a book of pages bound together with a

front and back cover like our modern books. From here on out we'll call it a scroll, regardless of which Bible version we pull from.

The scroll was rolled up and sealed with seven seals. No mention was made of the material or shape of the seals, though melted wax pressed and embossed with a royal signet ring is a common assumption given the context and historical period in which the words were written. In ancient Roman times, a wax signet seal might be used to demonstrate authorship or ownership, to legitimize a document as legally binding, or to restrict viewership to a particular party. In the case of this scroll sealed with seven seals, all of those applications are in play.

Many eschatological theories pivot around the placement and function of the scroll's seals, so it is interesting—and perhaps instructive—that John did not give a more detailed physical description of the scroll or its seals. Was it a single roll with seals positioned on the outside in a way that required all seven seals to be broken before the scroll could be opened? Or, did it have only one seal on the outside, and the rest were somehow positioned progressively within each layer so that a little more of the scroll could be unrolled and read each time a seal was broken? John didn't say, which either means the truth is meant to be reasoned from the context or that detail has no bearing on the flow of Christ's Unveiling. Personally, I imagine seven seals on the outside that must all be broken before the scroll can be opened (see the illustration at the beginning of the chapter), but I also think that detail has little bearing either way. We'll see why in book 3.

We also don't know how big the scroll was. Was it a thick roll indicating a long document? Or thin, indicating a short one? Again, those details are absent, which probably means they are irrelevant. All we know is that the scroll was written on both sides—inside and outside—which is a fascinating detail. How could John know this if the inside of the scroll was hidden?

We are told that no one was found worthy to open it or to look inside, but that doesn't mean that no one could see the outside writing. Perhaps John saw the writing on the outside, but the fact that it was held by God and sealed with seven seals portended to him that something immensely important was written inside.

Regardless of how he knew, it is significant that the scroll was written both inside and out. That means it was a double-sided document, or two pages worth of writing. We can also infer that the two sides have different purposes, since one was visible to all and one was not. For that reason, as we move forward we should be thinking about how the fractal of two may inform the purpose of the inside and outside of the scroll. In particular, we should be searching for how the scroll will impact our role as both sons of God and the Bride of Christ, as well as its different impacts on the "sons of day" compared to the "sons of night." We'll discuss this further in book 3.

## THE MYSTERY

So what is this scroll? It seems to appear out of nowhere. No explanation. No origin story. Just a sealed scroll in the right hand of God. John didn't mention it when He first saw the One on the throne, so that means either it wasn't there at first, or it was there but John didn't notice it until later.

Let's assume that John described things in the order in which he saw them, and that the order of his observation is significant to the message. In that case, perhaps John could only see the scroll after receiving the necessary context. First, he needed to see the One on the throne, set apart in His otherness. Then, he needed to hear the living creatures expressing the singular nature of God's set-apart-ness ("holy, holy, holy …") across all of time (Revelation 4:8). Then he needed to experience the awe of the elders worshiping the Holy One for His choice to initiate creation ("because of Your will they existed, and were created," Revelation 4:11).

All of that is necessary context for seeing and understanding the mystery of the sealed scroll. And it *is* a mystery. A mystery whose very appearance arrests the attention of heaven and begs the question of the ages: "Who is worthy to open the scroll and to break its seals?"

Many theologians suggest the scroll represents the mystery of God's plan for the universe. I agree with that general assessment, as it aligns well with the crimson thread and border of our map. In another sense, we could also say that the scroll contains the entirety of the Revelation of Jesus Christ. Not the *words* of the book of Revelation, but the ultimate unfolding of it in time and space. In other words, the scroll represents the actual Unveiling of Jesus Christ. In that way, it mirrors the opening verse of Revelation:

> The Revelation of Jesus Christ, which God gave Him to
> show to His bond-servants, the things which must soon take
> place ...
> —*REVELATION 1:1*

Likewise, the sealed scroll sits in the right hand of God the Father, and [spoiler alert] it is eventually given to Jesus Christ to open. More on that in a moment.

In book 3, we'll find that with the breaking of each seal, Christ will reveal a certain aspect of truth to His Bride about the reality of their engagement. And as you might expect, those truths follow the familiar fractal of seven pattern that correlates with the seven principles of God's character sown into creation from the beginning. The impact of Christ's sevenfold unsealing of truth will have a profound impact on the maturation of His bondservants. It will also cause other things to take place, especially in physical creation, as the earth groans and travails in anticipation of the revealing of the sons of God. Again, very similar to the dynamic described in Revelation 1:1.

In book 3, we'll also talk about the timing of the breaking of the seals, and we'll consider whether any have already been broken over the last two thousand years or whether they are all still to be broken in the future. And because I can't leave you hanging like that, here's a quick sneak peak: I believe both of those perspectives are true at the same time. Especially when we consider that there are two different applications of Daniel's prophecy of the seventieth week: one for the natural branches and one for the wild branches of the Body of Christ. Remember, the seed nature of the Word of God often causes biblical prophecy to unfold in cyclical stages on multiple levels. So it's possible that some of the seals have already been broken on some level while there still remains an ultimate unsealing for all seven at the end.

One more thing about our exploration of the sealed scroll in book 3:

> The impact of Christ's sevenfold unsealing of truth will have a profound impact on the maturation of His bondservants. It will also cause other things to take place, especially in physical creation, as the earth groans and travails in anticipation of the revealing of the sons of God.

Despite the scroll seeming to appear out of nowhere, it does not exist in a vacuum. God chose the symbolism partly for the rich biblical context it engenders. One of the ways we'll dig deeper into its meaning is by layering in other examples of scrolls from Revelation, Ezekiel, and Daniel. For now, though, let's just look at one other scroll that appears in Revelation to reinforce everything we just learned. This will also propel us into the final step of this section of our journey.

## JOHN'S SCROLL

Remember the first scroll we saw at the beginning of Revelation? Here are the verses again from a version that renders it as scroll rather than book:

> I was in the Spirit on the Lord's day, and I heard behind me a loud voice like the sound of a trumpet, saying, **"Write on a scroll** what you see, and send it to the seven churches ..."

> "Therefore write the things which you have seen, and the things which are, and the things which will take place after these things."
> —*REVELATION 1:10-11, 19, NAS*

John was commanded to record his prophetic experiences on a scroll and send it to the seven churches. That recording was to include the initial vision of Christ among the lampstands. It would also include the personalized invitations addressed to the angels of the seven churches, John's subsequent throne room experience, the drama surrounding the sealed scroll, and everything that would flow out of that drama that we haven't yet discussed.

Now, let's skip to the end of John's experience where he was given further instruction about his scroll (again, *biblion,* though translated as "book" in this verse):

> And he said to me, "Do not seal up the words of the prophecy of this book, for the time is near."
> —*REVELATION 22:10*

John's prophetic chronicle *about* the Unveiling of Jesus Christ was not to be sealed up. Rather, it was to be left open and available to be read by anyone, though it would only be heeded by Christ's bondservants. Notice how that contrasts with the sealed scroll in the right hand of the One on the throne. The sealed scroll contains more than just words *about* Christ's Unveiling. The breaking of its seals represents the commencement of the initial stages of His Unveiling. And as we're about to see, there is only one being in the universe who is worthy to breaks its seals and look upon its contents.

The difference between John's recording of the book of Revelation and the sealed scroll in the hand of God is like the difference between "book knowledge" and experience. Or the difference between reading a treasure map and actually embarking on the adventure. The first is meant to lead to the second. If you don't know there is a hidden treasure, and if you don't have a map to help you pursue it, the treasure will remain forever buried. But once you discover the map and understand its purpose, you are drawn into its quest. We have seen that Jesus is currently waiting for His people to fully accept His invitation to the treasure hunt (the letters to the seven churches) before He initiates the beginning stages of unveiling His treasure (the breaking of the seven seals). So it stands to reason that our proper engagement with John's scroll, which contains the record of his vision (the treasure map), is the primary missing ingredient that leads to the unsealing of Christ's Unveiling.

## THE QUESTION OF THE AGES

Back to the throne room scene and the question that perplexed the universe:

> And I saw a strong angel proclaiming with a loud voice, "Who is worthy to open the scroll and to break its seals?" And no one in heaven or on the earth or under the earth was able to open the scroll or to look into it. Then I began to weep greatly because no one was found worthy to open the scroll or to look into it.
> —*REVELATION 5:2-4, NAS*

No one in heaven or on earth or under the earth was found worthy to open the scroll or to look into it. This might be difficult to accept, but that statement suggests that not even the One on the throne was found worthy to open the scroll. He held it, but He couldn't open it.

How can that be?! Hadn't the twenty-four elders just proclaimed Him worthy because He had created all things? How could He be worthy as the initiator of creation to "receive glory and honor and power" but not be worthy to open the sealed scroll that would unleash His ultimate intention for creation (Revelation 4:11)?

If you are offended by that thought, you are not alone. Consider that the very idea was so troubling it caused John to "weep greatly." If not even the Father Himself could loose the seals binding the scroll's unfolding, then there truly was no answer to its mystery and no hope of God's great plan ever being fulfilled.

You can almost feel John's dismay at the realization that humanity—and therefore all of creation—might be forever stuck, separate from God and less than His ultimate desire for them. And that meant the One on the throne would remain forever alone. Perhaps the chasm really was too great?! Fortunately, the conundrum was only temporary:

> And one of the elders said to me, "Stop weeping; behold, the Lion that is from the tribe of Judah, the Root of David, has overcome so as to be able to open the scroll and its seven seals."
> —REVELATION 5:5, NAS

Notice the odd sequence. First, no one was found worthy. Then the Lion of the tribe of Judah, the Root of David, was found worthy because He "has overcome." Putting aside the fact that we already know this is talking about Jesus (we'll come back to His title as the Lion of the tribe of Judah in the next chapter), why was the vision presented in this way? Why all the consternation about no one being found worthy if Christ was actually worthy? Did God withhold the information about Jesus just to toy with John's emotions?

No, this scenario was crafted for more than just theatrical melodrama. The whole point was to underscore the reality that there was only ever one possible way for God to derive a suitable companion for His Son and fulfill His purpose for the universe. And that one way required the most improbable and impossible sequence of events imaginable. It required the unthinkable incarnation and willing sacrifice of the Word of God.

Only through the perfect, sinless, flawless execution of that plan would the Word of God *become* worthy to open the scroll. Without the incarnation and Christ's work on the cross, not even Father God could forcibly take humanity—who are the crown and the representation of the first creation—and make them partakers of the divine nature as suitable companions for His Son in the new creation. At least not in any way that didn't require Him to violate human free will. And violating free will would have violated His own nature.

Becoming worthy required God to become a human so that He could (among other things) prove the path of sonship that leads to the perfection of free will. Indeed, the drama surrounding the question of the scroll harkens back to the peculiar sequence God chose when creating Eve:

> Then the LORD God said, "It is not good for the man to be alone; I will make him a helper suitable for him." Out of the ground the LORD God formed every beast of the field and every bird of the sky, and brought them to the man to see what he would call them; and whatever the man called a living creature, that was its name. The man gave names to all the cattle, and to the birds of the sky, and to every beast of the field, but for Adam there was not found a helper suitable for him. So the LORD God caused a deep sleep to fall upon the man, and he slept; then He took one of his ribs and closed up the flesh at that place. The LORD God fashioned into a woman the rib which He had taken from the man, and brought her to the man.
> —*GENESIS 2:18-22*

As we discussed in book 1, this passage previews God's original and wholly irrepressible plan. God created Adam first and left him alone for a period of time on purpose. Not because Eve was inferior or second-rate in any way, but because this scenario best demonstrated His own aloneness. And because it previewed the process He would follow to fulfill His ultimate intention for the new creation.

Notice that Adam surveyed all of creation to find there was no helper suitable for him in existence. The same conclusion applied to God as well. God had already made everything and called everything good, and yet this one important gap remained. How could such a monumental problem be solved? This is the same basic question that caused John to weep greatly in the throne room.

Likewise, the deep sleep, the removal of Adam's rib, and the closing up of the flesh at that place, all represented Christ's incarnation and work on the cross. That was how the Son of God would become worthy to open the scroll. Therefore, the subsequent fashioning of the woman from the rib and the bringing of Eve to Adam represent the general story and purpose of the sealed scroll.

W ithout the incarnation and Christ's work on the cross, not even Father God could forcibly take humanity— who are the crown and the representation of the first creation— and make them partakers of the divine nature as suitable companions for His Son in the new creation. At least not in any way that didn't require Him to violate human free will.

## CHAPTER 20

# THE THRONE ROOM - PART 5:
# THE LION OF THE TRIBE OF JUDAH

Now that we understand the intensity of the drama surrounding the question of the ages and appreciate the stakes involved, let's talk about the hero with the singular answer. We know that Christ is the only one worthy to open the scroll, but notice the peculiar way He is finally introduced. The form in which the protagonist enters the throne room foreshadows everything that will happen afterward:

> And one of the elders said to me, "Stop weeping; behold, the Lion that is from the tribe of Judah, the Root of David, has overcome so as to be able to open the scroll and its seven seals."
>
> And I saw between the throne (with the four living creatures) and the elders a Lamb standing, as if slaughtered, having seven horns and seven eyes, which are the seven spirits of God sent out into all the earth.
>
> —REVELATION 5:5-6, NAS

Jesus was called a lion, but then He actually appeared as a lamb. And not just any lamb, but one that showed visible signs of having been slain. Considering sacrificial lambs were typically slaughtered by having their throats slashed and their blood drained, it may have been a very gruesome picture. There is no mention of blood, though, so perhaps the Lamb merely had visible scars, or looked limp and weak. Either way, despite external appearances, this Lamb was very much alive!

The Lion and the Lamb: two iconographic images of Christ that are often melded together in our minds. Two pictures from the animal kingdom that couldn't be more polar opposite.

The picture of Christ as a lamb makes perfect sense in this context, considering everything we've discussed about His willing sacrifice being the catalyst that earns Him authority to open the scroll. We'll unpack the Lamb's specific features in a moment. But first, what about the Lion? Why is He verbally introduced as a lion but seen as a lamb? The answer to this question is an immense statement about the true nature of the Unveiling of Jesus Christ, so let's take care to understand it.

> Why is He verbally introduced as a lion but seen as a lamb? The answer to this question is an immense statement about the true nature of the Unveiling of Jesus Christ ...

## THE LION OF THE TRIBE OF JUDAH

The idea of Jesus as a lion is a popular concept in modern Christianity. A roaring lion projecting power in spiritual warfare, or the serene King of the beasts exuding stately authority are both common pictures. Some of that may be thanks to the cultural ubiquity of *The Chronicles of Narnia* series by C.S. Lewis and his beloved depiction of Christ as Aslan the lion.

I've heard many sermons claim that Christ's first coming was like a lamb and His second coming will be like a lion. Maybe that's a good comparison, considering that Jesus came as a bondservant to earn authority and will return as a King to rule the nations with a rod of iron. So there is certainly some truth in that statement. But without further unpacking, it also risks oversimplifying and even misrepresenting the nature of Christ's rule when He returns. And it does so in a similar way to how first-century Israel epically misunderstood His first coming.

It is interesting that this verse in Revelation 5:5 is the first and last time that Jesus is ever directly referred to as a lion in Scripture, let alone "the Lion of the tribe of Judah, the Root of David." There are a couple of references in the Old Testament to God roaring like a lion, and there is an important reference in Revelation 10:3 about a shout that sounds like the roar of a lion, but nothing specifically about the Lion of the tribe of Judah. Do we really understand what that title represents?

In contrast, Jesus is called the Lamb almost thirty times in the book of Revelation alone, including at the very end, during the eternal state of the universe, after He has handed over the perfected kingdom to His Father. Yet He is only called "the Lion of the tribe of Judah" this one time in Revelation 5:5, in relation to His worthiness to open the sealed scroll. Why?

The word lion (or lions) appears well over one hundred times in Scripture, but this is the only time it is directly and clearly referring to Jesus. Virtually every other reference to lions is either talking about a harrowing encounter with literal lions, or it is metaphorically describing the ferocious, ruthless, and violent actions of a person or group—usually for evil, though there are a few notable exceptions for good.

There are a couple of times where God describes His own actions as that of a lion, but even those are in the context of His fierce wrath against wickedness or in protection of His people. Always the image is invoked to speak of wrath and an untamable, unassailable, ferocious force. After all, the lion was at the top of the food chain as the apex predator in that part of the world.

## THE ORIGINAL LION

The very first mention of a lion in Scripture is found in a prophecy spoken by the patriarch Jacob (Israel) over his son Judah, and it is the sole inspiration for the Lion of the tribe of Judah title mentioned in Revelation 5:5:

> Judah, your brothers shall praise you; your hand shall be on the neck of your enemies; your father's sons shall bow down to you.

> **Judah is a lion's whelp**; from the prey, my son, you have gone up. He couches, he lies down as a lion, and as a lion, who dares rouse him up?
>
> The scepter shall not depart from Judah, nor the ruler's staff from between his feet, until Shiloh comes, and to him shall be the obedience of the peoples.
>
> He ties his foal to the vine, and his donkey's colt to the choice vine; He washes his garments in wine, and his robes in the blood of grapes. His eyes are dull from wine, and his teeth white from milk.
>
> —GENESIS 49:8-12

Here, the picture of a young lion (a lion's whelp) is used to describe Judah's role among his brothers, and the tribe of Judah's eventual role within the nation of Israel. Judah's prowess in battle and forceful subjugation of his enemies would make him a leader to be followed.

Early fruit from this prophecy is most evident in the life of David and in the royal line of kings that God established through David. In that sense, David can certainly be seen as a young lion following the pattern of Judah. Notice, though, that when Revelation calls Jesus "the Lion of the tribe of Judah," it also calls Him "the Root of David." Not the descendent of David, or the branch of David, but the *root* of David.

The root of David is a phrase that only appears twice in Scripture: first in Revelation 5:5 and later in Revelation 22:16, when Jesus calls Himself "the root and descendent of David." Many other messianic prophecies in the Old Testament referred to Christ as "the branch of David" when describing attributes that the Messiah would spiritually or physically inherit as David's descendent. But in the context of the Lion of the tribe of Judah, he is the *root* of David. Why?

Perhaps because we are not meant to view Christ as a lion in the exact same sense that David or Judah were lions. Please follow my logic here because I believe this is the heart of the message behind Christ's title as Lion of the tribe of Judah.

David was a warrior. He was a man of physical conquest and violence and force. That was good for David—he was designed by God to be those things at that time in history—but he was also specifically forbidden from building the temple of God because those attributes were inappropriate for the foundation of God's house.

David was a branch of Jacob's prophecy. So was Judah. In both cases, their expressions of rulership were incomplete and imperfect in some fundamentally humanistic ways that didn't reflect the true grace of the divine root. Yes, Christ is the descendant of David who will rule the earth from David's metaphorical throne, but His rule will be different from every other government in history in some immensely important ways that are alluded to in Jacob's prophecy but not seen in the life of David.

Ever since the fall of Adam and Eve, society is only held together by the threat of punishment. Despite our best efforts, the fallen nature is fundamentally selfish, rebellious, and poverty-minded. No matter how moral a people group, things eventually unravel when rules are not present and consequences for rule breaking are not enforced. Such coercion is a necessary tool because humanity is still tied to the fruit from the tree of the knowledge of good and evil. As a result, every human government and system must rely on the threat and deterrent of punishment to maintain civil society. The Bible even tells us that God grants them the authority to wield that sword for our own good (see Romans 13).

Now think of the symbolism of the lion as an expression of that same coercive, ferocious, often violent power to enforce one will over another, whether for righteousness or evil. That's the basic idea conveyed in Jacob's prophecy over Judah, and it is certainly how David ruled his kingdom. It's even the enforcing power behind the old covenant law of Moses, which temporarily mapped God's eternal righteous law to a system of punishment and reward because of humanity's fallen nature and hardness of heart. It's not wrong, but it's not the perfect expression of the whole heart of God as revealed in Christ, and it is not the end goal for creation.

## UNTIL SHILOH COMES

Now let's see how the reign of Christ, the Lion of the tribe of Judah, will be different:

> The scepter shall not depart from Judah, nor the ruler's staff from between his feet, until Shiloh comes, and to him shall be the obedience of the peoples.
> He ties his foal to the vine, and his donkey's colt to the choice vine; He washes his garments in wine, and his robes in the blood of grapes. His eyes are dull from wine, and his teeth white from milk.
> —*GENESIS 49:10-12*

Jacob's prophecy ultimately speaks of the coming of Shiloh—a messianic name for Christ that means either "He who brings peace" or "He who shall be sent," depending on who you ask. In the context of the prophecy, "He who brings peace" makes the most sense, considering the coming of Shiloh is mentioned as bringing "the obedience of the peoples." At first glance, that may sound like just a continuation of the kind of rulership demonstrated by Judah and David: obedience and peace through force. But that is not the kind of obedience this verse is talking about.

The Hebrew word translated as obedience (*yiqhah*) here is an obscure word used only one other time in Scripture:

> The eye that mocks his father, and scorns **obedience** to his mother, the ravens of the valley will pick it out, and the young eagles will eat it.
> —*PROVERBS 30:17, NKJV*

This proverb has a direct relevance to the return of Christ in more ways than one, but for now, let's just focus on the word *obedience*. Although conveyed in the negative sense, the obedience it describes is the kind that unwise children fail to exercise when they scorn their mothers. And notice the word is specifically used in relation to mothers but not to fathers. It's a jarring picture because a mother's love and wisdom are so tender and sacrificially given that the idea of scorning one's own mother is anathema in most civil cultures. This is especially true of a son's relationship to his mother.

The same ethos that ties us so deeply to our mothers and prevents us from scorning them will be present in "the obedience of the peoples" during Shiloh's reign. It's not an obedience out of coercion, but one freely and naturally given out of love, earned respect, and a deep recognition of the selfless sacrifice made by the "mother." It is more of an allegiance and an honoring than just an obedience.

> The same ethos that ties us so deeply to our mothers and prevents us from scorning them will be present in "the obedience of the peoples" during Shiloh's reign.

Speaking of the obedience to Shiloh, some other Bible translations actually render it as "the allegiance of the nations is his" (BSB), or "the one whom all nations will honor" (NLT), or "unto him shall the gathering of the people be" (KJV). So this is much more than just the forceful submission or obedience that comes from being conquered, and it is much more than the threat of punishment that keeps civil societies in line. It is the deepest voluntary devotion that flows out a heart of admiration and an alignment of vision arising from tender nurture.

In contrast to the nature of a lion who uses strength, violence, and fear to lord it over others, Shiloh's rule will be marked by free will (allegiance of the nations) and unprecedented peace and prosperity:

> He ties his foal to the vine, and his donkey's colt to the choice vine; He washes his garments in wine, and his robes in the blood of grapes. His eyes are dull from wine, and his teeth white from milk.
> —*GENESIS 49:11-12*

The picture of "tying his foal to the vine" speaks of the prosperity available to all during the millennial reign of Christ. Grape vines typically only belong to the wealthy and affluent, but during Shiloh's reign they will be so abundant that even the common donkey associated with the lowest of citizens will be tied to their vines, with no anxiety over the vines being spoiled. And rather than horses for battle, people will live in peace, riding young donkeys (like the foal of a donkey that Christ rode into Jerusalem) and tie them to the abundantly available best vine branches.

Even the idea of washing "his garments in wine" and "his robes in the blood of grapes" draws a stark contrast between the violence that maintains the kingdoms of this world and the celebrations and carefree revelry that will accompany Christ's reign.

That's why Jacob's prophecy mentions Judah's lion nature as the foundation of Judah's leadership, but then says that the scepter will not depart from Judah *until* Shiloh comes. Shiloh will fulfill the prophecy of Kingship spoken over the tribe of Judah, but He will also be the end of the young-lion nature of human leadership. Or maybe it is better to say that He will not exhibit the nature of lions that we've come to expect since the fall of humanity in the garden when creation was subjected to the futility of the curse.

That kind of ferocious violence and fear-based coercion we associate with a lion's nature will no longer be necessary when Christ returns, because His Unveiling will shatter the illusion of our separation from God. It will sever humanity's connection to the fruit from the tree of the knowledge of good and evil, along with the associated selfishness and shame that prevents us from understanding the wisdom of His nature.

Of course, these things won't happen all at once. There will be a progressive build-up process for His Unveiling in the years preceding His return, and then, when He returns, there will be a healing process for the nations that takes some portion of His one-thousand-year reign, but none of that will leverage the fear of punishment or the violent coercion of a lion-like style of leadership to achieve.

Yes, He will rule the nations with a rod of iron. Yes, He will bash every last vestige of our ungodly world systems to pieces like unusable pottery, but His method of doing those things will not resemble the type of lord-it-over-others leadership that He clearly denounced during His first coming. Why would it? Why would He come as the Lamb the first time, going to the ultimate lengths to demonstrate humble, sacrificial servant leadership, only to return in an opposite spirit? It is nonsensical to expect Him to return as some benevolent dictator. A kind and generous dictator is still a dictator. And if Christ has to rule as a dictator, then what was the point of God's plan to perfect free will? He could have just sent Christ to rule with force at any time.

This is why Revelation consistently calls Him the Lamb throughout His Unveiling, including during His kingdom age and beyond. The authority earned through His sacrifice will win Him the allegiance of the nations when He returns. And as we'll begin to learn in book 3, the events that unfold on earth during the breaking of the seals, the blowing of the trumpets, and the pouring out of the bowls of wrath, will have an effect beyond preparing His Bride. They are also designed to prove to the nations that their way doesn't work. That their worldly knowledge devoid of God's wisdom isn't enough, and their only hope is Christ. To disabuse them of their reliance on the fruit from the tree of the knowledge of good and evil and the antichrist system it empowers.

Yes, He will rule the nations with a rod of iron. Yes, He will bash every last vestige of our ungodly world systems to pieces like unusable pottery, but His method of doing those things will not resemble the type of lord-it-over-others leadership that He clearly denounced during His first coming.

In keeping with the nature of the Lamb, He will remove those blinders by allowing the free-will choices of humanity to play out to their ultimate conclusion. He will do all of this while offering the grace of a better way for those who have ears to hear and eyes to see. And throughout the entire process, He will present the wisdom of His solution on earth in the form of a growing Bride who matures in the sight of all.

By the time Christ descends from heaven as King of kings and Lord of lords, only the beast and the deluded armies that worship him will oppose the Lamb's rule, and that will only be a subset of humanity alive on earth. The beast's armies will be quickly annihilated, not by strength of arms, but by the simple words of truth that come from Christ's mouth when He appears. The rest of the people still alive on earth will gladly celebrate their liberation from the failed and utterly disproven experiment of humanism, and they will willingly gather to Him—even to receive His judgments.

The power of His appearing is always about revealing Him as the Truth. Its just that the revelation of that truth will have different natural effects on different people based on how much of their life is built on the light versus the darkness. Even the physical return of Christ on a white horse, followed after by the armies of heaven, won't be the kind of military conquest and occupation we sometimes imagine it to be.

But I'm getting ahead of myself. We'll unpack these topics with more biblical evidence later in the series. My point right now is that Christ's method of transformation and dominion has always been about revealing truth that draws and convinces free will, not forcible conquest. That modus operandi will not change during or after the Unveiling. He is called the Lion of the tribe of Judah because He will fulfill the prophecy of Shiloh ruling over the nations, but He will not do so with the military prowess and aggressive coercion of David.

> The rest of the people still alive on earth will gladly celebrate their liberation from the failed and utterly disproven experiment of humanism, and they will willingly gather to Him—even to receive His judgments.

If anything, His lion nature is exercised through the compelling revelation of the beauty of His sacrifice that reconciles hearts to God's character and proves the wisdom of God's plan. If Christ is the Lion of the tribe of Judah, then shouldn't we expect Him to exhibit the characteristics of the lions of Messiah's kingdom, rather than the lions that are subjected to Adam's fall?

> Also the cow and the bear will graze, their young will lie down together, and the lion will eat straw like the ox …
>
> They will not hurt or destroy in all My holy mountain, for the earth will be full of the knowledge of the LORD as the waters cover the sea.
> —ISAIAH 11:7, 9

# CHAPTER 21

# THE THRONE ROOM - PART 6:
# THE LAMB THAT WAS SLAIN

J ohn didn't have the context of the entire book of Revelation nor the benefit of hindsight when he was in the throne room weeping over the sealed scroll, so I wonder what he thought when the elder first invoked the unfamiliar name of the Lion of the tribe of Judah. After all, it wasn't necessarily some long-expected title for the Messiah that carried clear connotations in the Hebrew mind.

Even if John immediately made the connection back to Jacob's prophecy over Judah, he probably wasn't imagining anything like an austere lion sitting in stately majesty, peacefully ruling over His kingdom like a nurturing mother. Given the overwhelming testimony of lions in Scripture, and his own cultural bias, he probably envisioned the unbridled, ferocious energy of a lion. Perhaps he thought of an unstoppable power to achieve God's purposes, and a violence and wrath toward His enemies. If anyone could open an unopenable scroll, it would be the One called the Lion of the tribe of Judah, the root of David, right?!

That, I believe, was the goal of the elder's introduction. It was the intended frame of reference—the mental image John was supposed to have when he turned to see the Lamb that was slain. In other words, we need to appreciate the ferociousness of lions to know why Christ is so special. Christ's nature as the Lion can only be understood through the picture of the Lamb, and the authority of the Lamb can only be fully grasped in light of what He endured to achieve it.

It's not just the love of God, nor the power of God, nor the wrath of God, nor even Christ's sacrifice that achieved the victory. It is all of these together that earned Him the unique authority, as Firstborn of the old and new creations, to open the sealed scroll, draw out a Bride, fulfill the plan of God, and to do so with an everlasting power and authority more effective to perfect human free will than anything available to the kingdoms of this world.

To understand how Jesus can and will be able to secure eternal free-will devotion by conquering hearts and minds rather than using ferocious coercion—we also need to understand that God does have the power and the right to judge the world like a ferocious lion of old. He could wipe the universe off the map. He could clean the slate, return everything to the void, and start over again from scratch. He even demonstrated a tiny fraction of that divine right during the flood. But hitting the ultimate reset button on creation would have been an indictment on His character and on the wisdom of His plan. At the same time, abandoning righteous judgement would have been an even greater indictment. Neither path would produce a suitable companion with a refined free will, a purified character, and a mature wisdom tested in adversity.

Instead, He developed the only possible solution. In concert with the rest of the Godhead, before the foundation of the world, He settled on a path that would allow Him to apply both the righteousness and the justice aspects of His character in the most constructive fashion.

The Word of God is absolute, inexorable, and unimpeachable. He saw the end from the beginning and knew exactly what needed to be done. Rather than pointing His well-deserved wrath at fallen creation, He became one of us so He could focus the wrath on Himself. He took the brunt of the judgment while leaving enough of life's difficulties to discipline and shape a Bride in His wake.

As the origin and destination of all prophecy—the root and the descendant of David, the Lion from the tribe of Judah—only Jesus could lay down His life as a representative of the first creation, satisfy God's wrath, and become the seed of the new creation in one fell swoop. And because He took the full force of God's wrath as a human on the cross, He now has full authority to pour out God's wrath against "all ungodliness and unrighteousness of men who suppress the truth in unrighteousness" (Romans 1:18).

Since He provided the path for the restoration and perfection of humanity, there can be no indictment of His char-

> Christ's nature as the Lion can only be understood through the picture of the Lamb, and the authority of the Lamb can only be fully grasped in light of what He endured to achieve it.

acter or His plan when He returns with the sword of His mouth. At that time, it will be fully appropriate for Him to speak the full truth of His nature in a way that destroys all who had foolishly spent their free will embracing wickedness and suppressing His Unveiling rather than accepting its provision. And such a revelation will be fully congruent with His Lamb nature.

That's the frame in which we are meant to see the Lamb taking the sealed scroll from the hand of the One on the throne. He's not going to open the scroll as a lion seeking to subjugate creation, since He already submitted to the Lion's full wrath so He could gain a different kind of authority. Instead, He will serve creation through the opening of the scroll, providing more and more light for humanity to understand God's heart and be transformed if they choose. Or reject God's heart and become ever more twisted if they choose. And just as the scroll is two-sided, only the Lion who became the Lamb has the authority to unleash these dual effects of its revelation.

In book 3 we'll learn more about the two sides of the scroll, and the different impacts the breaking of its seals and the opening of the scroll will have on the sons of darkness compared to the sons of light. It contains both the kindness and the severity of God; the provision and the accounting; the intimacy and the power necessary to fulfill all righteousness and justice while perfecting His Bride out of fallen humanity, restoring creation to heights far above its original expression, and eventually destroying all who intentionally set themselves against His glorious plan. And, as always, it will be accomplished through the progressive revelation of His nature. Even His wrath is simply the unveiling of aspects of His nature too pure and holy for creation to handle when not hidden in Christ behind "the cleft of the rock," so to speak (Exodus 33:22).

> E ven His wrath is simply the unveiling of aspects of His nature too pure and holy for creation to handle when not hidden in Christ behind "the cleft of the rock," so to speak.

## THE LAMB OF GOD

Let's wrap this chapter up by digging into the description of the Lamb who alone can accomplish all this:

> And I saw between the throne (with the four living creatures) and the elders a Lamb standing, as if slaughtered, having seven horns and seven eyes, which are the seven spirits of God, sent out into all the earth.
> —REVELATION 5:6

Unfortunately, this Bible version doesn't paint the clearest picture of the Lamb's position within the throne room, but other translations make it clear that He was standing in the center of the throne, encircled by the living creatures and the elders. Nothing was between the Lamb and the One on the throne—He was in a unique position of unity and equality with God.

Notice that the Lamb was standing, whereas the One was sitting. In other words, the One was at rest when He relinquished the scroll from His right hand of power over to the Lamb, and the Lamb was ready to take action. Thus the Father handed the keys of the Unveiling over to the Son, fully trusting the Son's worthiness to execute with excellence of wisdom and skill.

## SEVEN EYES OF THE LAMB

The Lamb had seven horns and seven eyes, which are the seven Spirits of God. There are two ways to read the text here, and it's not entirely clear which way God intended. Do just the eyes represent the seven Spirits of God? Or do the horns *and* eyes both represent different aspects of the seven Spirits of God? If the horns represent something different, what are they for and why are they mentioned in the same breath? More on that in a moment.

We know at least the eyes represent the seven Spirits of God. That means in the same scene we now have the seven lamps of fire (which are the seven Spirits of God) burning before the throne and the seven eyes of the Lamb, which are called "the seven Spirits of God *sent out into all the earth.*"

As we discussed in book 1, it seems the lamps stand before the throne of God giving light, while the eyes are "sent out into all the earth" to look for those whose hearts are completely His (see 2 Chronicles 16:9). The eyes of the Lord search for people who try to focus the eyes of their human spirit completely on Christ. His eyes do this so that He can strongly support His people with the internal illumination of God's character and provision that shines before the throne.

Let's drill down a little further. The Lamb is pictured with seven eyes to illustrate that He, as a man on earth, received the fullness of the Spirit's sevenfold illumination and provision because the eyes of His heart were completely synchronized with the Father. As a result, everything He did on earth He accomplished as a human endowed with the fullness of the Spirit of God. He didn't overcome the enemy by His innate divine power and the glory of His position in the Godhead. He temporarily laid those assets aside when He came to earth. Rather, He overcame by leveraging the same provisions available to every human through the seven Spirits of God.

Having said that, notice that the seven eyes are a part of Christ. *The Lamb* has the seven eyes. That means only the Lamb can access the fullness of the light of the seven lamps of fire shining before the throne of God. We must abide in Him—that is, learn to rest in oneness with His completed work—in order to receive the same illumination. There is no seeing the light of the seven lamps of fire outside of Christ, since the eyes are His alone.

## SEVEN HORNS OF THE LAMB

If the eyes are definitely the seven Spirits of God, surely the horns represent something different ... or at least some other aspect of the seven

Spirits of God. What would be the point of having two symbols that represent the exact same thing?

As we saw with the altar of burnt sacrifice, horns can represent strength, vigor, and authority. How does that idea mesh with what we learned about the Lamb's earned authority to perfect free will, and to conquer by winning the devotion of hearts and minds rather than using military might or the threat of punishment? If His lion-nature is meant to stand in direct contrast to the lions of this age, what role do the Lamb's horns play?

Hold that question for one moment. Now consider that in both Daniel and Revelation there are multiple prophetic visions of beasts with horns that are interpreted as earthly kings and kingdoms who are given (or will be given) a level of power and authority to rule for a season of history. We'll see some of that in more detail later in this series when we talk about the kingdom of the antichrist described in Revelation chapter 13.

I mention that because, in contrast to those horns, the Lamb's horns do not equate to kings or kingdoms. His authority is different. His kingdom is not dependent on this world's systems nor their strength of arms to subjugate. His authority is not brandished in horns as an external display or threat of power. His authority was earned by the wounds He received and is reflected in the scars He still bears as the Lamb that was slain. So again, what are His horns?

Like the altar, the Lamb's horns speak of His strength, vigor, and authority to accomplish the Father's will through powerful and effective giving that is sacrificial in nature. They are the seven aspects of God's provision for redemption and reconciliation expressed through Christ to the universe. In that way, the horns can be seen as His expression of the seven flames that are before the throne shining the sevenfold light of God outward. In other words, they are the power of God available to us through the Spirit of Christ for the building of His kingdom: the power to change hearts and minds and actions through the revelation of Jesus.

In a similar sense, the Lamb's seven horns also represent the result of Christ's own submission to the Father's discipline as a human. Remember, He learned obedience through the things that He suffered. He never sinned or disobeyed, but He did have to learn how to obey as a human. These horns represent His resulting strength in human sonship learned through the process of suffering. They are the proof of His maturity and worthiness to be the spotless Lamb of sufficient age and quality for the sacrifice. They are the strength and vigor of His Sonship that overcame the enemy, and they represent the same kind of sonship that His Body will demonstrate on earth as they participate in His Unveiling. They are the result of submitting to the conversion factor of the wilderness that teaches us to draw life from Him so that we can give it to others.

In that way, we can observe the appearance of the eyes and the horns of the Lamb during the story of His baptism when He was "birthed" into mature Sonship. Remember when He came up from the baptismal waters and the heavens opened, the Father spoke to Him, and the Holy Spirit descended on Him like a dove? That was Christ receiving the seven eyes of the seven Spirits of God. Then, after submitting to the forty-day testing in the wilderness and learning to rely completely on the Father's provision, He emerged from the wilderness full of the power of the Holy Spirit. That was the Lamb earning His seven horns. The lessons of the wilderness ensured He would not use the strength of His horns for selfish gain, but only to give and to liberate and to empower others according to the Father's will.

> The power of the Lamb's horns were often demonstrated in signs, wonders, and authority over darkness, but whether performing a miracle or preaching a sermon, the goal was always to bring the illumination of the knowledge of God.

The power of the Lamb's horns were often demonstrated in signs, wonders, and authority over darkness, but whether performing a miracle or preaching a sermon, the goal was always to bring the illumination of the knowledge of God. In the kingdom of Christ, only the treasures of wisdom and knowledge hidden in Him will eternally transform others. The kingdoms of this world become the kingdoms of our God through the Spirit's internal revelation, not through external might. Bad ideas are overcome by the skilled persuasion of better ideas, not by violence. Strongholds of the enemy are torn down by experiencing the knowledge of Christ, not by force. And as His Bride, we must allow the full reality of that truth to permeate our essence before we can be used to unleash it upon the rest of the world:

for the weapons of our warfare are not of the flesh, but divinely powerful for the destruction of fortresses. We are destroying speculations and every lofty thing raised up against the knowledge of God, and we are taking every thought captive to the obedience of Christ, **and we are ready to punish all disobedience, whenever your obedience is complete.**
—*2 CORINTHIANS 10:4-6*

So at the end of the day, the Lamb's horns represent His ability to reveal the fullness of the knowledge of God to creation in the only way that we can receive it without being utterly destroyed. Therefore, His eyes and horns work together in a way that is consistent with His unique expression of the Lion. They represent the two aspects of His authority earned on earth. They are the signs of His worthiness to open the two-sided scroll and unleash its dual effects on creation through the progressive revelation of His wisdom and knowledge.

Yes, some will resist His revelation right up to the end and therefore be destroyed by what they cannot comprehend, but that will be their choice. After all, creation will only reach the heights it was intended to reach through the knowledge of the Lord:

They will not hurt or destroy in all My holy mountain, for the earth will be full of the knowledge of the LORD as the waters cover the sea.
—*ISAIAH 11:9*

## THE LION LAMB

At the risk of belaboring the point, consider this final comparison like tying a bow around Christ's nature as the Lion Lamb. The lions of this fallen age are carnivorous beasts who survive by consuming the lives of others, and they use their strength for themselves, or at least to accomplish their own purposes. Sure, they typically exist in community, hunt in packs, and care for their young and wounded, but at the end of the day, even those things are utilities of self-preservation.

So too is the nature of every human system since Adam and Eve ate the fruit from the tree of the knowledge of good and evil. Even most expressions of the institutional church throughout history have leveraged this kind of strength in one way or another. And though God has tolerated and even blessed those systems at times, they are far from His end goal for us.

The strength of the lamb is different, at least in its utility to creation. Lambs don't consume the lives of other sentient beings to survive. The energy of their life is spent in producing wool and milk as sustenance for others. So too is the selfless nature of Christ's eternal kingdom, and the very nature of God's plan for the universe. The breaking of the seals on the scroll will help to unmask this truth to the Body of Christ and to the world in unmistakable ways.

Obviously, this idea is nothing new. Humans have always dreamed of utopian societies full of peace, prosperity, and harmony. But nobody has ever accomplished such paradise in reality because humanity is bound to the powerlessness and shame of the forbidden fruit, and we always devolve toward self-preservation.

Moreover, constant giving is unsustainable no matter how hard we try. God didn't make us to only give or to only receive. He created us to find fulfillment by receiving directly from His inexhaustible divine source of life and then learning to give to others out of that reserve. Only the full revelation of God's nature available in Christ's seven horns and seven eyes will enable us to walk in such a manner, freely and without coercion.

> Lambs don't consume the lives of other sentient beings to survive. The energy of their life is spent in producing wool and milk as sustenance for others. So too is the selfless nature of Christ's eternal kingdom, and the very nature of God's plan for the universe.

All of that can be summarized in this way: Christ is called the Lion of the tribe of Judah, not so that we will think of Him in terms of the lions that came before Him, but to force us to recontextualize God's desired expression of power and authority in leadership. And it is only in that unexpected frame that the Lamb stepped forward to answer the cry of creation and reveal the full splendor of God's plan:

And He came and took the scroll out of the right hand of Him who sat on the throne.
—*REVELATION 5:7, NAS*

Therefore, His eyes and horns work together in a way that is consistent with His unique expression of the Lion. They represent the two aspects of His authority earned on earth. They are the signs of His worthiness to open the two-sided scroll and unleash its dual effects on creation through the progressive revelation of His wisdom and knowledge.

## CHAPTER 22

# THE THRONE ROOM - PART 7:
# CREATION'S RESPONSE

W e've seen how John had to experience heaven's persistent praise of the One on the throne before he could comprehend the drama of the sealed scroll. Likewise, another epic response unfolded when the Lamb took the scroll, and it too was required viewing before John could grasp the breaking of the seals.

There were actually three separate responses from three unique groups, beginning with those closest to the throne and emanating outward in concentric ripples that consumed larger and larger groups of worshipers. Let's read through each response, making a few simple observations about the scope and impact of each, before moving into our final chapter where we will tie up this leg of our journey:

> When He had taken the scroll, the four living creatures and the twenty-four elders fell down before the Lamb, each one holding a harp and golden bowls full of incense, which are the prayers of the saints. And they sang a new song, saying, "Worthy are You to take the scroll and to break its seals; for

You were slaughtered, and You purchased people for God with Your blood from every tribe, language, people, and nation. You have made them into a kingdom and priests to our God, and they will reign upon the earth."
—*REVELATION 5:8-10, NAS*

## HOLY PLACE WORSHIP

The first response came from those closest to the throne: the four living creatures and the twenty-four elders. They had the clearest view of the action, and their reply was swift and harmonious. The creatures and elders fell down in reverence and began to sing a new song. They were also suddenly holding harps and golden bowls full of incense. More on those in a moment.

How John could see creatures like a flying eagle, a calf, or a lion holding harps and bowls is difficult to imagine. For this reason, some commentators have suggested that only the twenty-four elders held the harps and bowls and sang the new song, and the living creatures simply fell down before the Lamb. That is certainly possible. In some ways, that separation between the elders and the creatures would provide a tidier interpretation of their actions, but it also feels like an unnecessary stretching of the text. I mean, if we're applying that logic, how would *anyone* hold harps and bowls while falling down in reverence? In the mysterious visual language of the spirit, perhaps those physical mechanics don't matter any more than how a lamb could take a scroll and open its seals. What matters are the things John perceived and recorded about the symbols, not necessarily how the information was communicated into His consciousness.

## THE EVENING OFFERING

In any case, the golden harps and golden bowls full of incense are the keys to understanding this scene. The golden bowls of incense are the intercession and supplications of the saints, and the golden harps are for the thanksgiving and praise of the saints. In these two symbols we see a reference to the services performed on the heavenly version of the golden altar of incense.

Remember, in the Mosaic tabernacle, the altar of incense was positioned in the inner court right before the veil. Its incense rose perpetually before the mercy seat that stood behind the veil. To ensure that the sweet aroma was always present in the Holy Place, the priests would replenish the old incense with new incense twice a day, marking the time change from evening to morning and morning to evening.

Likewise, the continual worship that was offered day and night before the throne by the elders and living creatures in Revelation chapter 4 corresponds with the perpetual burning of incense upon the golden altar of incense. But now, in response to the Lamb taking the scroll, we see a brand new instance of worship that corresponds to the priests changing the old incense for new incense. This new song from the elders and creatures holding the golden bowls and golden harps also delineates a major changing of seasons in the schedule of the Unveiling.

Given the context, I believe it specifically represents the new incense of the evening offering that commences the twilight hours of God's end-time plan. I say that because what follows when the Lamb begins breaking the seals will bring increasing natural darkness for the world systems but increasing supernatural light for the saints as they shine brighter and brighter with the light of the seven Spirits of God.

In the Mosaic tabernacle, all seven lamps of the menorah were lit (or at least their oil was replenished) by the high priest at the time of the evening incense offering:

> When Aaron trims the lamps at twilight, he shall burn incense. There shall be perpetual incense before the LORD throughout your generations.
> —EXODUS 30:8

This verse is a perfect shadow of what will happen when the Lamb takes the scroll. It doesn't tell us which comes first, but the care of the menorah lamps and the evening incense offering are intimately linked. And although this specific verse in Exodus suggests that the high priest was the one who burned the incense, other verses make it clear that the daily services on the altar of incense were typically performed by Aaron's sons. Later in Israel's history they were performed by a weekly rotation of priests who descended from Aaron's line, divided by King David into ... you guessed it: twenty-four divisions (see 1 Chronicles 24:7-18).

So, in this metaphor, the high priest lighting each lamp of the menorah corresponds with the Lamb taking the scroll and (eventually) breaking its seven seals. As the darkness gradually increased outside of the tabernacle, the light gradually increased inside.

Likewise, the twenty-four elders and four living creatures (with harps and bowls of incense) will respond to the Lamb by singing a new song. This corresponds to the priesthood burning the evening incense to celebrate the time change.

To drill down one more step, remember that God considers a twenty-four hour day to run from sundown to sundown. A full day is divided into night and day periods, each containing twelve hours. In that same frame, this new incense offering welcomes the beginning of the night period that precedes the day of the Lord.

> The high priest lighting each lamp of the menorah corresponds with the Lamb taking the scroll and (eventually) breaking its seven seals. As the darkness gradually increased outside of the tabernacle, the light gradually increased inside.

Before the dawn of the day of the Lord, there will be a period of darkness that increases incrementally, like the darkening night plunging ever deeper toward midnight. We know that midnight corresponds to the middle of the seventieth week, but later in this series, we'll find that the dawn of the day of the Lord—those early hours preceding the full morning—will be marked by another burning of incense on the golden altar. That morning service will be slightly different than the evening service seen here in Revelation chapter 5, but we'll save those details for a later discussion.

## THE NEW SONG

Notice in Revelation 5:8 that the creatures and the elders were united in their worship of the Lamb, and that the prayer and praise of their offering in verses 9 and 10 was dedicated to describing His worthiness to take the scroll and break its seals. There are numerous ways to analyze the words of their song, and different lenses highlight different aspects of its message.

Because I tend to see things in groups of seven whenever possible, I prefer to parse this song into seven statements delineated by the seven actions described in the song. There is no reason to think this is the only right way to view the song, but it does open up some interesting avenues for analysis. Through that lens, we end up with the following sevenfold declaration about the Lamb's worthiness:

1. Worthy are You to take the scroll
2. And to break its seals
3. For You were slaughtered
4. And You purchased people for God with Your blood
5. You have made them into a kingdom
6. And [You have made them into] priests to our God
7. And they will reign upon the earth.

One way to look at these statements is, of course, through the fractal of seven. They contain at least tangential connections to the seven principles of God's character as described in the fractal of seven, though it takes a good deal of massaging to draw the connections out of these statements.

It is a little easier to see them as general descriptions of the authority contained in each of the Lamb's seven horns. In other words, His worthiness to open each seal. But even that requires the context of the seven seals to unpack.

Rather than taking the time to build all of that out, let's just keep it simple for now and view the whole of the song as a celebration of the Lamb's worthiness to initiate the final phase of God's plan for creation. The fact that the song was sung into the areas corresponding to the holy of holies and inner court suggests that the atmosphere of these parts of the throne room were being prepared for their role in the next phase of God's plan. More on that in book 3.

## OUTER COURT WORSHIP

After the new song was offered like evening incense in the Holy Place to welcome the beginning of Christ's Unveiling, the worship service extended outward:

> Then I looked, and I heard the voices of many angels around the throne and the living creatures and the elders; and the number of them was myriads of myriads, and thousands of thousands, saying with a loud voice, "Worthy is the Lamb that was slaughtered to receive power, wealth, wisdom, might, honor, glory, and blessing."
> —*REVELATION 5:11-12, NAS*

Encircling the throne and the creatures and elders, there was now an innumerable choir of angels standing in the outer court. I call this the outer court because they were likely in the general area occupied by the sea of glass and the yet-to-be-shown altar of burnt sacrifice (which we'll encounter in book 3). In response to the song of the living creatures and elders, the angel voices rang out with their own sevenfold proclamation of the Lamb's worthiness. Only this time, they spoke of what the Lamb would *receive* from the breaking of the seals because of what He gave. "The Lamb that was slaughtered" was "worthy to receive" the following:

1. Power
2. Wealth
3. Wisdom
4. Might
5. Honor
6. Glory
7. Blessing.

Like the previous song, at first glance, these seven gifts do not easily map to the principles seen on the seven days of creation. At least not in the order we have come to expect. Neither do they easily match the attributes of the seven Spirits of God in any obvious way. The connection is there, but it is hard to see and quite subjective. For now, let's keep it simple by saying that the angels are describing seven aspects of Christ's inheritance that He will receive through the opening of the sealed scroll as the old creation is made new through the process of His Unveiling.

Since these words are declared into the outer court before the breaking of the seals, I believe they specifically allude to the large part of Christ's inheritance that He will receive in the form of a great multitude of unbelievers from every tribe and nation and tongue that will flow into the outer court of His Body during the great tribulation.

Paul spoke of Christ's "inheritance in the saints" in a verse that echos a similar harmony:

> I pray that the eyes of your heart may be enlightened, so that you will know what is the hope of His calling, what are the riches of the glory of **His inheritance** in the saints …
> —*EPHESIANS 1:18*

Think of this concept of Christ's inheritance in the saints in light of the Revelation chapter 12 parable of the Unveiling that we discussed In book 1. We saw that the three parts of the Body of Christ will have widely different experiences with the great tribulation, and it is the outer court believers who will face the fiercest parts of the dragon's wrath.

We'll see all of those details in the greater context of the Unveiling in book 3, but the important thing to remember right now is that although the dragon will attempt to steal, kill, and destroy as much as possible during his short time on earth, a vast number of new converts will flow into the kingdom at that time because of Christ's ongoing Unveiling. Jesus encouraged His disciples with that reality right before drilling down on the difficulties of the great tribulation:

> This gospel of the kingdom shall be preached in the whole world as a testimony to all the nations, and then the end will come.
> —*MATTHEW 24:14*

Remember, by the time the great tribulation starts, the sons of God will have shaken loose the powers of darkness from their ruling perches in the second heaven, opening the minds of unbelievers to unprecedented levels of new light. We actually saw hints of that in the new song sung into the inner court and holy of holies right before this outer court proclamation: "You purchased people for God … from every tribe, language, people, and nation …" (Revelation 5:9).

In that way, the authority of the Lamb's seven horns will turn Satan's greatest heist into the folly of the ages:

> Men do not despise a thief if he steals
> To satisfy himself when he is hungry;

**But when he is found, he must repay sevenfold;**
He must give all the substance of his house.
—*PROVERBS 6:30–31*

Satan will be made to repay seven times more than what he has stolen from God's plan for creation. And the innumerable multitudes that flood into the kingdom of God during the great tribulation will be part of that repayment—the outer court part—bringing their power, wealth, wisdom, might, honor, glory, and blessing to the Lamb.

## ALL CREATION WORSHIPS

Finally, after the angel's celebration of the Lamb's outer court inheritance, a third worship set began:

> And I heard every created thing which is in heaven, or on the earth, or under the earth, or on the sea, and all the things in them, saying, "To Him who sits on the throne and to the Lamb be the blessing, the honor, the glory, and the dominion forever and ever." And the four living creatures were saying, "Amen." And the elders fell down and worshiped.
> —*REVELATION 5:13-14, NAS*

It is fitting that this final set emerged from creation because it is a preview of the impact Christ's Unveiling will have upon creation itself. Every spiritual and physical created thing: the rocks and trees, the rivers and mountains, the birds and fish, angels and demons, all of humanity, along with the very atoms, subatomic particles, and the forces of creation joined together in one glorious statement of faith about reality.

Perhaps it is hard to imagine everything "in heaven, or on the earth, or under the earth" participating in such worship, considering the statement is made *before* the perfection of all things. But remember that everything was created from the seed of the Word of God spoken into the void. The fundamental nature of Christ as the Word of God is, therefore, sown as a seed into the fabric of all things, and everything is held together by that nature. So in some mysterious way the light of Christ is in all things—even those sentient beings who have chosen to live in darkness and to oppose His plan.

Perhaps that is why, when the Pharisees tried to silence His disciples during His triumphal entry into Jerusalem, Jesus said, "If these become silent, the stones will cry out!" (Luke 19:40). It was a similar principle to what Paul described to the Romans:

> For the anxious longing of the creation waits eagerly for the revealing of the sons of God. For the creation was subjected to futility, not willingly, but because of Him who subjected it, in hope that the creation itself also will be set free from its slavery to corruption into the freedom of the glory of the children of God. For we know that the whole creation groans and suffers the pains of childbirth together until now.
> —*ROMANS 8:19-22*

Jesus and Paul weren't just using metaphorical language. There is a sense in which Christ's Unveiling is the light that will cause the seed of His Word that has been gestating in the fabric of all things to finally shed its prenatal husk and grow to maturity.

So here, right before the commencement of Christ's Unveiling, we see the seed of the Word of God—that which was sown into the fabric of all things—crying out in unison the truth of what it was designed to be. We may not always understand or agree with what we were made to be in Him, but the Word of God inside of us that holds our very atoms together cries out for His truth to be revealed in us. And the vibration of that anticipation within creation will approach a crescendo right before the Unveiling commences. It will be an internal testimony felt by all things—though many will try to ignore it—and it will create an atmosphere of anticipation suitable for the Lamb to take center stage.

---

The Word of God inside of us that holds our very atoms together cries out for His truth to be revealed in us. And the vibration of that anticipation within creation will approach a crescendo right before the Unveiling commences.

---

# CHAPTER 23

# FINAL COMPASS CHECK

W e're there! We've made it to the end of this leg of our journey, and now we stand on the brink of an exciting new
stage with the context and experience we need to truly appreciate what lies ahead!

Over the last seven chapters we've gotten acquainted with the main
players and objects in the heavenly throne room who will be involved in
the main drama of Christ's Unveiling. That drama commences in Revelation chapter 6, and that is where we'll pick up the trail of our treasure
hunt in book 3. But before we head off to our tents for some much-
needed recuperation in preparation for that phase of the journey, let's
perform one final compass check with the Song of Solomon to reorient
ourselves with the story of the Bride.

Last time we checked in, the Bride had just responded to her fiancé's
seven letters, inviting each part of her spirit to step into a new level of
devotion and maturity. He had challenged her to lay aside the sins that
had so easily entangled her and to refocus the eyes of her heart on Him.
And she had answered with seven statements of passionate abandon:

> May he kiss me with the kisses of his mouth!
> For your love is better than wine.
> Your oils have a pleasing fragrance,
> Your name is like purified oil;
> Therefore the maidens love you.
> Draw me after you and let us run together!
> The king has brought me into his chambers.
> —*SONG OF SOLOMON 1:2-4*

Now, remember what happened after Christ's letters to the seven churches, beginning in Revelation 4? John was called into the heavenly throne room where he witnessed the four living creatures and the twenty-four elders worshiping the One on the throne. Going forward, we'll view John as an ambassador of the Bride. What he sees and feels in Revelation will track with what the Shulamite experiences in Song of Solomon. Let's read the second half of verse four in the Song of Solomon narrative in light of that throne room scene:

> We will rejoice in you and be glad;
> We will extol your love more than wine.
> —*SONG OF SOLOMON 1:4*

As I mentioned earlier, it is not always obvious who is speaking in the Song of Solomon, but most Bible versions agree that this exultation comes from the daughters of Jerusalem—a group of onlookers who are emotionally invested in the budding romance between the king and his fiancée. As we move forward, I invite you to equate the company in the throne room—in this case, the four living creatures, the angels around the throne, and the twenty-four elders—with the daughters of Jerusalem in the Song of Solomon. They are onlookers and third-party assistants in the ultimate drama of the ages.

Depending on how you look at it, it is possible that the twenty-four elders should be considered part of the Lord's betrothed Bride instead. I wouldn't argue with that assessment, but since they are in heaven and seem to be ancillary to His Unveiling, we'll consider them part of the daughters of Jerusalem for now.

Just as we saw the four living creatures and the twenty-four elders giving glory and honor and thanks to God right after Christ sent the letters to the seven churches, the daughters of Jerusalem make a similar proclamation about Solomon's love right after hearing the Bride's seven-fold response: "We will rejoice in you and be glad; we will extol your love more than wine."

And when the Bride hears this proclamation from the daughters of Jerusalem, she replies in a way that perhaps mirrors whatever internal response John was feeling while observing the throne room worship:

> Rightly do they love you.
> —*SONG OF SOLOMON 1:4*

But then the initial throne room vision shifts when John sees the sealed scroll in the right hand of Father God. That's when the question of the ages is asked aloud, and all are found wanting: "Who is worthy to open the scroll and to break its seals?" (Revelation 5:2, NAS). For John, it was the ultimate gut punch after tasting the full glory of the One and realizing that the chasm between creation and God was still hopelessly uncrossable. John wept greatly at the realization that he didn't measure up … that nobody measured up.

Think of John's weeping in the context of what he had just experienced. He had seen a vision of the risen and glorified Christ among the lampstands. He had received Christ's personalized letters to His bond-servants, heard the encouragements and challenges and rebukes and promises they contained. The road to maturity would be hard, but hearing that the overcomers were called to sit with Christ upon His throne, which is the throne of the Father, likely elevated John's expectations for eternity to never-before-imagined heights.

And then he was transported to heaven, where he saw God in the splendor of His throne room. The awe and exhilaration he felt must have been overwhelming as he imagined living in God's presence for all eternity…but then it all came crashing down in a heartbeat with that unexpected question: "Who is worthy to open the scroll and to break its seals?"

Who was worthy to take fallen, rebellious, stubborn, sinful humanity—not to mention the rest of creation that humanity had defiled in their foolish attempts to reach heaven—and make them overcomers worthy of the rewards Christ had offered? Who could bridge the gap between what humanity had become and what they were called to be? Who could unveil and unleash God's plan to make the impossible into reality? It seemed that despite Christ's work on the cross to offer the path, humanity was too feeble and rebellious to follow it. So John wept bitterly.

In that frame, let's step through the corresponding response of the Bride in the Song of Solomon, recognizing that she too had just read the letters from her Bridegroom, had felt the agony and ecstasy of His words, and experienced the empowering hope of His promises. But now the reality of the question of the ages was setting in for her as well:

> I am black but lovely,
> O daughters of Jerusalem,
> Like the tents of Kedar,
> Like the curtains of Solomon.
> —SONG OF SONGS 1:5

First, notice the tone of this section: the afterglow has worn off as the Bride realizes how far she is from who she is meant to be.

"I am black but lovely" speaks of the dichotomy she is feeling. Other translations render this as "I am *dark*, but lovely" (NKJV). She is not so much describing her natural skin color as opining that her complexion has been darkened by a life of hard work under the sun as a farmer. She was beautifully designed by God, but her circumstances and actions had made her less so, at least in her own estimation.

"Like the tents of Kedar, like the curtains of Solomon." Again, she describes the tension between who she is and who she was designed to be. She is both dark like the tents of Kedar and lovely like the curtains of Solomon. To understand the rich spiritual allusions in these words, allow me a moment to build out another parallel. This might at first feel like a tenuous connection, but it fits perfectly with the overall theme of Revelation, and with the Bride's journey through the Unveiling.

> The awe and exhilaration he felt must have been overwhelming as he imagined living in God's presence for all eternity...but then it all came crashing down in a heartbeat with that unexpected question: "Who is worthy to open the scroll and to break its seals?"

## SLAVE OR FREE

Kedar was the second son of Ishmael (see Genesis 25:13). Hang on to that detail for a moment. Ishmael was the son of Abraham through the slave woman Hagar. As the apostle Paul pointed out to the Galatians, Ishmael represented the slave mindset of the old covenant:

> For it is written that Abraham had two sons, one by the bondwoman and one by the free woman. But the son by the bondwoman was born according to the flesh, and the son by the free woman through the promise. This is allegorically speaking, for these women are two covenants: one proceeding from Mount Sinai bearing children who are to be slaves; she is Hagar. Now this Hagar is Mount Sinai in Arabia and corresponds to the present Jerusalem, for she is in slavery with her children. But the Jerusalem above is free; she is our mother.
> —*GALATIANS 4:22-26*

Ishmael represents the old covenant; Isaac represents the new covenant. Ishmael, a mindset of slavery and the futility of human strength; Isaac, a spirit of sonship through the provision of the Holy Spirit and God's promise. Ishmael, the fruit from the tree of the knowledge of good and evil; Isaac, the fruit of the tree of life.

Okay, now Isaac's second son was Jacob, who became Israel. In our parallel, Jacob represents the true Body of Christ. Ishmael's second son was Kedar, who, in our parallel, represents the Church's attempt to use religious strength to accomplish God plan. It is the slave mindset that keeps us from following Christ into the wilderness and learning to lean on His provision for our lives.

Kedar can also be viewed as the institutional church system—at least when we embrace that system as a legitimacy crutch for self-righteousness. And at least as far as that system relies on the strength of the lion to subdue rather than the wisdom of the Lion-Lamb to empower. It is a system that ultimately keeps us wretched, poor, miserable, blind, and naked while thinking we are spiritually rich and have need of nothing. It is a system that keeps us weak and dependent on itself. We'll see how in a moment.

So when the Shulamite says, in one breath, that she is like the tents of Kedar and like the curtains of Solomon, she is describing the war within her between slavery and sonship, religion and freedom, futility and empowerment, shame and dignity. She knows who she is called to be, but she feels so far from that person.

## A FARMER OR A SHEPHERD?

Like John weeping profusely in the throne room, the Bride goes on to summarize the reason behind her mindset:

> Do not stare at me because I am swarthy,
> For the sun has burned me.
> My mother's sons were angry with me;
> They made me caretaker of the vineyards,
> But I have not taken care of my own vineyard.
> —*SONG OF SONGS 1:6*

"Do not stare at me because I am swarthy, for the sun has burned me." So she feels shame at her appearance and over the circumstances that made her this way—some of which were her own fault, but many were the fault of others.

"My mother's sons were angry with me; they made me caretaker of the vineyards." Who are "my mother's sons" in the context of the parallels we're drawing with the book of Revelation? Think back to the main characters from the Revelation chapter 12 parable of the Unveiling in book 1. We had the woman, the male child, and the woman's other children. Among other things, these three represent the three levels of maturity of the Body of Christ. All three are players in the Unveiling, and in a sense, all three are parts of the Bride.

The Song of Solomon is primarily a story about the Lord drawing His Bride

So when the Shulamite says, in one breath, that she is like the tents of Kedar and like the curtains of Solomon, she is describing the war within her between slavery and sonship, religion and freedom, futility and empowerment, shame and dignity.

through the levels of maturity, particularly from inner court to holy of holies. The outer court saints are, by definition, those who have not yet embraced the bridal relationship we see in Song of Solomon. He desires all of His people to know Him deeply in the holy of holies, but not everyone is willing to go on that journey with Him.

In that paradigm, "my mother's sons" is a reference to a particular portion of the outer court saints—the woman's other children. Specifically, they are those outer court saints who are entirely entrapped in an institutional church system that is offended by the creative and free exercise of godly sonship. That's why the Shulamite said her mother's sons were angry with her and forced her to take care of their vineyards.

Like the tents of Kedar, the vineyards represent the programs and systems of the institutional church that keep people busy and dedicated to its system but spiritually domesticated and weak. It is the one-size-fits-all, cookie-cutter Christianity that uses people as cogs in its machine rather than connecting them to the Bridegroom, helping them find what He designed them to be outside of religion, and releasing them to freely pursue the King in that area of life.

> Like the tents of Kedar, the vineyards represent the programs and systems of the institutional church that keep people busy and dedicated to its system but spiritually domesticated and weak.

It seems the Shulamite didn't want to work her brother's vineyards. She wanted to pursue her Bridegroom in a different way. Maybe she didn't sense His presence in the vineyard. Maybe she simply knew she was meant to meet Him elsewhere. There was nothing necessarily evil about the vineyard itself—it had its beneficial uses—but she was designed for something else. After all, her Beloved was a shepherd, not a farmer.

"But I have not taken care of my own vineyard." In other words, she had tried her best to do what was culturally acceptable to her family and the religious institutions, but there was no life in it for her—no grace or sense of fulfillment to help her be successful and fulfilled. The role required all her strength and left her feeling empty.

Like the difference between Cain (the farmer) and Abel (the shepherd), it seemed the works of her hands in the vineyard would never make her acceptable. The very life thrust upon her and begrudgingly embraced for lack of better options had proven unsustainable. She knew there was more but felt deep shame for falling short. What about the gloriously overcoming life her Beloved had spoken of and demonstrated so clearly in His own journey?! Her daily grind of futility left her hopeless and on the brink of despair. She wept once more as a dreaded thought landed in her soul: "*Is no one worthy to take the scroll and break its seals?!*"

## THE ONLY PATH

Just as the Shulamite began to spiral downward in despair, an answer came into her spirit like new oxygen for a gasping deep sea diver. From somewhere up in heaven the elder's voice echoed into her heart too: "Stop weeping! The Lion-Lamb is worthy!" And suddenly she knew it must be true of her beloved Shepherd. Surely, if anyone had the answer for her hopelessness it would be Him. After all, *He* had called *her*. Not the other way around. He had found her in the vineyard and reached into her world. Even in her sunburned, weary state, He had called her to Himself.

She knew He had the answer for her predicament, though she couldn't comprehend what it could be. Many questions still lingered in her soul, but with them now came expectation instead of doubt. So with renewed but cautious hope she called aloud:

> Tell me, O you whom my soul loves,
> Where do you pasture your flock,
> Where do you make it lie down at noon?
> For why should I be like one who veils herself
> Beside the flocks of your companions?
> —*SONG OF SONGS 1:7*

He was the beloved shepherd of her soul, and now she found herself longing to be with Him in His work. Participation in that job sounded so much more fulfilling than the vineyards of her brothers—even if it led into the wilderness instead of the safe and cultivated spaces of her family. And even in the dreaded heat of the noonday sun, surely her Beloved led His sheep beside streams of living waters, or into shaded groves to find their rest. That's what she needed! The work of His hands —the building of His kingdom—would look nothing like the toil in the tidy vineyards she had come to loathe. She was sure He could teach her to find wholeness in those wild places by His side!

But where?! He still seemed so far away. Surely He didn't want to do the job alone, leaving her to remain forever veiled, sunburned and less than His suitable wife? Always trailing behind, undignified, and merely following after those who followed Him?!

## HEAVEN'S RESPONSE

So we return to heaven's worship service after the Lamb had taken the scroll from the Father. Every earnest question of the Bride was about to be answered by the Bridegroom. And in preparation for that revelation, the attendants in the throne room let loose a response of celebration that demolished her anxiety and perfectly prepared her to receive His first few answers:

> If you yourself do not know,
> Most beautiful among women,
> Go forth on the trail of the flock
> And pasture your young goats
> By the tents of the shepherds.
> —*SONG OF SOLOMON 1:8*

Here, again, we have the daughters of Jerusalem speaking to the Shulamite about her Beloved. It may not be immediately obvious, but these words harmonize with the new song from the four living creatures and twenty-four elders. At least in as far as what John must have felt when their voices rang out on the heels of his weeping.

Remember, they sang their sevenfold song into the holy of holies and the inner court, and therefore their words most closely coincided with the Bridal narrative (the holy of holies and

> The work of His hands—the building of His kingdom—would look nothing like the toil in the tidy vineyards she had come to loathe. She was sure He could teach her to find wholeness in those wild places by His side!

311

inner court saints). Let's read their words one more time:

> Worthy are You to take the scroll and to break its seals; for
> You were slaughtered, and You purchased people for God
> with Your blood from every tribe, language, people, and
> nation. You have made them into a kingdom and priests to
> our God, and they will reign upon the earth.
> —*REVELATION 5:9-10*

They sang of the Lamb's authority to take the scroll and break its seals, but they also described His intention behind doing so: to take the people He had purchased with His blood and to make them into a kingdom of priests who would reign up on the earth. Like John, the Bride needed to hear this before she could experience her Beloved in a new way through the breaking of the seals.

Think of it like this: In Revelation and Song of Solomon, the Bride had just experienced a destabilizing rollercoaster. She had seen the glorious fullness of what she was meant to be and then crashed into the reality that it was an impossible pipe dream. And then Hope appeared when the Lion-Lamb took the scroll, reigniting the potential of her dreams and rocking her world even further. And into that emotional whirlwind, the Daughters of Jerusalem spoke words that reaffirmed the rightness of her desires, anchoring her soul to her Beloved's plan again, reassuring her that it would come to pass in Him. Such will be the general psyche of the Body of Christ on earth in the season leading up to the beginning of Christ's Unveiling.

"If you yourself do not know, most beautiful among women ...." In other words, "Yes, you are still the desire of His heart ... the reason He suffered so He could reveal the fullness of God's mysterious plan."

"Go forth on the trail of the flock and pasture your young goats by the tents of the shepherds." In other words, "Leave behind the vineyards and the culture of religious limitations from your mother's sons, and follow your Beloved into the thing for which you feel designed and called. It may lead you into the wilderness and require massive change, and you may feel ill-prepared and immature, but you will learn on the way from others who have left the comfort of domesticated systems in pursuit of free, creative sonship."

And that, my friends, is the posture that will lead us to maturity when Christ commences His Unveiling with the breaking of the seals.

Everything that happens in the first five chapters of Revelation is meant to bring us to that place. The letters to the seven churches, the throne room encounter, the question of the sealed scroll, truly beholding the Lion-Lamb who will open it—all these things must be read, experienced, and heeded by the Body of Christ to prepare us to engage with His Unveiling from the grounded but risky place of faith and courage. It was the place John found himself at the end of Revelation chapter 5. It was the place the Shulamite found herself at the end of Song of Solomon 1:8. And it is the edge of transformation to which He invites us now.

# What's Next?

Thank you for reading *Come Up Here: The Unveiling of Jesus Christ*, book 2 of *The Unveiling of Jesus Christ* series. I'm so glad you've chosen to come on this journey with me!

I hope you'll also join me in book 3, *Ballad of the Beloved: The Unveiling of Jesus Christ*, to follow the beloved Shulamite and John the beloved apostle into the heart of Christ's Unveiling where they experience the opening of the sealed scroll!

I'm currently targeting a mid-2026 release for book 3. Please visit my website at www.theunveiling.org to join my mailing list and stay up to date on my latest news. You can also read my blog, purchase watercolor artwork from my amazing wife, or ask me questions about anything I've written. I'd love to hear from you!

Lastly, would you please consider helping me spread the word about my books by leaving an honest book review? Reviews are one of the most impactful ways to help unknown indie authors like me get noticed. Scan the QR code below to see a list of book review sites from which you can choose.

Until next time, friends …

May the Father of glory give to you a spirit of wisdom and of revelation in the knowledge of Him. (Ephesians 1:18-19)

# OTHER BOOKS BY MICAH PAUL GAYLOR

The book of Revelation is more than a prophecy of future events. It is an invitation, a blessing, and a catalyst meant to equip creation for a Face to Face encounter with the King of Kings that will utterly transform the very fabric of reality.

Book 1 of the Unveiling of Jesus Christ series is all about preparation. No, not that "end of the world as we know it," doomsday kind of preparation. I mean the kind you make when you are about to go on an epic quest. Our quest is to understand and experience the true power of the book of Revelation—not as an oracle for survival but as illumination for transformation. Without this mindset, many previous eschatological expeditions have produced overconfident predictions while leaving their travelers empty-handed, unchanged, and jaded.

A better path is available. In this prelude to our journey through Revelation, we'll build a map for navigating end-times prophecy as God intended. With a fresh, sometimes out-of-the-box perspective, we'll unpack familiar Bible verses in unexpected ways that reveal God's beautifully consistent tapestry of truth. From Genesis to Revelation, we'll learn how God's plan connects the Old and New Testaments with a precision that will strengthen and deepen your faith.

Join me as we leverage the depth and breadth of Scripture to uncover a divine endgame that defies imagination. The goal is to adjust our focus, enlarge our perspective, and awaken an insatiable hunger for the Unveiling of Jesus Christ. Come prepared to be equipped for active participation in the consummating stages of God's eternal plan for His universe!

*Face to Face: The Unveiling of Jesus Christ*
Book 1 of *The Unveiling of Jesus Christ* series